NEW-SCHOOL
Sweets

*Old-School Pastries with an
Insanely Delicious Twist*

by

VINESH
JOHNY

*Pastry Chef & Co-Founder
of Lavonne Academy*

ANDRÉS
LARA

Global Pastry Educator

PAGE STREET
PUBLISHING CO.

PAGE STREET
PUBLISHING CO.

First published in 2021 by Vinesh Johny and Andrés Lara

Page Street Publishing Co.

27 Congress Street, Suite 105

Salem, MA 01970

www.pagestreetpublishing.com

Distributed by Macmillan, sales in Canada by The Canadian Manda Group.

25 24 23 22 21   1 2 3 4 5

ISBN-13: 978-1-64567-249-4

ISBN-10: 1-64567-249-2

Library of Congress Control Number: 2020944068

Cover and book design by Manek D'Silva for Page Street Publishing Co.

Photography by Manek D'Silva

Printed and bound in China

Page Street Publishing protects our planet by donating to nonprofits like The Trustees, which focuses on local land conservation.

DEDICATED TO JOONIE & MARIE,

for not only putting up with our madness
but also encouraging it. Thank you.

Contents

YUM-YUM COOKIES 72

OLD-SCHOOL ALFAJORES 74
SOUTH AMERICAN COOKIE SANDWICH WITH
A SALTED CARAMEL CREAM FILLING

BANANA OAT POWER COOKIE 77
WHOLESOME BANANA COOKIE DOUGH
PACKED WITH OVERNIGHT OATS

ROYAL COOKIES 'N' CREAM 79
MILKY AMERICAN CLASSIC WITH
A MOLDED HAZELNUT CREAM CROWN

PEANUT YUZU MARSHMALLOW COOKIE 83
MARSHMALLOW-TOPPED COOKIE MADE
WITH A FRAGRANT EAST ASIAN CITRUS FRUIT

MANGO CARAMEL PEANUT BUTTER COOKIE 85
NUTTY GOODNESS COVERED IN
A SMOOTH MANGO CARAMEL
AND RASPBERRIES

APPLE PECAN COOKIES 89
PECAN DOUGH LOADED WITH
PRALINE NUT PASTE AND
CARAMELIZED APPLES

ROCKY ROAD COOKIES 91
CHUNKY, DOUBLE-CHOCOLATE
CARAMEL COOKIE WITH A FLUFFY
MARSHMALLOW TOPPING

LET'S JAM LINZER 95
LIGHT, AUSTRIA-INSPIRED COOKIE SANDWICH
WITH GANACHE AND STICKY RASPBERRY JAM

THE BIG BOUNTY® 96
VEGAN CHOCOLATE COOKIE STUFFED
WITH SWEET COCONUT FILLING

MIDNIGHT LAYER CAKES

JAPANESE-SPICED MANGO BROWNIE CAKE
BANANA BROWNIE LAYERED WITH
MANGO-TOGARASHI AND
APRICOT-GINGER CONFIT

CRÊPE SUZETTE CAKE
TOWER OF CRÊPES LAYERED WITH
ORANGE CREAM, MARMALADE AND
BRANDY SAUCE

GERMAN CHOCOLATE STOUT CAKE
BEER-BATTER CAKE LAYERED WITH
COCONUT PECAN FILLING AND
CARAMEL PUFFED RICE

FIRST DATE CAKE
SPICED MIDDLE EASTERN DATE CAKE
LAYERED WITH HAZELNUT AND
COFFEE BUTTERCREAM

NINETIES BLACK FOREST CAKE
GRAND REIMAGINING OF THE
CHOCOLATE CLASSIC WITH
CHERRY CONFIT AND WHIPPED GANACHE

A CHOCOLATE CAKE
PERFECTLY MOIST DARK CHOCOLATE
CAKE LAYERED WITH RICH CHOCOLATE
FILLING

PANDAN PUMPKIN CHIFFON
FRAGRANT MALAYSIAN COCONUT CAKE
WITH JAGGERY-PUMPKIN CUSTARD

LEMON MERINGUE CAKE
FRESH SPONGE LAYERED WITH
LEMON CURD AND LOADED WITH MERINGUE

PINEAPPLE INSIDE-OUT CAKE
VANILLA BLUEBERRY CAKE WITH
YOGURT CHANTILLY AND A
CARAMELIZED PINEAPPLE CROWN

MASCARPONE COMFORT CAKE
DELICATE SPONGE LAYERED WITH
FRESH STRAWBERRY CONFIT AND
WHIPPED MASCARPONE

TRES LECHES MOUSSE CAKE
MEXICAN CAKE SOAKED IN THREE MILKS,
TOPPED WITH DULCE DE LECHE MOUSSE

SHOP-STYLE DESSERTS   194

Forewords

One of the most interesting things in any trade is when a professional transitions from student to teacher almost without realizing it. A teacher is someone who experiments and learns while teaching, not someone who believes that theirs is the only true way. The latter is neither my philosophy nor that of Andrés and Vinesh, who share their knowledge in a way that encourages the reader to explore and create their own path.

In my 35 professional years, I have had the privilege of working with several hundred young cooks. Today, many of them are great professionals, but there are no more than a dozen who I keep a fond memory of and associate with my own career. Andrés Lara is one of them. As soon as he entered El Bulli, I realized that we were going to have a great season together. In his expression, extreme humility was combined with a desire to absorb everything we could teach him. That was many years ago and now it is Andrés and his good friend Vinesh who show us the way of the current pastry world with their casual and playful recipes that are adapted to the palates of today.

Vinesh and Andrés told me, "Albert, this is a book that arises from friendship and travel; a simple book showing who we are." No, dear friends, I must tell you that they are wrong. Books are like movies, music and art in general. They are not simple or complicated, they are good or bad, and this is one of the good ones. The book you are holding is like the beginning of a thrilling story, and we can't wait to know what happens next.

Sweet dreams,

ALBERT ADRIÀ

Pastry chef and author of *A Day at El Bulli* and *Tickets Evolution*

This book is a tribute to passion. It is the fruit we get from all the years of work by two young talented chefs, Vinesh Johny and Andrés Lara, who delight our senses with this blend of foods from so many different countries and cultures. The flavors presented in this book range from coconut and mango to pandan and peppercorns, and the resulting combinations are unique because they are based on moments, places and experiences from both of their lives. The extraordinary techniques and presentation used in each creation is a reflection of their effort, discipline and passion for pastry.

These pages take us on a sweet journey through 73 recipes from two chefs with individual styles and careers, bringing their ideas together to create something new. Vinesh and Andrés have my admiration and respect for inspiring the next generation of pastry chefs across the world with this work, and I wish them many more successes.

Sincerely,

ANTONIO BACHOUR

Pastry educator and author of *Bachour the Baker* and *Bachour in Colour*

Introduction

Change is the only constant. Food has been part of our lives and cultures for so long it's easy to forget how much our habits and ingredients have evolved over the years. Each generation passes down their most hallowed recipes to the next in line, and along the way, new dimensions get added, methods get tweaked, entire dishes get reimagined. Rather than resist this constant evolution, we've decided to embrace it wholeheartedly. As pastry chefs, we hope to take the wide range of pastries and cakes and breads and bakes, all of which a long history of chefs have contributed to, and push them along a little further: pull in a glorious new texture to tease the palate, pair an exciting flavor, discover an innovative format, a novel method, a fresh look, infuse magic into every corner. And once we've finally found our favourite version of each dessert, we pass it on to you.

Andrés Lara is a globe-trotting Colombian pastry teacher who's always looking for the tastiest ingredients, and Vinesh Johny is the founder and chef of the award-winning Lavonne Academy of Baking Science & Pastry Arts in India. So how did two pastry chefs from opposite sides of the world even meet? In Japan of course, completely by coincidence! Vinesh was on holiday wandering around the streets of Tokyo, probably in search of something delicious to eat, and walked into a pastry school where Andrés was teaching a class. We started chatting about pastries, workouts and beaches in Goa and we haven't stopped talking since! It was love at first bake. Soon after, Andrés visited Lavonne Academy in India to teach a class. It went so amazingly, he started returning every single year, and each time we ended up going on little trips, trying new foods, becoming closer friends and dreaming up pastry ideas along the way. Even from across the world we kept swapping recipes until we realized this stuff shouldn't just be on our phones, it should be out there, in every home oven!

Home-baking has become a massive part of food culture today, but it also ends up retreading the same ol' classics. There's nothing wrong with going back to recipes you love, but we're here to encourage you to take that extra step, to add that extra ingredient, to push your experience in the kitchen just a little bit further; even just changing up the proportions in a recipe can result in something thoroughly joyful and fresh. Across these seven inventive chapters, we hope to bring the excitement of desserts straight to your kitchen. The recipes are accessible enough for casual chefs to follow, while the unconventional pairings and techniques aim to serve as fresh inspiration for even the highest level of pastry professionals.

We've peppered the recipes with little notes along the way, and there's a section dedicated to explaining some of the more uncommon terms and methods used in several of our desserts, so if you ever need a little help, feel free to jump ahead to the Quick Reference Notes section (page 218). The fields of baking and pastry essentially deal with many different ingredients reacting to each other in wondrous ways, and for these reactions to work perfectly each ingredient needs to be portioned out precisely, so for best results we always recommend having a digital scale with you in the kitchen and using gram measurements wherever possible. You'll also notice each recipe is made up of individual components being layered or combined in some way—we've designed these combinations to feel surprising at first, and then come together perfectly as if they were always meant to be. But this book is about you, so if you find a delicious component that you think would be perfect in your own recipe, go ahead and try it, indulge yourself, create something new; the real excitement of food lies in that playful experimentation.

Our goal was to honor the practiced traditions of baking and pastry, while introducing inventive new concepts and under-explored flavors from every single country that's influenced us so far. This globe-trotting, culturally diverse approach has helped create unique products like the Miso-Maple Sandwich (page 142) and the Vegan Banana Tahini Cake (page 47) and bring new dimensions to classics like Caramel Candy Apple Pie (page 14) and A Chocolate Cake (page 115). The biggest questions we ask ourselves are: What would truly make this the most delicious thing we've ever eaten? What flavours and textures would delight our friends? What twist would make our guests fall helplessly in love with this dish? We hope you find the answers in these wild, creative and blissfully unpretentious desserts. Welcome to *New-School Sweets*.

DRAMATIC
Pies & Tarts

When Andrés first got to America, he was struck by how the approach to food was so warm and homey, as compared to the very formal traditions of French cuisine. Both of us first started associating America with pies from those classic cartoons where the freshly baked pie would lie on the windowsill to cool and the smells wafting up from it would make everyone around go crazy! And when we finally got to eat at classic American diners and visit friends' homes, suddenly we could properly appreciate how much of a cultural phenomenon pies were, and still are, in the country.

Pies and tarts have also quickly become a central part of the classes we teach all over the world, constantly picking up new tricks and developing new recipes. When the two of us finally met, things started getting really wild and we started using all sorts of exciting ingredients to create every pie we could ever dream of, from the more traditional doughs with gentle fillings, to the impressive gastronomic delights of today. We wanted to represent that spectrum here, so we've got homey recipes like the Raspberry Gâteau Basque (page 23) and truly exotic cultural treats like the Mango Yogurt Pie (page 38). We'll walk you through creating a variety of crusts, lining and baking them, layering different fillings and topping it all off with garnishes, with each product boasting unique looks and flavor combinations. You're in for the ride of a lifetime with this tasty, crumbly collection.

CARAMEL CANDY APPLE PIE

Yield: 6 (3½-inch [7-cm]) pies
Mold: 3½-inch (7-cm) ring

It doesn't get any more old-school than biting into one of those classic caramelized apples at the local carnival. Our take on this childhood favorite combines some sinfully creamy and crumbly textures, with a balance of sweet and salty flavors. To fully explore the different sides of caramel, we'll be using it in three distinct ways—coated around the apples, inside the chewy filling and, of course, as a light chantilly on top. This pie guarantees you'll feel like a kid again.

Caramel Chantilly

¾ cup (150 g) granulated sugar

1¼ cups (300 g) heavy cream

Pie Dough

½ cup (120 g) butter, plus more for greasing rings, at room temperature

⅓ tsp sea salt

¾ cup (90 g) icing sugar

½ cup (30 g) almond flour

1 egg

1¾ cups + 1 tbsp + 1 tsp (230 g) all-purpose flour

Chewy Vanilla Caramel

½ vanilla bean pod (see Quick Reference Notes, page 219)

½ cup + 2 tbsp (150 g) heavy cream

⅛ cup + 2 tsp (40 g) milk

⅓ tsp sea salt

⅓ cup + 1 tsp (115 g) corn syrup, divided

⅓ cup + 2 tsp (75 g) granulated sugar

3½ tbsp (50 g) butter

Caramelized Apples

3 tbsp + ½ tsp (45 g) butter

3 Granny Smith apples, peeled and diced

½ cup + 2 tsp (120 g) brown sugar

Caramel Crunch

¾ cup (100 g) pie crust, baked

1 tbsp (15 g) butter

2 tsp (10 g) brown sugar

¼ vanilla bean pod

⅛ cup + 1 tbsp (35 g) milk chocolate

Toasted hazelnuts, for garnish

Edible gold leaf, for garnish

For the Caramel Chantilly. Caramelize the granulated sugar by spreading it in a saucepan and heating it evenly until it takes on a deep amber color. Add in the cream to help deglaze the saucepan, and use a spatula to mix it well and form a smooth caramel cream. Refrigerate the chantilly overnight.

For the Pie Dough. Starting things off in a stand mixer with a paddle attachment, cream the butter along with the salt, icing sugar and almond flour. Add in the egg gradually and mix for 1 to 2 minutes to get an even mixture. Next add the all-purpose flour and mix until there is a smooth dough, 1 minute. The dough should then be placed between two sheets of baking paper and flattened slightly before resting in the refrigerator for 1 hour.

Line a tray with baking paper and then grease the rings with extra butter and place them on the prepared tray. Roll the dough out into a sheet ⅛ inch (3 mm) thick, and cut out 6 (4-inch [10-cm]) discs of dough for the base of the pies. Place a disc inside each greased ring and press it gently, starting from the bottom and working your way up the sides. If the edges are above the rim, carefully trim them with a small knife, then refrigerate the tart shells for 1 hour. Preheat the oven at 320°F (160°C) and bake the tart shells for 20 to 25 minutes. You'll have some leftover dough trimmings, which need to be refrigerated and baked in the same way. Store these baked crust trimmings so they can be used while making the caramel crunch.

(continued)

Note from the Chefs:

The chewy caramel process might feel tricky at first, but as long as you have two pans and a thermometer handy, you'll be fine!

For the Chewy Vanilla Caramel. In a saucepan, add the vanilla, cream, milk, salt and 2 tablespoons (40 g) of corn syrup. Heat over medium heat, 2 minutes, until it turns nice and warm. In another saucepan, heat the granulated sugar along with the remaining 3 tablespoons + 2 teaspoons (75 g) of corn syrup, until it caramelizes to a light amber color, then pour the warmed cream mixture into the caramel to help deglaze the saucepan. Continue to cook the mixture until it reaches 225°F (107°C) before turning off the heat and letting it cool for 10 minutes. Mix in the butter, and use a hand blender to mix it into a beautiful, thick caramel. Strain and reserve the caramel in an airtight container at room temperature until assembly.

For the Caramelized Apples. In a saucepan, melt the butter and then add in the apples and brown sugar, cooking until they're evenly coated to give them a nice intense caramel feel, about 8 to 10 minutes.

For the Caramel Crunch. Bring out those baked crust trimmings, measure the amount needed for the recipe and blend them in a food processor until they form a crumbly texture. Heat the butter gently in a saucepan until it's melted, then add it into the crumble. Transfer this to a mixing bowl and add in the brown sugar and scraped vanilla as well. To finish things off, melt the milk chocolate and combine it into the crunch.

Time for assembly. First, spread a generous layer of the caramel crunch inside each baked pie crust. Next, pipe a layer of chewy vanilla caramel over the crust with a piping bag. Gently place the caramelized apples over the caramel piping, and follow that with another layer of chewy caramel. You can use a palette knife to flatten out the top of the caramel into a smooth surface. Finally, whip the caramel chantilly in a stand mixer with a whisk attachment to get it nice and airy, and use a piping bag fitted with a leaf nozzle to make neat lines across the top surface of the pie. Use a palette knife to neaten the edges, and finish up with toasted hazelnuts and gold leaf to give it an exquisite look.

These perfect caramelized apple pies are ready to eat. You can store them in the refrigerator for up to 2 days.

CARROT CONFIT PUMPKIN PIE

Yield: 6 (3½-inch [7-cm]) pies
Mold: 3½-inch (7-cm) ring

Thanks to its firm bite and delicate sweetness, the carrot is one of the few vegetables that's widely embraced as an ingredient in desserts! Of course, the West has carrot cakes; similarly, the East has enjoyed gajar halwa for ages: a thickened pudding made with grated carrots, milk and spices. Being one of Vinesh's local favorites, we wanted to use carrot halwa as the filling for this pie and build it up with a stunning crème brûlée to create a truly East-meets-West experience.

Pie Dough

½ cup (120 g) butter, plus more for greasing rings, at room temperature

½ tsp sea salt

¾ cup (90 g) icing sugar

½ cup (30 g) almond flour

1 egg

1¾ cups + 1 tbsp + 1 tsp (230 g) all-purpose flour

Carrot Halwa

3 tbsp + 1½ tsp (50 g) clarified butter, divided

2½ cups (300 g) carrots, shredded

½ cup (100 g) granulated sugar

⅓ cup + 1½ tsp (90 g) milk

Pinch of cardamom powder

¼ cup + 2 tsp (70 g) heavy cream

Pinch of sea salt

Zest of 1 orange

½ tsp saffron

1 tbsp (10 g) raisins

1 tbsp (10 g) cashews

Pumpkin Purée

2 cups (300 g) pumpkin

1½ tbsp (20 g) olive oil

2 tbsp (30 g) butter

Pumpkin Pie Brûlée

1¼ cups (300 g) heavy cream

⅛ cup + 1 tbsp + 2 tsp (50 g) brown sugar

¼ tsp ground nutmeg

⅓ tsp ground cinnamon

¼ tsp ground ginger

⅓ tsp sea salt

1 cup (250 g) pumpkin purée

6 egg yolks

¾ tsp cornstarch

Brown sugar, for brûléed garnish

Microgreens, for garnish (optional)

For the Pie Dough. In a stand mixer with a paddle attachment, kick things off by mixing the butter with the salt, icing sugar and almond flour. Gradually add in the egg a little at a time until fully incorporated. Follow that by folding in the all-purpose flour, mixing it until you get a smooth dough. Place this between two sheets of baking paper and flatten it slightly before resting in the refrigerator for 1 hour.

Grease the rings with extra butter and place them on a tray lined with baking paper. Roll the dough out into a sheet ⅛ inch (3 mm) thick, and cut out 6 (4-inch [10-cm]) discs of dough for the base of the pies. Place a disc inside each greased ring and press it gently, starting from the bottom and working your way up the sides. If the edges are above the rim, carefully trim them with a small knife, then pop them in the refrigerator for 1 hour. Preheat the oven at 320°F (160°C) and bake the crusts for 20 to 25 minutes, until they turn golden brown.

For the Carrot Halwa. Heat 2 tablespoons (30 g) of clarified butter in a saucepan, then add in the shredded carrots and cook over medium heat for 20 minutes, mixing continuously until the carrots are tender. Now add in the granulated sugar, milk and cardamom to get some interesting flavors going. As the mixture reduces, add in the cream and continue to cook for 5 minutes to get a thick, creamy consistency. Turn off the heat, and add in the salt, orange zest and saffron to give it some delicate aromas.

(continued)

CARROT CONFIT
PUMPKIN PIE *(continued)*

In another saucepan, heat the remaining 4½ teaspoons (20 g) of clarified butter and just before it begins to boil, add in the raisins and cashews. Sauté them until the mixture turns golden brown and starts giving off a stunning fragrance. Then drop these sautéed raisins and cashews into the carrot halwa, and reserve it in the refrigerator until we're ready to assemble.

For the Pumpkin Purée. Preheat the oven to 356°F (180°C). Peel and dice the pumpkin, making sure to scoop out the unnecessary seeds and strings. On a tray lined with baking paper, lay the pumpkin pieces out and drizzle the olive oil over them. Roast about an hour; you'll know it's done when the pumpkin has turned really soft and tender. Let the pumpkin cool a bit at room temperature.

Meanwhile, let's make some brown butter: Place the butter in a saucepan over medium heat until it begins to boil, turns brown and releases a nutty aroma. Turn off the heat and let the butter cool to room temperature. In a food processor, place the brown butter and roasted pumpkin and run them together to get a beautiful, thick pumpkin purée.

For the Pumpkin Pie Brûlée. Preheat the oven to 320°F (160°C). In a saucepan, start heating the cream, brown sugar, nutmeg, cinnamon, ginger and salt, bringing the mixture to a boil before adding in the pumpkin purée. In a separate bowl, mix the egg yolks and cornstarch, and pour one-third of the warmed pumpkin cream into the egg mixture to help temper the eggs. Pour this yolk-cream mixture back into the saucepan with the rest of the pumpkin cream, and with a hand blender, blend everything together into a smooth mixture, then strain it to get rid of any lingering lumps.

Pour the mixture into 3-inch (7.5-cm) disc silicon molds to form ½-inch (1.3-cm) layers. Place the mold in a tray filled with hot water, and put the tray in the oven for 35 minutes, until a gentle shake of the tray shows the custard is well set. After the pumpkin pie discs have baked, allow them to cool for 15 minutes and then put them in the freezer for 1 hour to set.

Note from the Chefs:

Silicon molds are useful in adding clean, interesting shapes to your desserts, but if you prefer to keep things classic, feel free to use a greased tin of an appropriate size and shape.

Time for assembly. Take each fully-baked pie crust and fill it up all the way with the carrot halwa, before placing the baked pumpkin pie on top. Sprinkle some brown sugar over the top, and blow-torch carefully to create that iconic caramelized surface. To make these treats look even more impressive, decorate them with a ring of microgreens for that extra pop of color.

This delicate and unique pie is best eaten immediately when all those textures are just right. You can store them in the refrigerator for up to 2 days.

CRUNCHY POTATO CHIP TART

Yield: 8 tarts
Mold: 2½-inch (6-cm) ring

It's hard to overstate how much we love chips—we're positively obsessed. They are eaten before meals, after meals, during meals, at tea-time, in the middle of the night and especially with a cold beer on a humid evening in Bangalore. Andrés used to make homemade potato chips as part of his plated desserts, but now they've come alive in this wild, crunchy, chocolate tart. No matter how hard Vinesh tries to stick to a low-calorie diet, as soon as these potato chips turn up, the mere idea of moderate consumption goes straight out the window. This is the perfect tart for an evening of indulgence.

Chocolate Tart Dough

½ cup (120 g) butter, plus more for greasing rings, at room temperature

½ cup (60 g) icing sugar

Pinch of sea salt

⅛ cup (30 g) milk

1¾ cups + 1 tbsp + 1 tsp (230 g) all-purpose flour

⅛ cup + 1 tbsp + 2 tsp (20 g) cocoa powder

Chewy Vanilla Caramel

½ cup + 2 tbsp (150 g) heavy cream

⅛ cup + 2 tsp (40 g) milk

1 vanilla bean pod (see Quick Reference Notes, page 219)

⅓ cup + 1 tsp (115 g) corn syrup, divided

Pinch of sea salt

⅓ cup + 2 tsp (75 g) granulated sugar

3½ tbsp (52 g) butter, at room temperature

Dark Chocolate Ganache

¾ cup + 1½ tsp (188 g) heavy cream

1¼ cups (165 g) dark chocolate, chopped

1 tbsp (18 g) invert sugar

¼ cup (68 g) butter

Chaat Masala Potato Chips

½ lb (250 g) baby potatoes

2 pints (1 L) vegetable oil

2 tsp (5 g) sea salt

2 tsp (5 g) chaat masala

For the Chocolate Tart Dough. Starting off in a stand mixer with a paddle attachment, mix together the butter, icing sugar and salt until combined. Now gradually add in the milk, and gently fold in the flour and cocoa powder, bringing it all together. The dough should be placed between two sheets of baking paper and flattened slightly before resting in the refrigerator for 1 hour.

Grease the 2½-inch (6-cm) rings with extra butter and place them on a tray lined with baking paper. Roll the dough out into a sheet ⅛ inch (3 mm) thick, and cut out 8 (4-inch [10-cm]) discs of dough for the base of the tart. Place a disc inside each greased ring and press gently starting from the bottom and working your way up the sides. If the edges are above the rim, carefully trim them with a small knife. Freeze these for an hour. Preheat the oven at 320°F (160°C) and bake them for 20 to 25 minutes, until they turn a nice, deep brown.

For the Chewy Vanilla Caramel. In a saucepan, add the cream, milk, vanilla, 2 tablespoons (40 g) of corn syrup and salt. Mix over medium heat until it's nice and warm. In another saucepan, heat the granulated sugar along with the remaining 3 tablespoons + 2 teaspoons (75 g) of corn syrup until it starts to caramelize and take on a deep amber color. Pour the warmed cream mixture into the caramel to help deglaze, and continue to cook the mixture until it reaches 225°F (107°C). That's when you turn off the heat and let it cool for 10 minutes. Finish things off by mixing in the butter using a hand blender, then strain the caramel and reserve it for later.

(continued)

For the Dark Chocolate Ganache. In a saucepan over medium heat, bring the cream to a simmer. Add the dark chocolate to a heatproof bowl. Pour the cream into the chocolate bowl, allowing it to melt with the heat. Let the creamy chocolate cool to room temperature before incorporating the invert sugar and butter and using a hand blender to bring it all together to form a perfectly smooth ganache.

Note from the Chefs:

Making your own potato chips is easier than it sounds, and also super fun. But if you want to focus on the goodies inside, then grab your favorite pack of crunchy salted chips and continue with the recipe. Just make sure you don't eat them all before you decorate the tart.

For the Chaat Masala Potato Chips. Slice the baby potatoes with a mandoline and lay the slices between a set of tissues for 15 minutes to help absorb the excess moisture. We want them to be light and crispy, and too much water content is going to prevent that.

Now for the fun part, actually frying those chips! Start heating the vegetable oil in a pan, making sure the oil reaches about 347°F (175°C) before adding in the potato slices. Gently fry the potatoes until they look golden and crispy, 5 to 8 minutes, and then put them in a mixing bowl and toss them in a mixture of salt and chaat masala, evenly coating the chips with these spices.

Time for assembly. Spread a generous layer of the chewy vanilla caramel into each of the baked tart shells until they're about half full. Follow that by filling dark chocolate ganache right to the top. You can use a palette knife to flatten the ganache and get a nice smooth surface on which to arrange the fried potato chips. Place them one by one to form an impressive rose pattern, starting from the inside and working your way out. This crispy crown is going to give your tart that unforgettable texture.

You can store the individual ingredients in the refrigerator for up to 2 days, but once these tarts are assembled, you'll want to eat them right away so those chips have the perfect crunch.

RASPBERRY GÂTEAU BASQUE

Yield: 1 cake
Mold: 6-inch (15¼-cm) ring, with 1½-inch (3.8-cm) height

You don't have to be an expert on pastry to know that a lot of it comes from France. Treats like the croissant and the soufflé have become staples in bakeries and homes across the world, but we think there are some underrated gems that deserve more of the limelight . . . which brings us to our version of the Gâteau Basque, a perfectly buttery, crumbly pie dough, stuffed with pastry cream. We've decided to take things further with a sweet and tangy raspberry jelly inside. It's among the most comforting things you can sink your teeth into.

Basque Dough

¾ cup + 1 tbsp + 1 tsp (50 g) almond flour

1 cup + 1 tbsp + 1 tsp (135 g) all-purpose flour

⅛ tsp baking powder

½ cup (105 g) butter, at room temperature

⅓ cup + 2 tsp (75 g) granulated sugar

Pinch of sea salt

Zest of 1 lemon

2 egg yolks

Pastry Cream

3 egg yolks

2 tbsp (15 g) cornstarch

3 tbsp + 1 tsp (40 g) granulated sugar, divided

⅔ cup + 2½ tsp (175 g) whole milk

½ vanilla bean pod (see Quick Reference Notes, page 219)

Raspberry Jelly

1 cup (110 g) raspberries

Pinch of sea salt

¼ cup (50 g) granulated sugar, divided

1 tsp pectin NH

½ tsp lemon juice

Butter, at room temperature, for greasing rings

Egg Wash

2 egg yolks

2 tsp (10 g) heavy cream

Pinch of sea salt

Icing sugar, for garnish

For the Basque Dough. Sift the almond flour, all-purpose flour and baking powder into a medium bowl. Using a stand mixer with a paddle attachment, start by combining the butter, granulated sugar, salt and lemon zest until it's evenly mixed. Gradually add in the egg yolks a little at a time, followed by the sifted dry ingredients. Mix it all together to get a nice dough, then place the dough between two sheets of baking paper and roll it out into sheets ¼ inch (6 mm) thick. Rest the sheet of dough in the refrigerator overnight.

For the Pastry Cream. Take the egg yolks, cornstarch and 1 tablespoon + 2 teaspoons (20 g) of granulated sugar together in a mixing bowl. Mix them well to form a paste and set it aside for a bit. Now, in a saucepan, heat the milk, vanilla and the remaining 1 tablespoon + 2 teaspoons (20 g) of granulated sugar until it's nice and warm, then pour one-third of it into the yolk mixture, while stirring continuously to help temper the egg yolks. Strain this mixture back into the saucepan containing the milk, and cook until it begins to boil. Once it's turned nice and thick, in about 30 seconds, turn off the heat, wrap it with cling film, and set it aside in the refrigerator until assembly.

For the Raspberry Jelly. Drop the raspberries in a saucepan with salt and ⅛ cup (25 g) of granulated sugar, and start to cook them over medium heat. Once the mixture is warm, add in the pectin and remaining ⅛ cup (25 g) of granulated sugar, and let it boil for a good 2 minutes. Then mix in the lemon juice and turn off the heat, allowing it to cool. Pour the cooked raspberry mixture into a 5-inch (13-cm) ring forming a ½-inch (1.3-cm) layer of jelly, and leave it in the freezer for 2 hours to set.

(continued)

> ### Note from the Chefs:
>
> We use pectin NH to keep the jelly softer. In case you can't get your hands on it, even ordinary pectin that is used for jam-making will work just fine; you just might end up with a slightly thicker consistency for your jelly.

Time for assembly. Preheat the oven to 320°F (160°C). Grease the ring with butter and place it on a tray lined with baking paper. Cut out a 9-inch (23-cm) disc of dough to serve as the base of our pie. Place the disc in the center of the ring and press gently, starting from the center of the base and working your way up the sides. If the edges are above the rim, carefully trim them with a small knife. Now use a palette knife to spread a layer of delicious pastry cream into the pie. Place the disc of raspberry jelly on top, and then follow it with a second layer of pastry cream to fill it up. Cut out a 6-inch (15¼-cm) disc from the remaining basque dough to cover the top of the pie—place it over the filling and gently seal the edges of the dough together.

Finally, in a small bowl mix the egg yolks, cream and salt for the egg wash, and brush it gently over the surfaces of the dough to give it a nice shine. Pick up a small knife and make some decorative slashes on the top surface to give it a distinctive look. Pop it into the oven for 40 minutes, until it turns a delicious golden brown, and finish it off with a handsome dusting of icing sugar.

This comforting, traditional pie is best served straight out of the oven, obviously. You can store it in the refrigerator for up to 3 days.

RICE PUDDING BABA TART

Yield: 8 tarts
Mold: 2.5-inch (6-cm) ring

One of the joys of having a friend visit your country is being able to introduce them to all the foods you grew up with. On Andrés' first visit to India, Vinesh took him around to the local traditional sweet vendors. These are tiny shops with dozens of trays lined with countless sweets and confections—honestly the hardest part is just deciding what to eat. But once the gulaab jamun came out, Andrés instantly fell in love with the soft, fried dough soaked in an aromatic rose syrup. It immediately reminded him of the classic baba doughs of France, so we found a way to honor the jamun in our own cafe-style tart that's filled with rice pudding and topped with baked, soaked baba.

Coconut Rice Pudding

½ cup (105 g) arborio rice

2½ cups (600 g) whole milk

½ vanilla bean pod (see Quick Reference Notes, page 219)

½ cup (112 g) coconut milk

½ cup (100 g) jaggery

Zest of 1 lime

Pinch of sea salt

½ tsp ground cardamom

½ tsp ground cinnamon

Baba Dough

½ cup + 2 tsp (75 g) bread flour

1 tbsp + 2¼ tsp (25 g) butter, at room temperature

¾ tsp granulated sugar

¼ tsp sea salt

1 tsp instant dry yeast

2 eggs, whole

Spiced Rose Syrup

¾ cup + 1½ tbsp (200 g) water

½ cup (100 g) granulated sugar

2 pieces whole cardamom

2 pieces cinnamon bark

2 pieces whole cloves

1½ tbsp (20 g) rose water

Pistachio powder, for garnish
Rose petals, for garnish

Coconut Ganache

¾ cup (180 g) coconut cream, divided

2 tsp (14 g) corn syrup

2½ tsp (14 g) invert sugar

⅞ cup (150 g) white chocolate

4 tsp (20 g) coconut rum (We recommend Malibu®)

1 cup + 2 tsp (250 g) heavy cream

Pinch of sea salt

Tart Dough

½ cup (120 g) butter, plus more for greasing rings, at room temperature

Pinch of sea salt

¾ cup (90 g) icing sugar

1 egg

1¾ cups + 1 tbsp + 1 tsp (230 g) all-purpose flour

½ cup (30 g) almond flour

For the Coconut Ganache. In a saucepan, heat 6 tablespoons (90 g) of coconut cream, the corn syrup and the invert sugar until the mixture is nice and warm. Then pour it out into a narrow container with the white chocolate, and emulsify well using a hand blender. Add in the last 6 tablespoons (90 g) of coconut cream along with the coconut rum, cream and salt, and continue to blend into a smooth ganache. Wrap in cling film and keep this in the refrigerator overnight for it to set perfectly.

For the Tart Dough. In a stand mixer with a paddle attachment, start by mixing the butter with salt and icing sugar. Gradually add in the egg a little at a time, making sure it's well combined. Next, fold in the all-purpose flour and almond flour, and gently mix everything into a nice dough. Place this between two sheets of baking paper and flatten slightly, before resting the dough in the refrigerator for 1 hour.

(continued)

RICE PUDDING BABA TART *(continued)*

Grease 8 rings with extra butter and place them on a tray lined with baking paper. If you don't have 8 rings you can bake these in batches. Roll the dough out into a sheet ⅛ inch (3 mm) thick, and cut out 8 (4-inch [10-cm]) discs of dough for the base of the tart. Place a disc inside each greased ring and press gently, starting from the bottom and working your way up the sides. If the edges are above the rim, carefully trim them with a small knife, then pop these in the refrigerator for 1 hour. Preheat the oven at 320°F (160°C) and bake for 20 to 25 minutes, until they turn a delicious golden brown.

For the Coconut Rice Pudding. Start by blanching the rice: Take a bowl of water with about a teaspoon of salt dissolved in it, and submerge the rice into it, washing the grains and removing the starch until the water turns a pale white. Then pour out the starch water and add in fresh salt water, repeating the process a total of 3 times.

Now that the rice is ready, add it to a saucepan along with the whole milk and vanilla, and cook it until the mixture starts to turn thick and creamy. Once it's done, turn off the heat and mix in the coconut milk and jaggery, then season the pudding with the lime zest, salt, cardamom and cinnamon to give it a warm, spiced flavor. Mix so everything combines well, and set it aside for later.

For the Baba Dough. Preheat the oven to 338°F (170°C). In a stand mixer with a paddle attachment, take the flour, butter, granulated sugar, salt and yeast and combine evenly. Add in the eggs a little at a time while mixing continuously, combining the ingredients into a thick, elastic dough. Once

the dough is ready, it's time to fill it into 8 (1-oz [30-ml]) spherical molds. If you don't have 8 molds you can bake in batches. Fill them about halfway, then let them proof at room temperature for 15 minutes, until the dough has risen to just below the surface of the mold. Pop them in the oven for 15 minutes, until golden brown. After baking, allow them to cool and demold; you may notice some excess on the top of each sphere, which can be trimmed with a small knife to get a beautiful, rounded shape.

For the Spiced Rose Syrup. Make sure that everything else is ready for assembly before we start soaking the babas in the spiced rose syrup. Never keep soaked babas lying around! Start by heating the water and granulated sugar in a saucepan along with the cardamom, cinnamon and cloves. Let it boil for a couple of minutes to let the spice flavors open up, then add in the rose water. Turn off the heat and pour it into a small but slightly deep container, and pop those freshly baked babas in so they're completely submerged in the rose syrup. Leave them to soak for about 20 minutes so they're nice and juicy.

Time for assembly. Bring those baked tart shells out, and fill them completely with a generous helping of rice pudding. Whip the coconut ganache in a stand mixer with a whisk attachment until it's nice and fluffy, and using a piping bag with a large, round tip nozzle, form a neat dome of ganache over each tart. Finally, take a soaked baba and carefully place it right on top, with a sprinkling of pistachio powder and rose petals to finish the look.

These incredible India-inspired tarts are best served chilled. You can store them in the refrigerator for up to 2 days.

PEPPERCORN HAZELNUT TART

Yield: 4 tarts
Mold: 2.5-inch (6-cm) ring

If you haven't been to China yet, you probably haven't been privy to all the mind-bending ways in which peppers can be used. The moment you taste an amazing quality sichuan pepper, you realize it's not just about being hot or spicy, it's so much more complex. This exotic Eastern tart manages to pair the lingering aroma of a sichuan-hazelnut ganache with the sweet, fruity notes of a jasmine-infused strawberry jelly.

Gluten-Free Flour Mix

¼ cup (35 g) brown millet flour

2½ tbsp (20 g) tapioca flour

2½ tbsp (20 g) brown rice flour

¼ tsp xanthan gum

Gluten-Free Tart Dough

3½ tbsp (50 g) butter, plus more for greasing rings, at room temperature

1 tbsp + 2 tsp (20 g) granulated sugar

1 tbsp + 1 tsp (10 g) icing sugar

⅔ cup (40 g) almond flour

Pinch of sea salt

¼ vanilla bean pod (see Quick Reference Notes, page 219)

⅔ cup (75 g) gluten-free flour mix

1 egg yolk

Strawberry Crunch

⅛ cup + 1 tsp (25 g) white chocolate, melted

⅛ cup + 1 tbsp (50 g) 100% almond paste

1 tbsp + ¼ tsp (15 g) butter, at room temperature

1 cup (25 g) freeze-dried strawberries

Pinch of sea salt

Zest of 1 lime

Strawberry Jelly

¾ tsp gelatin

2½ tsp (12 g) cold water

½ cup (125 g) strawberry purée

2 tsp (10 g) jasmine tea

½ tsp pectin NH

1 tbsp + 2 tsp (20 g) granulated sugar

½ tsp lemon juice

Hazelnut Ganache

½ tsp gelatin

1¾ tsp (9 g) cold water

¾ cup + 2 tsp (190 g) heavy cream

½ tsp sichuan pepper

Zest of 1 lemon

¼ cup (40 g) caramelized white chocolate (see Quick Reference Notes, page 218)

⅛ cup (35 g) 100% hazelnut paste

Tempered white chocolate, for garnish (see Quick Reference Notes, page 219)

Freeze-dried strawberries, for garnish

Hazelnuts, toasted and chopped, for garnish

Gold leaf, for garnish (optional)

For the Gluten-Free Flour Mix. Before we get down and dirty with the tart crust, mix the brown millet flour, tapioca flour, brown rice flour and xanthan gum together in a large bowl. Or you could use a food processor for an even easier mix.

For the Gluten-Free Tart Dough. In a stand mixer with a paddle attachment, start combining the butter with the granulated sugar, icing sugar, almond flour, salt, vanilla and of course, the gluten-free flour that we just made. Mix the ingredients well, then incorporate the egg yolk a little at a time until it comes together as a nice dough. Place this between two sheets of baking paper and flatten slightly before resting in the refrigerator for 1 hour.

Preheat the oven to 320°F (160°C). Grease the rings with the extra butter and place them on a tray lined with baking paper. Roll the dough out into a sheet ⅛ inch (3 mm) thick, and cut out 4 (4-inch [10-cm]) discs of dough for the base of the tart. Place the disc inside the greased ring and press gently, starting from the bottom and working your way up the sides. If the edges are above the rim, carefully trim them with a small knife, then pop these in the refrigerator for 1 hour. Bake for 20 to 25 minutes, until they turn golden brown.

(continued)

Note from the Chefs:

The strawberry crunch is a fat-based recipe, which means the crunchy stuff we put inside (the freeze-dried strawberries) will maintain its crispy texture and not get soggy because there isn't any water present!

For the Strawberry Crunch. In a mixing bowl, add the melted white chocolate, almond paste and butter, mixing it all together well. Drop in the strawberries, salt and lime zest, and stir to combine. Reserve this fruity mixture at room temperature until we're ready for assembly.

For the Strawberry Jelly. In a small bowl, add the gelatin and water, letting the gelatin bloom for 5 minutes, until it swells. Now, in a saucepan, heat the strawberry purée until it starts to boil, then add in the jasmine tea. Turn off the heat and let the mixture infuse for 2 hours to really absorb those jasmine aromas. Then strain the purée and start heating it again. Once it's nice and warm, add in the pectin and granulated sugar, and continue to boil for about a minute. Add in the lemon juice and the bloomed gelatin and stir the mixture well. Pour it out into a dome-shape mold and freeze for an hour to set. If you can't get your hands on a dome mold, grab a 6-inch (15¼-cm) square cake frame, pour the gel into it and freeze to set, then use a cookie cutter to get nice round discs of jelly.

For the Hazelnut Ganache. Start this process by soaking the gelatin in ice cold water for 5 minutes. Now, in a saucepan, heat the cream until just before it starts to boil. Turn off the heat and add in the sichuan pepper and lemon zest, and let it infuse for an hour. Once infused, resume heating the cream to bring it to a simmer, and mix in that bloomed gelatin, stirring to make sure it dissolves completely. In a large bowl, combine the white chocolate and hazelnut paste, and pour the hot cream through a strainer over the chocolate to help it melt. Use a hand blender to mix it all into an even emulsion, and store in the refrigerator for 6 hours so it sets well.

For the garnish. We've used white chocolate sticks as an elegant decoration. If you'd like to do the same, just spread tempered white chocolate on an acetate sheet and allow it to cool. While the chocolate is still semi-set, use a knife and metal ruler to cut it into some straight, thin sticks.

Time for assembly. Now that all the components are ready, let's put these amazing tarts together! Heat the strawberry crunch slightly before layering it onto the base and inner walls of each tart shell. Put these in the refrigerator for 15 minutes to set. Now, in a stand mixer with a paddle attachment, whip the hazelnut ganache to bring it to a light and airy consistency. Use a piping bag to pipe whipped ganache into the tart shells until they're about three-fourths full. Place a disc of strawberry jelly inside, and continue to pipe a stunning double rosette of ganache over it. We used a star nozzle on the piping bag to achieve that lovely, elegant look. Finally, garnish with white chocolate sticks, freeze-dried strawberries, a sprinkling of toasted, chopped hazelnuts and a touch of gold leaf, if desired.

Serve up these classy tarts chilled. They're just as stunning to look at as they are to eat. You can store these in the refrigerator for up to 2 days.

SUMMER LEMON MASCARPONE TART

Yield: 2 tarts
Mold: 6-inch (15¼-cm) tin

Mascarpone seems to get all its fame and reputation from the Italian tiramisu. And while we love that layered dessert as much as anyone, we're glad to have found countless other ways in which the ultra-rich soft cheese can be used. Take this tart, for example. Sure, it has the makings of greatness with the wild lemon cream filling and the hazelnut crunch subtly layered into the crust, but really, it's the decorative mascarpone crown that completes the picture—both for your eyes and for your salivating mouth.

Tart Dough

½ cup (120 g) butter, plus more for greasing rings, at room temperature

¼ tsp sea salt

¾ cup (90 g) icing sugar

½ cup (30 g) almond flour

1 egg

1⅞ cups (235 g) all-purpose flour

Meringue

1 egg white

⅛ cup (40 g) corn syrup

Pinch of cream of tartar

Vanilla Mascarpone Cream

⅓ tbsp (2.5 g) gelatin

1 tbsp (15 g) cold water

⅜ cup + 2½ tsp (105 g) milk

1 tbsp + 2½ tsp (38 g) corn syrup

½ vanilla bean pod (see Quick Reference Notes, page 219)

2 egg yolks

½ cup (128 g) mascarpone cheese

½ cup (65 g) meringue

Almond Sponge

⅓ cup (65 g) granulated sugar, divided

2 eggs, separated

1 tbsp + 1 tsp (20 g) milk

⅔ tsp vanilla extract

1 tbsp + 1 tsp (10 g) all-purpose flour, sifted

1¼ cups (75 g) almond flour

1 tbsp + 2¼ tsp (25 g) butter, melted

Zest of 1 lemon

Lemon Cream

⅓ tbsp (2.5 g) gelatin

1 tbsp (15 g) cold water

¼ cup + 1 tsp (65 g) lemon juice

⅓ cup + 1 tsp (70 g) granulated sugar, divided

2 eggs, whole

Zest of 1 lemon

¼ cup + 2¾ tsp (70 g) butter

Hazelnut Crunch

½ cup (55 g) pie crust, baked

½ cup (70 g) whole hazelnuts, roasted (see Quick Reference Notes, page 219)

¼ cup + 1 tsp (50 g) milk chocolate, melted

⅞ cup (25 g) crispy rice cereal (We recommend Rice Krispies®)

Pinch of sea salt

Raspberries, for garnish

Lemon zest, for garnish

Microgreens, for garnish

For the Tart Dough. In a stand mixer with a paddle attachment, start off by mixing the butter with salt, icing sugar and almond flour. Gradually add in the egg a little at a time until it's fully incorporated. Fold in the all-purpose flour and combine everything together to get a nice dough. Place the dough between two sheets of baking paper and flatten slightly before resting it in the refrigerator for 1 hour.

Preheat the oven to 320°F (160°C). Grease the rings with the extra butter and place them on a tray lined with baking paper. Roll the dough out into a sheet ⅛ inch (3 mm) thick, and cut out 2 (4-inch [10-cm]) discs of dough. To line the rings, place a disc inside and press gently, starting from the base and working your way up the sides. If the edges are above the rim, carefully trim them with a small knife, then pop it in the refrigerator for 1 hour. Bake 20 to 25 minutes, until they turn golden brown. You'll also have some leftover trimmings of dough, which should be refrigerated and baked in the same way. Keep these baked crust trimmings to use in the hazelnut crunch.

(continued)

For the Meringue. Warm the egg white, corn syrup and cream of tartar over a double-boiler. Once it reaches 162°F (72°C), stop the heat and let the mixture cool to room temperature. Transfer it to a stand mixer with a whisk attachment, and whip until it forms a meringue with medium peaks. Measure out ½ cup (65 g) of meringue to use in the vanilla mascarpone cream.

For the Vanilla Mascarpone Cream. First, in a small bowl, add the gelatin and water, letting the gelatin bloom for 5 minutes, until it absorbs the water and swells. Make a crème anglaise in a saucepan by warming the milk, corn syrup and vanilla. In a separate dish, add the egg yolks and then add in about one-third of the heated milk mixture to help temper the yolks. Pour the tempered eggs back into the first saucepan, and heat until it reaches 180°F (82°C). Turn off the heat and add in the bloomed gelatin, stirring until it's completely dissolved. Let this mixture cool before folding in the mascarpone cheese, followed by the meringue. Finally, cast it into a decorative mold like we've done, or a 6-inch (15¼-cm) cake ring, and freeze for 4 hours to set perfectly.

For the Almond Sponge. Preheat the oven to 320°F (160°C) and line a 9 x 9–inch (23 x 23–cm) tray with baking paper. In a stand mixer with a whisk attachment, add 2 tablespoons + 2 teaspoons (32.5 g) of granulated sugar, the egg yolks, milk and vanilla extract, and whip them together until it reaches a nice ribbon consistency. Now fit a fresh whisk and bowl to the stand mixer, and whip the egg whites and the remaining 2 tablespoons + 2 teaspoons (32.5 g) of granulated sugar. Once you get a light meringue with medium peaks, use a spatula to gently fold it into the whipped yolk mixture, bringing it all together. Then mix in the all-purpose flour, almond flour, butter and lemon zest. Spread this batter out into the prepared tray and bake 15 to 20 minutes. We're looking to get a beautiful, thin sponge that's soft and springy to touch.

For the Lemon Cream. To begin with, in a small bowl add the gelatin and water, letting the gelatin bloom for five minutes, until it swells. In a saucepan, heat the lemon juice and 2 tablespoons + 2½ teaspoons (35 g) of granulated sugar until it's nice and warm. Combine the eggs, lemon zest and the remaining 2 tablespoons + 2½ teaspoons (35 g) of granulated sugar in a separate dish, and pour one-third of the heated lemon juice in to help temper the eggs. Then pour this mix back into the first saucepan with the remaining lemon juice, and bring the whole mixture to a boil. Turn off the heat and add in the bloomed gelatin, stirring well and allowing it to cool. Mix in the butter, and use a hand blender to get a gorgeous, smooth lemon cream. Store the cream in the refrigerator until assembly.

For the Hazelnut Crunch. Grab the baked crust trimmings and crush them to a chunky crumble. Make a 100 percent hazelnut paste by blending the roasted hazelnuts into a paste. In a mixing bowl, add the milk chocolate, hazelnut paste, crispy rice cereal, crumbled pie crusts and salt. Mix all these amazing textures together.

Time for assembly. In the fully baked tart shells, first spread an even layer of hazelnut crunch, then cut out a disc of almond sponge slightly smaller than the tart and cozily fit that inside. Next fill the tart all the way up with lemon cream and use a palette knife to help flatten the top of the cream to a neat surface. Carefully demold the disc of mascarpone cream, and place it on top of the tart. At the very end, finish off with fresh raspberries, lemon zest and some microgreens to complete the look.

These elaborate tarts are going to be super tasty when served up chilled and fresh. You can store them in the refrigerator for up to 2 days.

STRAWBERRY CHEESE RHUBARB PIE

Yield: 2 pies
Mold: 6-inch (15¼-cm) ring with 1½-inch (3.8-cm) height

Rhubarb pie is one of those timeless classics, and each generation creates their own interpretation. The titular leaf stalk gives its iconic red color and blend of sharp, tangy and sweet flavors to the filling, while the cheesecake cream, lightened by a soft meringue, forms a blanket across this layered and comforting pie. We've decided to give this pie some additional textures to make each bite more interesting with crispy rice cereal chocolate crunch and almond sponge, while the fresh strawberries and crumble help add that extra punch.

Pie Dough

½ cup (120 g) butter, plus more for greasing rings, at room temperature

¼ tsp sea salt

¾ cup (90 g) icing sugar

½ cup (30 g) almond flour

1 egg

1⅞ cups (235 g) all-purpose flour

Chocolate Crunch

¾ cup (100 g) pie crust, baked

1 tbsp + ¼ tsp (15 g) butter, melted

¼ vanilla bean pod (see Quick Reference Notes, page 218)

2 tsp (8 g) brown sugar

⅔ cup + 2 tsp (20 g) crispy rice cereal (We recommend Rice Krispies)

3 tbsp + 1 tsp (35 g) white chocolate, melted

Almond Sponge

⅓ cup (65 g) granulated sugar, divided

2 egg yolks

1 tbsp + 1 tsp (20 g) milk

⅔ tsp vanilla extract

2 egg whites

1 tbsp + 1 tsp (10 g) all-purpose flour, sifted

1¼ cups (75 g) almond flour

1 tbsp + 2¼ tsp (25 g) butter, melted

Zest of 1 lemon

Rhubarb Compote

1 cup (125 g) rhubarb

2 tbsp + 2½ tsp (35 g) granulated sugar, divided

¼ tsp pectin

1 tsp lemon juice

Pastry Cream

1 egg yolk

1 tbsp (8 g) cornstarch

1 tbsp + 2 tsp (20 g) granulated sugar, divided

⅜ cup (95 g) whole milk

¼ vanilla bean pod (see Quick Reference Notes, page 219)

Meringue

2 egg whites

¼ cup (80 g) corn syrup

Pinch of cream of tartar

Cheesecake Cream

⅝ cup (150 g) cream cheese

½ cup (130 g) pastry cream

⅔ cup (90 g) meringue

Zest of 1 lemon

Crumble

3½ tbsp (50 g) butter, cold

1 tbsp + 2 tsp (20 g) granulated sugar

⅜ cup + 1 tbsp (55 g) all-purpose flour

Zest of 2 lemons

Fresh strawberries, for garnish

Orange zest, for garnish

For the Pie Dough. Starting things off in a stand mixer with a paddle attachment, mix the butter with salt, icing sugar and almond flour. Gradually add in the egg a little at a time, mixing until everything is fully incorporated. Follow that by folding in the all-purpose flour, and combine gently into a nice dough. Place this between two sheets of baking paper and flatten slightly before resting in the refrigerator for 1 hour.

Preheat the oven to 320°F (160°C). Grease the rings with butter and place them on a tray lined with baking paper. Roll the dough out into a sheet ⅛ inch (3 mm) thick, and cut out 9-inch (23-cm) discs of dough. To line the rings, place a disc inside and press gently, starting from the base and working your way up the sides. If the edges are above the rim, carefully trim them with a small knife, then pop it in the refrigerator for 1 hour. Bake for 20 to 25 minutes, until they turn golden brown. You'll also have some leftover trimmings of dough, which should be refrigerated and baked in the same way. Keep these baked crust trimmings aside to use in the chocolate crunch.

(continued)

For the Chocolate Crunch. In a food processor, pulse the baked pie dough trimmings to a crumbly consistency, then add in the melted butter and continue to mix. Transfer it to a bowl. Add the vanilla seeds to the pie dough–butter mixture, and then add in the brown sugar and crispy rice cereal. Finally add in the melted white chocolate to bring this delicious crunch together.

For the Almond Sponge. Preheat the oven to 320°F (160°C) and line 2 (5-inch [13-cm]) circular tins with baking paper. In a stand mixer with a whisk attachment, add 2 tablespoons + 2 teaspoons (32.5 g) of granulated sugar, along with the egg yolks, milk and vanilla extract, and whip them together until it reaches a nice ribbon consistency. Now fit a fresh whisk and bowl to the stand mixer, and whip the egg whites with the remaining 2 tablespoons + 2 teaspoons (32.5 g) of granulated sugar. Once you get a light meringue with medium peaks, use a spatula to gently fold it into the whipped yolks mixture, bringing it all together. Then mix in the all-purpose flour, almond flour, melted butter and lemon zest. Spread this batter out into the prepared tray and bake for 15 to 20 minutes. We're looking to get a beautiful, thin sponge that's soft and springy to touch.

For the Rhubarb Compote. First chop up the rhubarb into small ½-inch (1.3-cm) chunks, and begin to heat it with 1 tablespoon + 1¼ teaspoons (17.5 g) of granulated sugar in a saucepan to about 104°F (40°C). Combine the remaining 1 tablespoon + 1¼ teaspoons (17.5 g) of granulated sugar and pectin together, and then mix them into the rhubarb, continuing to boil the mix until it thickens to take on a jam-like consistency. Turn off the heat, and add in the lemon juice to round out the flavors.

For the Pastry Cream. In a mixing bowl, take the egg yolk, cornstarch and 2½ teaspoons (10 g) of granulated sugar, and mix to form a paste. Then in a saucepan, heat the milk, vanilla and the remaining 2½ teaspoons (10 g) of granulated sugar until it's warm and fully dissolved. Pour one-third of the milk mix into the yolk mix while stirring to help temper the eggs. Strain that mixture back into the saucepan containing the rest of the milk, and cook until it begins to boil and thicken. Remove from the heat and set it aside in the refrigerator.

For the Meringue. Over a double-boiler, heat the egg whites, corn syrup and cream of tartar until it reaches 162°F (72°C). Stop the heat and let the mixture cool to room temperature. Transfer it over to a stand mixer using a whisk attachment and whip until it forms a meringue with medium peaks. Measure out ⅔ cup (90 g) of meringue for the cheesecake cream.

For the Cheesecake Cream. Mix the cream cheese in a stand mixer with a paddle attachment until it turns nice and smooth, then add in the pastry cream and whipped meringue, gently combining it all together. Mix in the lemon zest.

For the Crumble. In a food processor, add the cold butter along with the granulated sugar, flour and lemon zest, and blend until a crumble texture begins to form. Then freeze those chunks of crumble for 2 hours to get them firm. While the crumble is in the freezer, preheat the oven to 320°F (160°C). Bake the crumble for 15 to 20 minutes, until it's a delightful golden brown.

Time for assembly. In the fully baked tart shell, first spread a layer of chocolate crunch, then cut out a disc of almond sponge slightly smaller than the tart and cozily fit that inside. Spread some rhubarb compote all over the sponge, and pipe a generous layer of cheesecake cream over that. For the final touches, stack some fresh strawberries in the center surrounded by a circle of lemon crumble, and season it all with orange zest.

You can store this in the refrigerator for up to 2 days.

MANGO YOGURT PIE

Yield: 2 pies
Mold: 6-inch (15¼-cm) tart ring

Summers in India can be brutal. With temperatures reaching dizzying heights, there's a tendency for the foods people consume during the hottest months of the year to be incredibly refreshing. Goa, a state that finds itself on the majority of holiday itineraries in India, is known for its abundant mango season during summer, while the state of Punjab is known for lassi: the most OG creamy yogurt smoothie in the world. We decided to take both these legendary summer treats and put them together in one smashing beat-the-heat pie.

Pie Crust

⅝ cup + ¾ tsp (80 g) all-purpose flour

2½ tbsp (20 g) buckwheat flour

¼ cup (45 g) yellow corn flour

2 tbsp (15 g) cornstarch

¼ tsp sea salt

½ cup (115 g) butter, plus more for greasing rings, cold

⅓ cup + 1 tsp (70 g) granulated sugar

Mango Jelly

½ cup + 1 tbsp (135 g) mango purée

1 tbsp + 1 tsp (20 g) water

2 tsp (10 g) lime juice

2 tbsp (25 g) granulated sugar

2 tsp (4 g) gellan gum

Yogurt Filling

¾ cup (180 g) Greek yogurt, divided

2 tsp (5.5 g) cornstarch

2 eggs, whole

¼ cup (50 g) granulated sugar

½ tsp sea salt

1 tsp vanilla extract

1 tbsp + ¼ tsp (15 g) butter, melted

Zest of 1 lime

Mango, cubed, for garnish

Microgreens, for garnish

Gold leaf, for garnish

Honey, for garnish

Desiccated coconut, for garnish

For the Pie Crust. To a food processor, add the all-purpose flour, buckwheat flour, yellow corn flour, cornstarch, salt, butter and granulated sugar, and mix to get a nice crumble consistency. Now line the bottom of the rings with aluminum foil and grease the insides with butter. Sprinkle the pie crumble into the rings, filling them with a ⅛-inch (3-mm) layer. Gently press down to form an even pie crust. Rest them in the refrigerator for 2 hours. Preheat the oven at 320°F (160°C) and bake for 20 to 25 minutes, until they turn a lovely, deep brown.

For the Mango Jelly. Have the pie crusts in the rings, ready for filling. In a saucepan, combine the mango purée, water, lime juice, granulated sugar and gellan gum and whisk until everything is evenly combined. Heat the mix until it starts to boil for about 15 seconds, then cast it immediately into the rings over the pie crust. Pop these in the freezer for 2 hours for the jelly to set perfectly.

For the Yogurt Filling. Preheat the oven to 347°F (175°C). Portion out 3 tablespoons (45 g) of the yogurt, and mix it with the cornstarch. Then, in a separate bowl, mix together the eggs, granulated sugar, salt and vanilla extract, and add that into the yogurt-cornstarch mixture. Combine gently while gradually adding in the remaining ½ cup + 1 tablespoon (135 g) of yogurt, warm, melted butter and lime zest. Pour this lovely, tangy, creamy yogurt filling over the pie crusts to form a ½-inch (1.3-cm) layer, and pop them in the oven to bake for 15 to 20 minutes, until the top of the filling is well set.

Time for assembly. When you're ready to serve, grab the freshest, sweetest mangoes you can find and slice them into neat cubes to use as a fresh topping, along with some microgreens and gold leaf. Then to finish the look, brush the sides with honey and dust a delicate coating of desiccated coconut on the sides to get that textural look.

For the best flavor of fruit and yogurt, you'll want to serve these beautiful pies chilled. You can store this pie in the refrigerator for up to 2 days.

PECAN BUTTER TART

Yield: 2 tarts
Mold: 6-inch (15¼-cm) ring, with
1½-inch (3.8-cm) height

Easily one of the most quintessentially Canadian desserts you could ever lay your eyes on: the butter tart. Andrés spent only a few brief years in Canada, but the friendships made and the recipes learned will last a lifetime. This is a traditional tart recipe that we tried and loved, and then added our own madness by drowning all those pecans in a rich and decadent maple-butter syrup. Even just the nutty buttery aroma of a tart like this can give you goosebumps.

Tart Dough

¼ cup + 2¾ tsp (70 g) butter, cubed, plus more for greasing rings

3 tbsp + 2 tsp (45 g) granulated sugar

1 egg

1 tsp milk

1⅓ cups + 1 tsp (170 g) all-purpose flour

⅓ tsp baking powder

Pinch of sea salt

Maple Butter Filling

¼ cup + 2¾ tsp (70 g) butter

1 tbsp + 1½ tsp (40 g) honey

2 tbsp (40 g) maple syrup

⅔ cup (150 g) brown sugar

1 tbsp (12 g) vanilla extract

1 tbsp (12 g) sea salt

3 eggs

2 tbsp + 1 tsp (35 g) heavy cream

1½-2 cups (150-200 g) pecans

For the Tart Dough. Starting in a stand mixer with a paddle attachment, cream the butter along with the granulated sugar. Gradually add in the egg and milk a little at a time, and mix until it all comes together. Finally, fold in the flour, baking powder and salt, to get a lovely, smooth dough. Chill this dough in the refrigerator for about 2 hours.

Grease the rings with extra butter and place them on a tray lined with baking paper. Roll the dough out into a sheet about ¼ inch (6 mm) thick, and cut out 2 (4-inch [10-cm]) discs of dough so we get a nice heavy crust. To line the mold, place a disc inside the ring and press gently, starting from the base and working your way up the sides. If the edges are above the rim, carefully trim them with a small knife, then put these in the refrigerator for an hour. Preheat the oven at 338°F (170°C) and bake for 20 to 25 minutes, until they turn a light golden brown.

For the Maple Butter Filling. In a saucepan, melt the butter over medium heat, add in the honey and maple syrup, and stir. Then mix in the brown sugar until it's completely dissolved, followed by the vanilla extract and salt. Now place the eggs in a separate dish, and add in about one-third of the heated maple mixture to help temper the eggs. Then add the tempered eggs back into the first saucepan and mix to get an even consistency. Finally, add in the cream, mix and strain to get a beautiful, smooth sauce we can use as a filling.

Time for assembly. Preheat the oven to 320°F (160°C). Toast the pecans for 10 minutes, then turn the oven down to 248°F (120°C). Fill the tart crusts almost all the way to the top with the toasted pecans. Next, pour in the maple sugar sauce and allow it to coat the pecans evenly. Let it settle for a few minutes, and top up with more maple butter filling since we're feeling generous. Bake for 90 to 120 minutes, until the filling looks just about set. Finally to finish the look, use a circular stencil to dust icing sugar along the sides of this gorgeous tart.

These nutty, buttery tarts are going to give your taste buds something to remember. You can store them in an airtight container for up to 5 days.

NEXT-LEVEL
Travel Cakes

Let's make one thing clear: we love to travel. We've done a lot of trips both together as friends and individually for classes or projects, and with every new destination there's always the excitement that something new will be discovered—some dessert we hadn't heard of, or some flavor combination we hadn't yet considered. Whether it's the Mediterranean influence on the Vegan Banana Tahini Cake (page 47) or the tropical fruit in the Pistachio Pineapple Gourmandise (page 71), the experiences one has while traveling somehow always find their way back to the kitchen table.

But our love for travel isn't actually why these are called travel cakes. By avoiding too many perishable ingredients, these products will be easy to carry around to a classy high tea or on a family road trip. Basically, they travel well and last longer than other recipes in the book, often up to 5 days, though we've never been able to resist finishing them before that. This is a selection of our favorite travel cakes; we'll be using some traditional baking techniques but will try to take every product a notch higher with some yummy glazes and toppings. So put the kettle on and bring out the picnic basket—let's make some tasty travel cakes.

San Marc
Atitlan

On the road...

FAB BAG

"MY L

CHILDHOOD BANANA COCONUT CAKE

Yield: 2 cakes
Mold: 6 x 3 x 2-inch (15¼ x 7½ x 5-cm) loaf tin

We became pastry chefs as adults, but our flavor choices go back all the way to our childhoods. Since Vinesh is always reminiscing about the tender coconuts his mom used to prepare for him after school, and Andrés is always smiling thinking about the sweet baby bananas he'd eat every morning, we wanted to make a cake that would link our hometowns—all the way from Kerala to Colombia. So make yourself a cup of coffee, grab a slice of this beautiful teacake, and let hundreds of years of banana-coconut culture wash over you!

Banana Cake

1 cup (150 g) ripe bananas

1 egg

½ vanilla bean pod (see Quick Reference Notes, page 219)

½ cup + 1 tsp (115 g) brown sugar, divided

⅓ cup + 2 tsp (75 g) granulated sugar

⅜ cup + 1 tbsp + 1 tsp (100 g) grapeseed or olive oil

3 tbsp (40 g) buttermilk

⅝ cup + ¾ tsp (80 g) all-purpose flour, sifted

½ tsp baking soda

⅓ tsp sea salt

⅓ cup (35 g) grated fresh coconut

Manié butter, for greasing the tin (see Quick Reference Notes, page 218)

1¼ cups (150 g) cocoa nibs, for coating the tin

Caramel Cream

½ cup + 1 tbsp + 1 tsp (140 g) heavy cream, divided

1 tbsp + 1 tsp (10 g) cornstarch

¼ vanilla bean pod (see Quick Reference Notes, page 219)

3 tbsp + 2 tsp (45 g) granulated sugar

½ cup + 1½ tbsp (100 g) milk chocolate

¼ tsp sea salt

Hazelnut Praline Paste

1⅛ cups (150 g) whole hazelnuts

½ cup (100 g) granulated sugar

Hazelnut Glaze

2½ tbsp (25 g) milk chocolate

¼ cup + 1½ tsp (40 g) dark chocolate

1½ tbsp (25 g) cocoa butter, finely chopped

1 cup (250 g) hazelnut praline paste

Desiccated coconut, for garnish

For the Banana Cake. Preheat the oven to 302°F (150°C). Our first order of business is getting these bananas roasted perfectly. Roasting bananas in their own skin helps retain moisture and develop flavors, so we're going to put the unpeeled bananas in the oven for 20 to 30 minutes, until the peels turn black. Then cool 'em, peel 'em, mash 'em into a paste using a fork, and measure out the amount we need for the batter.

Now let's get the batter going. In a stand mixer with a whisk attachment, whip the egg, vanilla, ¼ cup + 2 teaspoons (65 g) of brown sugar and granulated sugar until it's light and airy. It should look like a thick ribbon falling from the whisk. Use a spatula to slowly mix in the oil and buttermilk, followed by the mashed bananas. After this, fold in the all-purpose flour, baking soda, salt and grated coconut to get a thick, textural batter with some gorgeous aromas.

(continued)

CHILDHOOD BANANA COCONUT CAKE *(continued)*

Preheat the oven to 320°F (160°C). Grease the loaf tins with manié butter and coat them with a mixture of the ground cocoa nibs and 3 tablespoons + 2 teaspoons (50 g) of brown sugar; this is going to give an incredible finish to our cake. Portion out the batter equally between the loaf tins so they're each about two-thirds full and bake them for 25 to 30 minutes. Use a cake tester to know if the baking is done, or use a probe thermometer to check when the cakes reach 203°F (95°C). After baking, let the cakes cool before flipping them out from the tins.

For the Caramel Cream. Start by mixing ¼ cup + 1 tablespoon + 2 teaspoons (70 g) of cream with the cornstarch in a bowl and keep it ready. Then in a saucepan, add ¼ cup + 1 tablespoon + 2 teaspoons (70 g) of cream and the vanilla over a low heat: you want to keep this mixture nice and warm. Meanwhile, spread the granulated sugar evenly in another saucepan, and start heating until it begins to caramelize around the edges, then gently stir the granulated sugar to get rid of any lumps and obtain a smooth, light-amber caramel.

Remove the caramel pan from heat, and pour in that warm vanilla-cream preparation to help deglaze the caramel. Follow this by adding in the cornstarch-cream mixture, and boil the entire mix for about a minute until it thickens. Make sure to continuously stir while boiling so nothing sticks to the bottom of the pan. Pour the hot, creamy mixture into a bowl containing the milk chocolate, and allow the chocolate to melt. Toss the salt in as well, and use a hand blender to emulsify the mix into a beautiful caramel cream. Let this rest for 2 hours in the refrigerator before using it. Then use a piping bag to pipe three neat lines of the caramel cream on the top surface of the cakes along the center, and place the cakes in the freezer for 4 hours to properly harden before glazing.

For the Hazelnut Praline Paste. Line a tray with baking paper. With the oven still at 320°F (160°C), on another tray, toast the hazelnuts for 10 to 15 minutes. Don't rush this by turning up the heat; keep it low and slow. Once they're golden brown, spread them out on the prepared tray to allow them to cool. Meanwhile, start heating the granulated sugar in a saucepan, gently stirring until it caramelizes and takes on a medium amber color, then pour evenly over the toasted hazelnuts. Allow the mix to cool for about 15 minutes, then, in a food processor, blend the caramel-coated nuts to get a smooth praline paste.

For the Hazelnut Glaze. The milk chocolate, dark chocolate and cocoa butter all need to be melted before we use them. Pop all three into a microwave-safe bowl and microwave for 40 seconds, then give it a little mix, and heat for another round of 40 seconds. Repeat this process until they all look and feel evenly melted. Allow the melted chocolate mixture to cool to room temperature before combining it into the hazelnut praline paste.

Time for assembly. Bring the cakes out of the freezer and arrange them on a wire rack with a plate beneath to catch excess glaze. Pour the hazelnut glaze evenly over the cakes. Finish things off by sprinkling desiccated coconut over the top and allowing the glaze to set for 15 minutes.

This banana coconut teacake is best served at room temperature so all the ingredients have their natural flavor. You can store the cakes in the refrigerator for up to 5 days.

VEGAN BANANA TAHINI CAKE

Yield: 2
Mold: 6 x 3 x 2-inch (15¼ x 7½ x 5-cm) loaf tin

Bananas are a staple fruit in India; you get them big, you get them small, you get them green, yellow and red. We'd say stick to the classic Robusta bananas that are easily available and have a gentle sweetness to them. If you haven't come across tahini before, it's a creamy Mediterranean condiment made with ground sesame, which, along with the hazelnut praline glaze, gives this wholesome cake an incredible flavor and texture.

Banana Cake

2⅓ cups (350 g) roasted bananas, mashed

⅝ cup (96 g) oats

⅔ cup + 2 tsp (60 g) desiccated coconut

1¼ tsp (6 g) baking soda

⅓ tbsp (6 g) apple cider vinegar

1½ tbsp (24 g) tahini

¼ cup (60 g) coconut oil

⅛ cup + 1½ tsp (50 g) maple syrup

2 tsp (8 g) vanilla extract

⅓ tsp sea salt

⅔ cup + 1 tbsp + 2 tsp (96 g) dark chocolate

Manié butter, for greasing tins (see Quick Reference Notes, page 218)

Black sesame seeds, for topping

White sesame seeds, for topping

Hazelnut Praline Paste

1⅛ cups (150 g) whole hazelnuts

½ cup (100 g) granulated sugar

Sesame Glaze

2½ tbsp (25 g) milk chocolate

¼ cup + 1½ tsp (40 g) dark chocolate

1½ tbsp (25 g) cocoa butter, finely chopped

1 cup (250 g) hazelnut praline paste

½ cup (75 g) sesame seeds, toasted

For the Banana Cake. Preheat the oven to 302°F (150°C). Start off by roasting the unpeeled bananas for 20 to 30 minutes, until they turn black. Roasting bananas with their natural skins on helps retain more moisture so the fruit inside develops an amazing flavor. Then cool 'em, peel 'em, mash 'em into a paste with a fork, and measure out the amount we need for the batter.

In a food processor, blend the roasted, mashed bananas together with the oats, desiccated coconut, baking soda, apple cider vinegar, tahini, coconut oil, maple syrup, vanilla extract and salt. Blend until you have a nice smooth batter, then pour it out into a mixing bowl. Chop the dark chocolate into small chunks and gently combine into the batter with a spatula.

Preheat the oven to 320°F (160°C). Grease the loaf tins with manié butter and portion out the batter equally between them so they're each about two-thirds full. Sprinkle a mix of black and white sesame seeds over the top surfaces, then pop them in the oven to bake for 25 to 30 minutes. Use a cake tester to check if the baking is done, or use a probe thermometer to know when the cakes reach 203°F (95°C). After baking, let the cakes cool before you flip them out of their tins and freeze for about 4 hours to harden.

> ### Note from the Chefs:
>
> As lovers of interesting ingredients, we find tahini contributes so much to the deliciousness of this cake, but if you can't find it, try using peanut butter instead to get a more classic peanut butter and banana combination.

(continued)

VEGAN BANANA TAHINI CAKE

(continued)

For the Hazelnut Praline Paste. Line a tray with baking paper. With the oven still at 320°F (160°C), on another tray, toast the hazelnuts for 10 to 15 minutes. Don't rush this by turning up the heat; keep it low and slow. Once they're golden brown, spread them out on the prepared tray to allow them to cool. Meanwhile, in a saucepan, start heating the granulated sugar, gently stirring until it caramelizes and takes on a medium amber color, then pour evenly over the toasted hazelnuts. Allow the mix to cool for about 15 minutes, then, in a food processor, blend the caramel-coated nuts to get a smooth praline paste.

For the Sesame Glaze. In a microwave-safe bowl, add the milk chocolate, dark chocolate and cocoa butter. Microwave for 40 seconds, then give it a little mix and heat for another round of 40 seconds. Repeat this process until they all look and feel evenly melted. Allow the mixture to cool for about 10 minutes before mixing in the hazelnut praline paste and popping in those toasted sesame seeds.

Time for assembly. Line a tray with baking paper. Glaze each cake by inserting a small knife into the top, and dipping the cake into the sesame glaze almost all the way, until just the top crust is left exposed. Then scrape any excess from the bottom and place them on the prepared tray to set for about 10 minutes. Use this time to properly admire your gorgeous sesame-covered creation.

These bangin' Banana Tahini Cakes are ready for you to slice up and serve. You can store them covered in the refrigerator for up to 5 days.

CHEWY
CARAMEL
CAKE

Yield: 2 cakes
Mold: 6 x 3 x 2-inch (15¼ x 7½ x 5-cm) loaf tin

Here's a great dessert cake for those who enjoy the deep, rich flavors of caramel. We're going to be dipping it into a nutty chocolate glaze to add some fun crunchy textures, and the soft and chewy deliciousness of the topping makes it an absolute delight to take a bite out of. Honestly, sometimes we eat a spoon of that chewy caramel before it even makes its way onto the cake. Some folks enjoy pairing a rich caramel cake like this with a little scoop of ice cream on the side. Or a large scoop—we're not here to judge.

Salted Caramel

½ cup + 2 tbsp + 2 tsp (135 g) granulated sugar

⅓ cup + 1 tbsp + 1 tsp (100 g) heavy cream

¼ cup + 1¾ tsp (65 g) butter

⅓ tsp sea salt

Caramel Cake

Butter, for greasing tins

2 eggs

1 tbsp (15 g) brown sugar

1½ tsp (6.5 g) amaretto liqueur

1 tsp vanilla extract

⅜ cup + 2 tsp (25 g) almond flour

1 cup (300 g) salted caramel

2½ tbsp (35 g) clarified butter

⅞ cup + 2 tsp (115 g) all-purpose flour, sifted

1⅓ tsp (6.5 g) baking powder

2 egg whites

2¾ tsp (15 g) invert sugar

Soft Chewy Caramel Topping

⅔ cup (160 g) heavy cream

1 vanilla bean pod (see Quick Reference Notes, page 219)

¾ cup + 2½ tsp (160 g) granulated sugar

½ cup (125 g) butter

Hazelnut Chocolate Glaze

1¾ cups (300 g) caramelized white chocolate, melted (see Quick Reference Notes, page 218)

⅜ cup (85 g) cocoa butter, melted

¾ cup + 1 tbsp (110 g) hazelnuts, chopped and toasted

For the Salted Caramel. In a saucepan over low heat, caramelize the granulated sugar until it starts turning medium amber. In another saucepan, heat the cream until it's nice and warm. Once the caramel has formed, add in the butter, followed by the warmed cream and salt. Continue to boil the mixture for about half a minute, while stirring throughout to get a beautiful, thick, salted caramel. Let it cool to room temperature.

For the Caramel Cake. Preheat the oven to 320°F (160°C). Grease the tins with butter. Use a food processor to blend the eggs, brown sugar, amaretto, vanilla extract, almond flour and salted caramel. Once it's all come together evenly, add in the clarified butter. Then use a spatula to fold in the all-purpose flour and baking powder. In a small bowl on the side, whip the egg whites and invert sugar together to make a medium-stiff meringue, and fold this into the batter as well. Fill the loaf tins about two-thirds full of batter, then immediately bake for 25 to 30 minutes. Use a cake tester to check if the baking is done, or use a probe thermometer to know when the cakes reach 203°F (95°C). After baking, let the cakes cool before you flip them out of their tins and freeze for about 4 hours to harden.

For the Soft Chewy Caramel Topping. In a heavy-bottom saucepan, heat the cream and vanilla. In another saucepan caramelize the granulated sugar to a medium amber, and mix in the heated vanilla-cream. Cook over medium heat for 5 minutes, until it reaches 226°F (108°C), then turn off the heat, and add in the butter while mixing vigorously. You can leave it aside at room temperature to cool.

(continued)

CHEWY CARAMEL CAKE *(continued)*

For the Hazelnut Chocolate Glaze. In a bowl, combine the white chocolate and cocoa butter. Let it cool to below 86°F (30°C) and then mix in the hazelnuts to add some crunch to our chocolate coating.

Time for assembly. Line a tray with baking paper. Let's get the hardened cakes out of the freezer and coat them in this chocolatey goodness. Use a small knife inserted into the top of the cake to dip it into the caramel-chocolate mixture almost all the way, keeping just the top crust exposed, then scrape any excess from the bottom and leave them on the prepared tray to set. For the finishing touch, generously spread that delicious chewy soft caramel over the top to form a shiny, sugary wave.

This stylish Chewy Caramel Cake can be sliced and served immediately. Store well-wrapped or in a sealed container at room temperature for up to 5 days.

TROPICAL CARROT CAKE

Yield: 2 cakes
Mold: 8 x 2 x 2-inch (20⅓ x 5 x 5-cm) loaf tin

On Andrés' first trip to India, we took a bike trip to the infamous coastal paradise of Goa for a mini-vacation. On our very first day by the ocean, we tasted what will always be remembered as the most seductive, cold, spicy and fresh carrot-pineapple salad ever made. Simple ingredients were transformed to pure bliss. That's when the idea for the Tropical Carrot Cake was born. With its chunks of pineapple, orange zest and light chantilly, this cake instantly gets you in a vacation mood.

Mascarpone Chantilly

1 tbsp + 1 tsp (20 g) cold water

1½ tsp (3 g) gelatin

½ cup + 2 tbsp (150 g) heavy cream

2 tbsp (25 g) granulated sugar

½ vanilla bean pod (see Quick Reference Notes, page 219)

⅔ cup (150 g) mascarpone cheese

Carrot Cake

1 egg

½ cup + 3 tbsp + 2 tsp (145 g) granulated sugar

1½ tsp (10 g) corn syrup

⅓ cup + 1½ tsp (75 g) grapeseed or olive oil

1 tbsp (15 g) orange marmalade

⅞ cup + 1½ tsp (100 g) grated carrots

¼ cup (45 g) canned pineapple, drained

1 cup (125 g) all-purpose flour, sifted

⅔ tsp baking soda

⅔ tsp baking powder

½ tsp ground cinnamon

Pinch of sea salt

2½ tbsp (55 g) candied orange peel

Zest of ½ orange

Manié butter, for greasing tins (see Quick Reference Notes, page 218)

Yogurt Crumble

3½ tbsp (50 g) butter, cold

1 tbsp + 2 tsp (20 g) granulated sugar

⅜ cup + 1 tbsp (55 g) all-purpose flour

2 tbsp (25 g) yogurt powder

Desiccated coconut, for coating

For the Mascarpone Chantilly. Add the water to a small bowl and bloom the gelatin in the water for 5 minutes, until it absorbs the water and swells. Next up, in a saucepan heat the cream with the granulated sugar and vanilla over medium heat and bring it to a simmer. Stir in the bloomed gelatin and allow it to fully dissolve. Pour the mascarpone cheese in as well, and use a hand blender to whip everything up to a smooth, creamy texture. Store this in the refrigerator overnight.

For the Carrot Cake. In a stand mixer with a whisk attachment, whip the egg and gradually add in the granulated sugar and corn syrup until it turns light and airy. With a spatula, gently fold in the oil, orange marmalade, carrots and pineapple pieces. Follow this by mixing in the all-purpose flour, baking soda, baking powder, cinnamon and salt. Finally, add in the candied orange peel and orange zest for those glorious bursts of flavor. Rest the batter in the refrigerator for 4 hours before baking.

Preheat the oven to 320°F (160°C). Grease the loaf tins with manié butter and portion the batter equally between them until they're about half full, then bake for 25 to 30 minutes. Use a cake tester to check if the baking is done, or use a probe thermometer to know when the cake reaches 203°F (95°C).

(continued)

> *Note from the Chefs:*
>
> Yogurt crumble is one of our favorite additions to dessert; it adds just the right kind of texture and acidity. You can find tangy yogurt powder online these days, but in case it isn't available, a bit of toasted almond flour will do just fine!

For the Yogurt Crumble. In a food processor, add the butter, granulated sugar, all-purpose flour and yogurt powder, and process until a crumbly texture begins to form. Freeze your little chunks of yogurt crumble for 2 hours to get them firm. While they're freezing, preheat the oven to 320°F (160°C). Bake the yogurt crumble for 15 to 20 minutes, until it takes on a delightful golden brown. Keep the crumble aside to use on top of the cake for some real glorious texture and flavor.

Time for assembly. Once the cakes have baked and cooled, flip them out of the tins onto a board and get ready to dress them up. Coat the sides of the cake with desiccated coconut: this stuff adds a heavenly texture to the cake, so be generous. Now, in a stand mixer with a whisk attachment, whip the mascarpone chantilly until it's light and airy. Place the chantilly into a piping bag fitted with a petal nozzle and pipe a delicate ruffle pattern across the top surface of the cake. Last up, garnish with some yogurt crumble to give it a rustic finishing touch.

Serve this Tropical Carrot Cake either chilled or at room temperature for the tastiest results. You can store it refrigerated for up to 5 days.

ROCKY CHOCOLATE FINANCIER

Yield: 2 pastries
Mold: 6-inch (15¼-cm) cake ring

The simple and under-appreciated financier will always hold a place in Andrés' heart as one of the first recipes he ever made in pastry school—it was the start of an endless fascination with brown butter. He often recounts the feeling of wonder seeing butter caramelize for the first time, accompanied by that unforgettable nutty aroma. We've taken this French classic and loaded it with massive flavors and textures, from the poached strawberries inside to the rocky chocolate crumble on top.

Chocolate Cake

⅔ cup (125 g) butter

1 cup (115 g) icing sugar

⅓ cup + 1 tsp (45 g) all-purpose flour

1 tbsp + 2½ tsp (10 g) cocoa powder

1¼ cups (75 g) almond flour

2¾ tsp (15 g) invert sugar

4 egg whites

4 tsp (20 g) rum

⅔ cup (90 g) dark chocolate

Cocoa Nib Crumble

⅛ cup + 1 tbsp + 2 tsp (50 g) brown sugar

3½ tbsp (50 g) butter, cold

¾ cup + 1 tbsp + 1 tsp (50 g) almond flour

¼ cup + 1½ tsp (35 g) all-purpose flour

2½ tbsp (15 g) cocoa powder

⅕ tsp salt

2 tbsp + 2 tsp (20 g) cocoa nibs

Poached Strawberries

1⅝ cups + 2 tbsp (250 g) fresh strawberries

¾ cup + 1 tbsp + 1 tsp (100 g) icing sugar

Manié butter, for coating the rings (see Quick Reference Notes, page 218)

1¼ cups (150 g) cocoa nibs

⅛ cup + 1 tbsp + 2 tsp (50 g) brown sugar

Cocoa powder, for garnish

For the Chocolate Cake. We'll need to start browning our butter before using it—trust us, this is worth it. Add the butter to a saucepan and put it over medium heat until it begins to boil and release a gorgeous, nutty aroma. These are just the kind of inspirational smells one needs when making a financier. Once the butter has browned, remove it from the heat and strain it before using it in the batter.

Now onward to the cake batter! Sift the icing sugar, all-purpose flour and cocoa powder into a large bowl. Mix in the almond flour. Then gradually add in the invert sugar, egg whites and rum, mixing until it's perfectly combined. Melt the dark chocolate and brown butter, and mix those into the batter as well. Leave this lovely chocolate batter to rest overnight in the refrigerator; this helps with even hydration and lets the flavors mature before baking.

For the Cocoa Nib Crumble. Preheat the oven to 320°F (160°C) and line a tray with baking paper. In a food processor, add the brown sugar, butter, almond flour, all-purpose flour, cocoa powder and salt. Process the mix in short bursts until you achieve a breadcrumb consistency. Then add in the cocoa nibs slowly and continue mixing to get beautiful cocoa crumble rocks. Reserve two-thirds of these cocoa rocks for the topping. But let's go a step further with the remaining one-third, and transform it into a cocoa clay. Lay it out on the prepared tray and bake for 15 to 20 minutes, then blend it in the food processor until it starts to become soft and pliable. Time to get artistic! Roll the chocolate clay in your hands to form smooth, rounded, cocoa pebbles about 1 inch (2.5 cm) in diameter. These will be decoration at the very end.

(continued)

ROCKY CHOCOLATE FINANCIER *(continued)*

For the Poached Strawberries. Let's slice the strawberries in half and, in a saucepan, mix them with icing sugar, letting them marinate for an hour. Then bring them to a boil for about a minute for the fruit to get tender. Once cooked, remove from heat and leave in the refrigerator to cool.

Time for assembly. Preheat the oven to 320°F (160°C). Line the bottom of each cake ring with aluminum foil and grease the insides with manié butter. Sprinkle a mixture of the cocoa nibs and brown sugar into the rings so the cakes get a nice coating. We're going to pour the batter one part at a time. To start off, fill each ring with a ½ inch (1.3 cm) of batter. Now strain the poached strawberries and layer just the fruit over the batter. Then add another ½ inch (1.3 cm) of batter into the ring to cover the strawberries, followed by a generous sprinkling of those unbaked cocoa crumble rocks over the surface. Don't hold back; this stuff makes all the difference.

We're ready to bake these for 25 to 30 minutes. Use a cake tester to check if the baking is done, or use a probe thermometer to see when the cakes reach 203°F (95°C). Let them cool before carefully releasing your cakes from the rings. Dust some cocoa powder all over, and place one of those smooth cocoa pebbles on top of each cake to complete the look.

Voila! This Rocky Chocolate Financier is ready to knock everyone's socks off. You can store it in the refrigerator for up to 5 days.

CITRUS BLUEBERRY WINTER CAKE

Yield: 2 cakes
Mold: 8 x 2 x 2-inch (20⅓ x 5 x 5-cm) loaf tin

We love starting with simple recipes and then taking them up a notch with complementary flavors and toppings. A citrus tea cake would be great by itself, but adding in that chopped blueberry gel (which is similar to a jelly but firmer) really makes every bite sing, while the soothing creamy ganache on top wraps those cool, tangy flavors up in a soft, comforting blanket.

Blueberry Gel

⅔ cup (150 g) blueberry purée

⅔ tsp gellan

3 tbsp + 1 tsp (40 g) granulated sugar

2 tbsp (30 g) water

Orange Cake

⅔ cup + 1 tbsp (160 g) butter

¾ cup (150 g) granulated sugar

2 eggs

1 egg yolk

1⅜ cups + 1 tbsp (180 g) all-purpose flour

1½ tsp (7.5 g) baking powder

½ tsp salt

⅜ cup + 1½ tsp (100 g) milk

Zest of 1 orange

3 tbsp (45 g) orange juice

½ vanilla bean pod (see Quick Reference Notes, page 219)

Manié butter, for greasing tins (see Quick Reference Notes, page 218)

Cream Cheese Ganache

½ cup + 1 tbsp + 1 tsp (100 g) white chocolate, chopped

3 tbsp + 1 tsp (50 g) heavy cream

⅝ cup (150 g) cream cheese

Lemon zest, for garnish

For the Blueberry Gel. To start things off, add the blueberry purée to a saucepan and use a whisk to dissolve the gellan into it completely so you get a smooth consistency. Now mix in the granulated sugar and water, and bring these ingredients to a vigorous boil for about a minute, watching this fruity mixture thicken. Now let's grab a 6-inch (15¼-cm) square cake frame, pour the blueberry gel into it, and leave it in the refrigerator to set for 1 hour. Once it's taken on a fun jelly-like consistency, dice it into little ⅓-inch (8-mm) cubes and keep them close by for the batter. If you're finding it hard to get your hands on gellan to make blueberry gel cubes, feel free to simplify the process by using 1 cup (150 g) of fresh blueberries in the batter instead.

For the Orange Cake. Preheat the oven to 320°F (160°C). In a stand mixer with a paddle attachment, cream the butter and granulated sugar until it turns pale and fluffy. Gradually add in the eggs and the extra yolk, while continuing to mix. In a separate bowl, mix the all-purpose flour, baking powder and salt. Alternate adding the dry mix with the milk to the batter to maintain a nice consistency. Once that's done, let's give it some aromatic citrus flavors by mixing in the orange zest, orange juice and vanilla.

Time to start layering the blueberry gel cubes into the batter—pour the batter into a large bowl a little at a time, stopping intermittently to sprinkle in some blueberry gel cubes so the cubes are well distributed in the batter.

Grease the loaf tins with manié butter and portion out the batter equally between them so they're each about two-thirds full before popping them in the oven to bake for 25 to 30 minutes. Use a cake tester to check if the baking is done, or use a probe thermometer to know when the cakes reach 203°F (95°C). After baking, let the cakes cool before you flip them out of their tins. Leave them in the refrigerator for 2 hours.

(continued)

CITRUS BLUEBERRY WINTER CAKE *(continued)*

For the Cream Cheese Ganache. Add the white chocolate to a bowl. In a saucepan, heat the cream to a simmer and then pour it into the bowl with the white chocolate, allowing it to melt the chocolate. Use a hand blender to emulsify it well, and leave it aside to cool. When it's at about 104°F (40°C), add in the cream cheese and blend to get a beautifully smooth ganache. Once it's cooled, cover this with cling film and keep it in the refrigerator for 2 hours before using it on the cake.

Time for assembly. Use a piping bag to pipe the cream cheese ganache as kisses of varying sizes, across the entire top surface of each cake. Now lay a strip of stiff plastic on top of the ganache and use a light weight, something like a baking tray, to gently press down and flatten the kisses. Put these cakes in the freezer to set for 30 minutes before taking the plastic strip off, leaving a nice, clean, creamy pattern. To finish up, use a microplane to add a delicate sprinkling of lemon zest over the top.

This zesty citrus cake can now be sliced and served chilled to adoring guests. You can also store it in the refrigerator for up to 5 days.

ROASTED NUT FRUIT CAKE

Yield: 2 cakes
Mold: 6 x 3 x 2-inch (15¼ x 7½ x 5-cm) loaf tin

Fruit cake has been a tradition for hundreds of years—the Romans used it for sustenance, the British used it for royal occasions, and now the dish is considered a gastronomic icon of the Christmas season. The magical thing about fruit cake, though, is that every bakery and every household seems to have their own amazing recipe: some are fruitier, some are spicier, or nuttier, crumblier, juicier. Personally, we never really enjoyed those timid little cakes with a meager sprinkling of fruits; we like ours moist, boozy and full of delicious surprises like toasted nuts, berries and apricots in every bite, rather than the usual raisins. So when it comes making this recipe, the most important thing to remember is . . . don't hold back on the good stuff!

Soaked Dried Fruit

1 vanilla bean pod (see Quick Reference Notes, page 219)

⅝ cup (75 g) dried apricot

⅔ cup (75 g) dried blueberry

⅝ cup (75 g) dried cranberry

½ cup (50 g) toasted pecans, chopped

⅓ cup (50 g) toasted hazelnuts, halved

½ cup (50 g) toasted almond slivers

⅓ cup (50 g) toasted pistachios, de-skinned

1 tsp ground cinnamon

½ tsp nutmeg

⅔ tsp ground anise

Zest of 1 orange

Zest of 1 lemon

Dark rum, enough to submerge fruit

Cake

1 tsp baking powder

½ tsp sea salt

1⅜ cups (175 g) all-purpose flour, divided

⅔ cup + 1 tbsp (160 g) butter

1⅓ cups (160 g) icing sugar

3 eggs

1 cup (140 g) soaked dried fruits

⅛ cup + 1 tbsp (70 g) candied orange peel

Manié butter, for greasing tins (see Quick Reference Notes, page 218)

Soaking Syrup

½ cup (100 g) granulated sugar

⅔ cup + 1½ tsp (165 g) water, divided

4 tsp (20 g) dark rum

Apricot jam, for glazing

For the Soaked Dried Fruit. When it comes to soaking fruit, we're fond of using rum and spices to get a classic wintery flavor. In a ziplock bag, add the vanilla, dried apricots, dried blueberries, dried cranberries, pecans, hazelnuts, almonds, pistachios, cinnamon, nutmeg, anise, orange zest and lemon zest. Pour in a generous amount of dark rum until the fruit mixture is fully submerged. Seal the bag and leave the fruits to soak for at least 24 hours—though honestly, we'd recommend longer. If you aren't in a hurry, go ahead and soak them for a full week so those flavors get really well-absorbed.

Once it's soaked to satisfaction, open up the bag and strain out the fruit to use inside the cake batter, as well as for the topping.

For the Cake. Preheat the oven to 320°F (160°C). Into a bowl, sift the baking powder, salt and 1 cup (131 g) of all-purpose flour. In a stand mixer with a paddle attachment, cream the butter, icing sugar and remaining ⅜ cup (44 g) of the all-purpose flour. Gradually add in the eggs a little at a time until they're fully incorporated. Follow that by mixing in the sifted ingredients, to get ourselves a nice thick batter. Finally, fold in the soaked dried fruits and candied orange peel, mixing so they're evenly distributed.

(continued)

ROASTED NUT FRUIT CAKE *(continued)*

Grease the loaf tins with manié butter and portion out the batter equally between them so they're each about two-thirds full, then pop them in the oven to bake for 25 to 30 minutes. Use a cake tester to check if they're well baked, or use a probe thermometer to know when the cakes reach 203°F (95°C).

For the Soaking Syrup. In a saucepan, add the granulated sugar and ⅜ cup + 2 teaspoons (100 g) of water. Boil the mix until the sugar is well dissolved. Then leave the syrup to cool to room temperature before mixing in the dark rum and the remaining ¼ cup + 1½ teaspoons (65 g) of water. This helps make the syrup lighter so it seeps into the cake even better when soaking.

Time for assembly. Warm the soaking syrup and keep it in a container large enough to comfortably fit the cakes. Once they're done baking, flip the cakes out of the tins and soak them in that heady rum-sugar syrup, getting them nice and moist. Let's take some more of that delicious soaked fruit mixture and arrange it all over the top of the baked fruit cakes, achieving a decadent, luxurious look. For the finishing touch, melt a little apricot jam and brush it over the fruit toppings to form a shiny, sugary glaze.

This delightful Christmas treat can be sliced and served warm to best bring out the flavors. You can store it at room temperature for up to 5 days.

HAZELNUT BROWNIE SANDWICH

Yield: 2 pastries
Mold: 5-inch (13-cm) square cake tin

On a somber rainy afternoon, we were taking a tour around Bangalore and visited one of our favorite coffee roasteries in town. While sipping on some amazing coffees with origins from all over the world, we looked at the pastry counter and grumbled about how every coffee shop seems to have the same ol' boring brownies. No one seems to do anything fun with these classic treats. We imagined the perfect pairing with that coffee to be a novel sandwich-style brownie, and that drove us straight back to the kitchen to actually construct this hybrid dessert fantasy. Complete with toffee and marmalade layers, and a gorgeous dacquoise topping, our radical Hazelnut Brownie Sandwich is all flavor and no fluff.

Toffee Shards

¼ cup + 1 tbsp + ¾ tsp (75 g) butter

⅓ cup + 2 tsp (73 g) granulated sugar

1 tbsp (15 g) water

Orange Marmalade

1 unpeeled orange, large

2 tbsp (30 g) orange juice

½ cup + 2 tbsp (125 g) granulated sugar, divided

½ tsp pectin

Brownie

½ cup (110 g) butter, plus more for greasing tins, at room temperature

½ cup + 1 tbsp + 1 tsp (130 g) brown sugar

¼ tsp sea salt

2 eggs, at room temperature

½ cup (60 g) dark chocolate

⅜ cup + 1 tsp (50 g) all-purpose flour

1 tsp cocoa powder

2½ tbsp (60 g) candied orange peel

1 tsp vanilla extract

Zest of ½ orange

Hazelnut Dacquoise

4 egg whites

2 tbsp + 1 tsp (30 g) granulated sugar

¾ cup (90 g) icing sugar, plus more for dusting

1 cup (100 g) hazelnut powder

For the Toffee Shards. Line a tray with baking paper. In a saucepan over high heat, add the butter, granulated sugar and water and allow it to caramelize, making sure to continuously mix vigorously to maintain a perfect emulsion. Once it's a deep amber color, about 4 to 5 minutes, pour it onto the prepared tray and allow it to cool. Use something hefty like a rolling pin to break the slab into smaller shards, and keep these yummy little heavenly fragments aside for later.

For the Orange Marmalade. In a large saucepan filled with water, place the whole orange and bring it to a boil for a good 2 hours, making sure to replace the water every 40 minutes to help get rid of the bitterness. Let the orange cool for a while before chopping it up into small, ³⁄₁₆-inch (5-mm) pieces, and removing all the seeds to get a nice mixture of pulp and rind. Take the cut up oranges into a new saucepan over medium heat, and add the orange juice and ¼ cup + 1 tablespoon (62.5 g) of granulated sugar. In a bowl, combine the pectin with the other ¼ cup + 1 tablespoon (62.5 g) of granulated sugar, and add that into the saucepan once the stewing orange pieces have reached 104°F (40°C), stirring to let it dissolve. Bring the mixture to a boil and watch as it reaches a thick jam-like consistency, then turn off the heat and set aside to use after baking.

(continued)

For the Brownie. Preheat the oven to 320°F (160°C). Grease the tins with extra butter and line them with baking paper. In a stand mixer with a paddle attachment, cream the butter with the brown sugar and salt. Once it's turned light and fluffy, gradually add in the eggs, a little at a time until they're fully incorporated. Melt the dark chocolate, and mix it into the batter as well, followed by the all-purpose flour, cocoa powder and candied orange peel. Finally, fold in the vanilla extract and orange zest to complete the brownie batter.

Portion out the batter between the prepared tins, then scatter toffee shards over the top surface for some beautiful crunch. Bake for 25 to 30 minutes. Use a cake tester to check if the baking is done, or use a probe thermometer to know when the cakes reach 203°F (95°C). Once baked, let the brownies cool a little before spreading a nice layer of orange marmalade over the surface. Turn the oven up to 356°F (180°C). As you can see, things have officially moved from good to great, and there's still more to come!

For the Hazelnut Dacquoise. In a stand mixer with a whisk attachment, whip those egg whites, gradually adding in the granulated sugar until you get a meringue of medium peak consistency. Fold in the icing sugar and hazelnut powder with a spatula; we do this gently so the meringue doesn't lose its form. Add the dacquoise to a piping bag, and pipe it evenly over the top of the baked brownies, then dust some icing sugar over the top. We'll want to put these in the oven again for 15 minutes, until the top turns a delicate, irresistible golden brown.

Cut these brownies into sandwich-style triangles and serve them warm if you prefer. You can store them at room temperature for up to 3 days.

THE JUICIEST VEGAN LEMON CAKE

Yield: 2 cakes
Mold: 8 x 2 x 2-inch (20⅓ x 5 x 5-cm) loaf tin

When we're in India we always end up working out together at the gym, and right outside there's this tiny stall that serves up the absolute best nimboo paani (Indian lemonade). We can think of nothing better when you're hot and tired than sipping on such a delightfully chill and tangy beverage. This elegant cake was dreamt up to recreate that refreshing feeling: it's simple to make but beautiful to behold and bursting with citrus flavors.

Lemon Yogurt Cake

Coconut oil, for greasing tins

3½ oz (100 g) silken tofu

1 cup + 2½ tsp (210 g) granulated sugar

Zest of 2 lemons

Zest of 1 orange

¾ cup (190 g) soy vanilla yogurt

¾ cup (160 g) grapeseed oil

1⅔ cups (210 g) all-purpose flour, sifted

1 tbsp (16 g) baking powder

½ tsp sea salt

¼ tsp guar gum

Soaking Syrup

¼ cup (60 g) lemon juice

1 tbsp + 1 tsp (15 g) granulated sugar

2½ tbsp (15 g) trehalose

Ginger Infusion

⅜ cup (90 g) water

3 tbsp (15 g) ginger, grated

Glaze

¼ cup (45 g) ginger infusion

2 tbsp (30 g) lemon juice

2¼ cups (270 g) icing sugar, sifted

Edible flowers, for garnish

Edible gold leaf, for garnish

For the Lemon Yogurt Cake. Preheat the oven to 320°F (160°C). Grease the tins with coconut oil. In a food processor, add the silken tofu, granulated sugar and zest of both lemons and orange. Blend for about 30 seconds to make sure the mixture is nice and fine. Add the soy vanilla yogurt and start to blend, slowly pouring in the grapeseed oil while mixing. Once the mixture is smooth as silk, use a spatula to fold in the all-purpose flour, baking powder, salt and guar gum, making sure there aren't any lumps.

Portion the batter equally between the tins until they're about two-thirds full, and bake for 25 to 30 minutes. Use a cake tester to check if the baking is done, or use a probe thermometer to know when the cakes reach 203°F (95°C). After baking, carefully flip them out of the tins onto a wire rack to cool, ready for soaking and glazing.

For the Soaking Syrup. In a saucepan, add the lemon juice, granulated sugar and trehalose and heat until the mixture turns warm. Use a brush to apply a nice layer of syrup to all surfaces of each cake, getting them moist and leaving them to cool to room temperature.

For the Ginger Infusion. Bring the water to a boil, add in the grated ginger, and let it sit over medium heat for 1 minute. Cover it with a lid and let it cool before straining out this potent ginger infusion. Of course, the longer the ginger steeps, the more intense it will be, so the duration depends on how much you love ginger!

For the Glaze. In a bowl, mix the measured ginger infusion, lemon juice and icing sugar to get a nice, smooth glaze. You can adjust the thickness of the glaze by adding more or less lemon juice than we've recommended.

Time for assembly. Preheat the oven to 356°F (180°C). Line a tray with baking paper. Put a plate below the cakes' cooling rack to catch extra glaze, and then pour the glaze evenly over the cakes. Transfer the glazed cakes onto the prepared tray. Turn off the oven and put the cakes in for just 2 minutes for the glaze to set. A good way to check if the glaze is just right is to touch it with a finger. If it doesn't leave much residue on your finger, the glaze is set. Finish off by garnishing the cakes with some vibrant edible flowers and gold-leaf for a stunning natural look.

These zesty lemon yogurt cakes can be served chilled or at room temperature. You can store them in the refrigerator for up to 5 days.

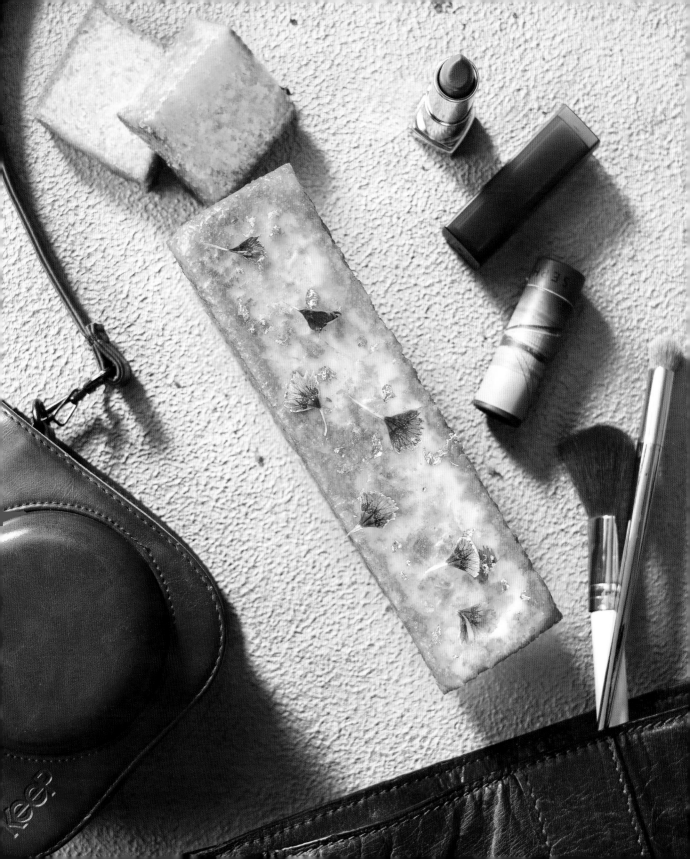

PISTACHIO PINEAPPLE GOURMANDISE

Yield: 1 pastry
Mold: 6-inch (15¼-cm) round cake tin

"Gourmandise" is defined as the unrestricted enjoyment of food, often in excess. You'll find that an accurate description, because one bite into this cake and the lavish pineapple topping immediately fills your face with flirty tropical flavors, while at the same time the lightness of the delicate pistachio sponge means you'll find yourself reaching for a second slice. With pineapple being a staple in so many Eastern countries, and pistachios a traditional gift during festivals in India, this cake is like a love letter from our travels across Asia.

Pistachio Sponge

¼ cup + 2¾ tsp (70 g) butter

1½ tsp (10 g) invert sugar

2 tbsp (30 g) pistachio paste

1 cup (115 g) icing sugar

¾ cup + 1 tbsp + 1 tsp (50 g) almond flour

⅜ cup + 1 tsp (50 g) all-purpose flour

½ tsp baking powder

4 egg whites

Pineapple Confit

1 cup (150 g) pineapple, fresh

1 tbsp (15 g) water

⅓ cup (85 g) pineapple juice

1 tbsp + 1 tsp (15 g) granulated sugar

¾ tsp pectin

Zest of 2 lemons

Juice of 1 lemon

¼ tsp sea salt

1 tsp coconut rum (We recommend Malibu)

Pistachio Powder

¾ cup + 1 tbsp (100 g) pistachios, toasted

For the Pistachio Sponge. In a stand mixer with a paddle attachment, beat together the butter, invert sugar and pistachio paste to get an even blend. Then gently mix in the icing sugar, almond flour, all-purpose flour and baking powder, and combine well to get a thick batter. Gradually add the egg whites a little at a time, while continuing to mix until they are fully incorporated.

For the Pineapple Confit. Chop up the pineapple into ½-inch (1.3-cm) cubes, throw them into a heavy-bottomed pan, and add in the water and pineapple juice. Bring this mixture to 140°F (60°C) before adding in the granulated sugar and pectin. Continue cooking to bring the pineapple mixture to a comfortable boil, until it turns to a thick jam-like consistency. Now let's remove it from the heat, and season the confit with lemon zest, lemon juice and salt. Mix gently, and add the coconut rum to perfectly round off those tropical flavors. This cake is gonna make you feel like you're on a beach vacation!

For the Pistachio Powder. In a food processor, add the pistachios and process for 20 seconds until they're finely ground.

Time for assembly. Preheat the oven to 320°F (160°C). Line the cake tin with baking paper and pour out the batter till the tin is about two-thirds full. Bake for 20 to 25 minutes. Use a cake tester to check if the baking is done, or use a probe thermometer to know when the cake reaches 203°F (95°C). After baking, allow it to cool before carefully removing the sponge from the mold. Coat the side surfaces of your cakes with the pistachio powder for some great color contrast. Bring that pineapple confit out, and use a spoon to layer it into a neat circle on the top surface.

Your pistachio pineapple cake is ready to be the target of everyone's gourmandise. Slice it up and serve chilled. You can store it in the refrigerator for up to 3 days.

YUM-YUM Cookies

Cookies have always been Vinesh's biggest weakness. Once he starts eating them there's just no stopping; one has to physically restrain him from finishing the whole platter. The logic with cookies seems to be: why keep for tomorrow what you can definitely eat today?

Cookie addictions aside, what still amazes us about these little treats is how versatile they really are. You could eat the simplest little cookie, like the Old-School Alfajores (page 74) and feel utter, blissful nostalgia. Or you can start getting creative by adding some wondrous flavors into the dough and some fun chunky toppings like with our Rocky Road Cookie (page 91). Of course, you could also go full-on gourmet with unique textures and astonishing toppings arranged upon a grand baked canvas, like with the stunningly elegant family-style Peanut Yuzu Marshmallow Cookie (page 83).

The following are a selection of recipes we've curated for different styles and moods, but there's always going to be a tasty base with which we start, and then build up each component from there. We think this set of circular delights are going to find a special place in your heart.

OLD-SCHOOL ALFAJORES

Yield: 12 cookies
Mold: 3-inch (7½-cm) cookie cutter

Walk into any Latin bakery and you'll likely be greeted by the smell of freshly baked bread. You may also notice in some of the more traditional shops, they put out rows of jars on the counter filled with all kinds of treats. Look in one of those jars and you're likely to find a version of alfajores: a crumbly cookie sandwich filled with a soft caramel cream. As a chubby kid in 1985, Andrés would go to a bakery in Colombia every weekend, and ask his mom to get him two alfajores. With this quick and simple recipe, you can make an endless supply of these caramel-filled delights!

Coconut Shortbread

½ cup (120 g) butter

¾ cup (90 g) icing sugar

1 egg

⅓ tsp sea salt

1⅞ cups (235 g) all-purpose flour

⅓ cup (30 g) coconut flour

Caramel Cream

⅔ cup + 2 tsp (120 g) caramelized white chocolate (see Quick Reference Notes, page 218)

Pinch of sea salt

⅔ cup (160 g) heavy cream, divided

¼ vanilla bean pod (see Quick Reference Notes, page 219)

3 tbsp + 1 tsp (40 g) granulated sugar

1 tbsp + 1 tsp (10 g) cornstarch

¼ cup (25 g) toasted coconut flakes, for garnish

For the Coconut Shortbread. Preheat the oven to 320°F (160°C). Line a tray with baking paper or a silicon mat. In a stand mixer with a paddle attachment, cream the butter and icing sugar together. Gradually add in the egg a little at a time until fully incorporated. Then fold in the salt, all-purpose flour and coconut flour, combining to get a nice cookie dough. Place the dough between two sheets of baking paper and flatten it a little before resting in the refrigerator for 1 hour. Once the dough is feeling cool and firm, roll it into a sheet ⅛ inch (3 mm) thick, and use the cookie cutter to cut out discs. Place them on the prepared tray; cover with an additional silicon mat if you have one, then bake for 15 to 20 minutes, until they turn a delicious golden brown.

> *Note from the Chefs:*
>
> If you can find a good quality store-bought caramelized white chocolate, then by all means, use it! Otherwise follow our steps in the Quick Reference Notes (page 218) to make your own, or simply just use normal white chocolate.

For the Caramel Cream. In a heatproof bowl, add the white chocolate and salt and set it aside. In a saucepan over medium heat, add ⅓ cup (80 g) of cream with the vanilla, and bring to a simmer. Then in another saucepan, start caramelizing the granulated sugar by heating and stirring until it turns a deep amber color. Pour the warmed cream into the caramel to help deglaze the pan. In a small bowl, mix together the remaining ⅓ cup (80 g) of cream with the cornstarch, and add that into the caramel as well, allowing it to boil for about a minute longer.

Pour this hot mixture into the bowl containing the white chocolate, and use a hand blender to form a smooth emulsion. Keep this in the fridge for 2 hours before using it.

Time for assembly. In a stand mixer with a paddle attachment, mix the caramel cream on medium speed until it's soft and creamy. Then using a piping bag, pipe the cream onto one coconut shortbread, and place another shortbread on top to form a sandwich. Repeat this process until we have a tray full of lovely cookie sandwiches. Now for the finishing touch, coat the sides of each cookie with toasted coconut flakes to give them a rustic, beautiful look.

These classic Latin treats are ready to be served. Eat them all immediately, or save some for later. You can store these in an airtight container at room temperature for up to 2 days.

BANANA OAT POWER COOKIE

Yield: 10 cookies
Mold: 3-inch (7½-cm) ring

We're both big fans of early morning exercise, and as pastry chefs, we're also fans of making bite-size treats that give you a boost in energy. So whenever we're in the same city, we meet on the night before to plan out our morning exercise and decide what to eat for breakfast. Over the years we've seen workout styles come and go, but oats have remained a classic, trusty power food!

To get this cookie right, you'll need to rest the batter overnight, so by the morning you're ready to bake and assemble. What better motivation to wake up early than the smell of fresh cookies?

Cookie Dough

1 cup + 1½ tbsp (140 g) all-purpose flour

⅓ cup (40 g) oat flour

½ tsp baking powder

½ tsp baking soda

½ tsp sea salt

Pinch of nutmeg

¼ cup + ¾ tsp (60 g) butter, plus more for greasing rings, at room temperature

½ cup + 1 tsp (115 g) brown sugar

¼ cup (55 g) ripe, peeled and mashed banana

3 tbsp (40 g) olive oil

1 egg

1¾ tsp (7.5 g) vanilla extract

½ cup + 1½ tsp (90 g) milk chocolate, chopped

½ cup (60 g) walnuts, toasted and chopped

Salted Caramel

2 tsp (10 g) cocoa butter, finely chopped

½ cup (60 g) dark chocolate, finely chopped

½ cup (120 g) heavy cream

1 vanilla bean pod (see Quick Reference Notes, page 219)

1½ tbsp (35 g) corn syrup

¾ cup (150 g) granulated sugar

2 tbsp (30 g) butter

½ tsp sea salt

½ cup (60 g) walnuts, toasted and chopped, for garnish

For the Cookie Dough. Sift together the all-purpose flour, oat flour, baking powder, baking soda, salt and nutmeg, then set it aside. In a stand mixer with a paddle attachment, start by creaming the butter and brown sugar. Add the banana then gradually mix in the oil, egg and vanilla extract, and combine well to form a batter. Add the sifted mix into the batter a little at a time, folding it in until fully incorporated. Finally, toss in the milk chocolate and walnuts, and mix gently to distribute. Let's allow the cookie dough to rest overnight in the refrigerator.

> *Note from the Chefs:*
>
> If you've ever eaten a bowl of healthy, creamy, overnight oats, you'll know it's worth the wait! Oats tend to have a pretty tough outer shell, so by resting the batter overnight we're allowing time for that starch to hydrate. It also gives the banana flavors time to mature so when the cookie is finally baked, it has this beautiful structure and aroma. All that from doing nothing!

(continued)

BANANA OAT POWER COOKIE *(continued)*

We sometimes enjoy making one huge mega-cookie for everyone to share, but lots of people prefer traditional smaller cookies, so let's go with that. Preheat the oven to 320°F (160°C). Grease the rings with extra butter and line a tray with baking paper. Once the dough has rested long enough, bring it out of the refrigerator and weigh out 60-gram portions, or one ice-cream scoop. Place them into the rings placed on the prepared tray, flattening slightly against the sides. Bake these for 20 to 25 minutes, until they're a nice deep brown. Allow them to cool, then demold with care.

For the Salted Caramel. In a heatproof bowl, add the cocoa butter and dark chocolate. In a saucepan, heat the cream with the vanilla and corn syrup until it's warm. Then in another saucepan, caramelize the granulated sugar by heating and stirring until it turns a deep amber. Pour the warmed cream into the caramel to deglaze the pan, and add in the butter. Let's cook this mixture to 225°F (107°C), then pour it into the bowl containing the cocoa butter and dark chocolate. Allow the chocolate and cocoa butter to melt, then add in the salt and use a hand blender to bring it to a luscious, smooth consistency. Cover with cling film, and store in the refrigerator for 2 hours.

Time for assembly. Let's use a piping bag to pipe some of that gorgeous salted caramel generously over the top of each cookie. Cover them with a layer of toasted, chopped walnuts to finish the look and add some great texture.

These chunky cookies are ready to serve or snack on throughout the day. You can store them in an airtight container for 2 days.

ROYAL COOKIES 'N' CREAM

Yield: 10 cookies
Mold: 2½-inch (6-cm) ring

Cookies 'n' cream is such a distinct comforting flavor, so we couldn't resist making our own twist on the classic combination. Imagine the most chunky chocolate chip cookie ever baked, with the most stylish molded hazelnut cream ever seen sitting on top as a crown. Now stop imagining, and make it a reality! This is easily one of our personal favorites, and a fitting tribute to all the cute cows that casually roam around the streets of Bangalore.

Chocolate Chip Cookie

½ cup (110 g) butter, plus more for greasing rings

¼ cup + 2 tbsp + 2 tsp (85 g) granulated sugar

½ cup (100 g) brown sugar

1 egg

2 tsp (10 g) vanilla extract

1½ cups (195 g) all-purpose flour

½ tsp sea salt

½ tsp baking soda

1½ cups (195 g) dark chocolate, chopped

Hazelnut Cream

2 tsp (4 g) gelatin

¾ cup + 1 tbsp (194 g) water, divided

2 egg yolks

½ cup (80 g) milk chocolate, melted

2 tbsp + 2 tsp (25 g) hazelnut paste (see Quick Reference Notes, page 219)

Velvet Spray (optional)

⅓ cup + 2 tsp (50 g) dark chocolate

1½ tbsp (25 g) cocoa butter

Hazelnut paste, for garnish

For the Chocolate Chip Cookie. In a stand mixer with a paddle attachment, cream the butter, granulated sugar and brown sugar. Gradually add in the egg and vanilla extract, followed by the all-purpose flour, salt and baking soda, to get a nice, even dough. Finally, fold in the dark chocolate and rest the dough in the refrigerator for 1 hour.

While the dough is resting, preheat the oven to 320°F (160°C). Grease the rings with extra butter and place on a tray lined with baking paper. Once the dough is well rested, weigh out 60-gram portions, or one ice-cream scoop, and place them in the prepared rings. Bake for 12 to 15 minutes, until the edges start to brown. Allow them to cool, then bring them out from the molds and keep them aside until we're ready to assemble.

> ### Note from the Chefs:
>
> The trick to getting this cookie perfectly gooey in the center with a bit of crust on the edges is to pull them out of the oven when they've reached an internal temperature of 192°F (89°C). So use a probe thermometer if you can; a little precision while baking makes all the difference!

For the Hazelnut Cream. We'll first need to bloom the gelatin. Add 1 tablespoon (24 g) of ice cold water to a bowl and add the gelatin, soaking it for 5 minutes, until it absorbs the water and swells.

In a saucepan, heat ¾ cup (170 g) of water until it's warm, and pour a little into a dish containing the egg yolks to help temper them. Then pour the tempered yolks back into the saucepan and continue stirring over a low heat, until it cooks to 180°F (82°C). Turn off the heat, and stir the bloomed gelatin into the heated yolk mixture until it's fully dissolved. Follow that by adding in the milk chocolate and hazelnut paste, combining everything together using a hand blender to form a rich hazelnut cream.

(continued)

Pour the cream into flat silicon molds and freeze for 4 hours to harden. If you don't have molds and want to keep it simple, just pour it out into a tray to get it ½ inch (1.3 cm) thick, then after freezing, use a cookie cutter to cut neat discs of hazelnut cream.

Note from the Chefs:

Silicon molds are useful in adding clean, interesting shapes to your desserts, but if you prefer to keep things classic, feel free to use a greased tin of an appropriate size and shape.

For the Velvet Spray. Skip this step if you don't have a spray gun. Your dessert will still look amazing; it just won't have the exact same matte finish. Otherwise, melt the dark chocolate and cocoa butter separately, then mix them together into a bowl.

Time for assembly. Demold the cream discs, and keep them on a tray to get them ready to spray. Make sure the dark chocolate cocoa butter mixture we made is at 84°F (29°C), then use a spray gun to coat all the cream discs and give them that professional velvet look. Gently place the coated cream discs directly on top of each baked cookie, then pipe a dollop of hazelnut paste right in the center to make them feel extra special.

These awesome cookies taste as good as they look. Eat them immediately at room temperature. You can store them in an airtight container for up to 1 day.

PEANUT YUZU MARSH-MALLOW COOKIE

Yield: 4 cookies
Mold: 5-inch (13-cm) ring

Yuzu is basically the God of all lemons. If you've never tasted it, you're in for a treat—it's aromatic beyond comparison, smells as fresh as the first day of spring, and adds a stunning jolt of acidity to the marshmallow in this recipe. The inspiration for this combination of elements came from Southeast Asian cuisine, where you'll find peanut-based noodle or rice dishes that are balanced with lime or lemongrass. So get ready for the most unique aromas and textures in this show-stopping dessert cookie!

Coffee Cacao Cookie Dough

¼ cup + 2 tsp (25 g) cocoa powder

1⅓ cups + 1 tsp (170 g) all-purpose flour

1 tsp baking powder

½ tsp baking soda

¾ tsp sea salt

3 tbsp + 2½ tsp (55 g) butter, plus more for greasing rings, at room temperature

½ cup + 1 tsp (115 g) brown sugar

¼ cup (50 g) granulated sugar

2 egg yolks

⅛ cup + 2 tsp (40 g) milk

1 tbsp (15 g) brewed espresso

1 tsp vanilla extract

2 tsp (10 g) grapeseed or olive oil

½ cup + 1 tsp (90 g) white chocolate, chopped

½ cup (60 g) dark chocolate, chopped

Peanut Crunch

⅜ cup (65 g) milk chocolate

⅜ cup + 5 tsp (125 g) peanut butter

½ tsp sea salt

1 cup (140 g) peanuts, toasted and chopped

Oil, for coating acetate strips

Yuzu Marshmallow

3 tbsp (20 g) gelatin

½ cup (120 g) cold water

¾ cup (110 g) dextrose

⅓ cup (90 g) yuzu purée

⅛ cup + 1½ tbsp (75 g) corn syrup

¾ cup + 3 tbsp + 1½ tsp (195 g) granulated sugar

½ tsp citric acid powder

Sesame seeds, for garnish

Matcha powder, for garnish

For the Coffee Cacao Cookie Dough. In a large bowl, sift together the cocoa powder, all-purpose flour, baking powder, baking soda and salt. Set it aside. In a stand mixer with a paddle attachment, combine the butter with the brown and granulated sugars on low speed for a minute. Then gradually add in the egg yolks and milk a little at a time until it's completely incorporated. Fold in the espresso and vanilla extract, followed by the oil, to form an even dough. Continue mixing in the sifted ingredients. Finally, fold in the white and dark chocolate, and let the dough rest in the refrigerator for 1 hour. While the dough is resting, preheat the oven to 320°F (160°C). Grease the rings with extra butter and place on a tray lined with baking paper. After the dough has rested, portion it out into 150-gram chunks, or three ice-cream scoops, and place them into the greased rings. Gently press and flatten to form a nice cookie base, then bake for 30 minutes, until the edges are firm to the touch. Allow to cool, then carefully demold.

For the Peanut Crunch. Melt the milk chocolate and mix it with the peanut butter in a bowl. Toss in the salt and the peanuts to give it a great texture. Allow this tasty, nutty mix to cool to room temperature before spreading a generous layer of it over each of the baked cookies. Now cut 2-inch (5-cm)-tall strips of stiff plastic, lightly coat them with oil, and wrap them around each cookie to make acetate rings. These thin walls are going to help us contain the marshmallow perfectly on top of the cookie.

(continued)

PEANUT YUZU MARSHMALLOW COOKIE *(continued)*

For the Yuzu Marshmallow. Have a piping bag ready to go; we'll need it as soon as the marshmallow is whipped. In a small bowl, bloom the gelatin in the cold water for 5 minutes, until it absorbs the water and swells. Place the bloomed gelatin in a stand mixer bowl and add the dextrose. Then in a saucepan, combine the yuzu purée, corn syrup and granulated sugar, and cook the mixture to exactly 230°F (110°C). Transfer the hot mixture to the stand mixer bowl containing the dextrose and bloomed gelatin. Use a spatula to stir well, ensuring that the gelatin is fully melted and dissolved. Then fit the mixer with a whisk attachment and whip the mix to get a light, airy marshmallow texture. We want a fluffy, delicious cloud. Then fit the mixer with a whisk attachment and whip the mix to get a light, airy marshmallow texture. Add in the citric acid powder, and whip a little more till it's evenly incorporated and you get a fluffy, delicious cloud of marshmallow.

Now is not the time to stop and admire! Immediately add the marshmallow to the piping bag and pipe a 1-inch (2.5-cm) layer of this yuzu marshmallow on top of each cookie base. Place these in an airtight container and leave them overnight at room temperature to give the marshmallow time to set.

Time for finishing. Once the marshmallow is perfectly set, peel those plastic strips off to reveal our beautiful, neat marshmallow-topped cookie. To finish this off, sprinkle toasted sesame seeds and dust matcha powder over the top and sides.

These incredible family-style cookies are ready to eat at room temperature. You can store them in the refrigerator for up to 2 days.

MANGO CARAMEL PEANUT BUTTER COOKIE

Yield: 2 cookies
Mold: 6-inch (15¼-cm) ring

Beneath the nutty, raspberry-studded exterior of this cookie, there's a wild hidden secret. We transformed this rustic peanut butter cookie base into a tangy tropical dream by using the king of Indian fruit: mango. Grab the best mangoes you can find so they can lend that signature natural sweet-n-sour-ness to the soft caramel layer inside. In our experience, once someone has tasted a slice of this jumbo-size cookie, they can't help but having a second serving.

Cookie Dough

⅓ cup + 1 tbsp (95 g) butter, plus more for greasing rings, at room temperature

1⅓ cups + 1 tsp (170 g) all-purpose flour

⅔ tsp baking powder

½ tsp sea salt

⅓ cup (90 g) creamy peanut butter

1¼ tsp (8 g) invert sugar

½ cup (110 g) brown sugar

1 egg

Cookie Crust

⅜ cup + 1 tbsp (65 g) toasted peanuts, chopped

⅜ cup (65 g) white chocolate, chopped

¼ tsp salt

Mango Caramel

¼ cup + 1 tsp (45 g) milk chocolate, chopped

½ cup + 1 tbsp + 2 tsp (120 g) granulated sugar

⅓ cup (90 g) butter

½ cup (120 g) mango purée, warm

Pinch of sea salt

½ vanilla bean pod (see Quick Reference Notes, page 219)

Caramelized Peanuts

3 tbsp + 2 tsp (45 g) granulated sugar

1 tbsp (15 g) water

⅞ cup (125 g) peanuts, toasted

1½ tsp (7.5 g) cocoa butter

Pinch of Madras curry powder

Pinch of sea salt (skip if using salted peanuts)

Fresh raspberries, for finishing

For the Cookie Dough. Grease the rings with extra butter and place them on a tray lined with baking paper. In a large bowl, sift the all-purpose flour, baking powder and salt. Set the bowl aside. In a stand mixer with a paddle attachment, cream the butter, peanut butter, invert sugar and brown sugar for a minute. Then slowly incorporate the egg, mixing well each time before adding more. After that, add in the sifted ingredients and mix to get an even dough. Portion the cookie dough equally between the prepared rings. Rest these in the refrigerator for an hour before we get to baking. Preheat the oven to 320°F (160°C).

For the Cookie Crust. In a bowl, mix together the peanuts and white chocolate and season with salt. Once the cookies are back out from the refrigerator, sprinkle this nut mixture generously over the top surface of each. Bake them for 25 to 30 minutes, until they turn a perfect golden brown.

For the Mango Caramel. In a heatproof bowl, place the milk chocolate. In a saucepan, caramelize the granulated sugar by heating and stirring it until it turns deep amber. Add in the butter and mango purée, and continue to cook until the mixture reaches 225°F (107°C). Pour this into the bowl containing the chocolate, allowing it to melt with the heat. Then drop in the salt and vanilla, and use a hand blender to get an incredibly smooth mango caramel. Put it in the refrigerator for 2 hours to allow it to set.

(continued)

MANGO CARAMEL PEANUT BUTTER COOKIE *(continued)*

For the Caramelized Peanuts. Line a tray with baking paper. In a saucepan, heat the granulated sugar and water to 241°F (116°C), then turn off the heat and toss in the peanuts. Mix continuously until the sugar syrup crystallizes and coats the peanuts. Now place the pan back over low heat, and continue stirring until the peanuts get coated with a nice layer of caramel. Then add in the cocoa butter, curry powder and salt (if the peanuts are unsalted), and give it a final mix to evenly distribute all those flavors. Spread these coated peanuts out onto the prepared tray, and allow them to cool.

Time for assembly. Spread a generous layer of mango caramel onto each cookie base. Carefully arrange fresh raspberries around the edge, and sprinkle those coated caramelized peanuts in the middle to help finish the look and add an unforgettable crunch.

These heavenly cookies are ready to slice and serve at room temperature, and since they've got fresh fruit you want to finish them off within a day.

APPLE PECAN COOKIES

Yield: 10 cookies
Mold: 3-inch (7½-cm) ring

This cookie is the descendant of another great American tradition: pies. Picture this: The apples are caramelized to perfection, just like in your favorite apple pie; the pecans are blended into a decadent chewy caramel, like the perfect pecan pie; and the cookie base itself is a crumbly dream reminiscent of the most buttery of pie crusts. These mini-discs of heaven perfectly balance out the decadence of dark chocolate and caramel, with the natural appeal of apples and nuts.

Pecan Cookie

½ cup (108 g) butter, plus more for greasing rings, at room temperature

1⅛ cups (110 g) pecan paste (see Quick Reference Notes, page 219)

⅓ cup (75 g) brown sugar

3 tbsp + 2 tsp (45 g) granulated sugar

1 tbsp (18 g) invert sugar

¾ tsp sea salt

1 egg

1 egg yolk

1 cup (130 g) dark chocolate, melted

1 cup + 1½ tbsp (140 g) all-purpose flour

1⅓ cups (130 g) pecans, roasted and chopped

Caramelized Apples

3 Granny Smith apples

1 tbsp + 1 tsp (20 g) butter

¼ cup (55 g) brown sugar

1 vanilla bean pod (see Quick Reference Notes, page 219)

Pecan Praline Paste

1 cup + 3½ tbsp (120 g) pecans

¼ cup + 2 tbsp + 2 tsp (80 g) granulated sugar

Chewy Pecan Caramel

½ tsp gelatin

1 tsp cold water

½ cup + 2 tsp (130 g) heavy cream

Pinch of sea salt

1 tbsp (20 g) corn syrup

⅓ cup + 2 tsp (75 g) granulated sugar

¼ cup (70 g) pecan praline paste

Pecans, roasted and chopped, for garnish

For the Pecan Cookie. Grease the rings with extra butter and place them on a tray lined with baking paper. Roast the pecans for 10 minutes and then grind them into a paste. Now kick things off with the cookie dough: in a stand mixer with paddle attachment, cream the butter, pecan paste, brown sugar, granulated sugar, invert sugar and salt on a low speed for 2 minutes. Then add in the egg and egg yolk a little at a time until fully incorporated. Melted dark chocolate goes in next, followed by the all-purpose flour and pecans. Mix each ingredient in well to end up with a nice chunky dough that we can rest in the refrigerator for an hour. Once the dough is ready, portion out 70 grams, or one heaping ice-cream scoop, for each cookie and place them into the prepared rings. Bake these for 15 to 20 minutes, until the edges are firm to the touch. Preheat the oven at 320°F (160°C) and bake these for 15 to 20 minutes, until the edges are firm to the touch.

For the Caramelized Apples. Cut the apples down into tiny cubes. Now, in a sauté pan over low heat, start melting the butter, brown sugar and vanilla together, then toss in those apple cubes. Cook the apples until they turn tender and are well-coated in juices, then turn off the heat and set them aside to use in the end.

(continued)

> ## Note from the Chefs:
>
> If you've never made praline paste at home, it will blow your mind how easy it is. Here we'll be using it to create that signature caramel topping, but once you make it, you can simply eat it on toast like any other nutty spread!

For the Pecan Praline Paste. Spread the pecan nuts out on a tray lined with baking paper and roast them for 10 minutes in an oven set to 320°F (160°C). In a saucepan, caramelize the granulated sugar by heating and stirring until it turns a light golden brown, then pour it over the toasted pecans and allow it to cool. Once the caramel has hardened, break it into shards and toss them in the food processor to blend into a lovely pecan praline paste.

For the Chewy Pecan Caramel. In a small bowl, add the gelatin and cold water, letting the gelatin bloom for 5 minutes, until it absorbs the water and swells. In a saucepan, warm the cream, salt and corn syrup until it's warm, then stir to get a nice homogenous mixture. Now in a heavy-bottomed pan, heat the granulated sugar while stirring continuously until it caramelizes, then add in the warmed cream mixture to help deglaze the pan. Continue cooking to 223°F (106°C). At this point, turn off the heat and add in the measured praline paste, followed by the bloomed gelatin. Use a hand blender to bring it all to a smooth consistency, then wrap and refrigerate the caramel for 1 hour to set.

Time for assembly. Bring out those baked cookies, and start topping them with caramelized apples in a ring shape, leaving some space in the center. Spoon the beautiful pecan caramel into that center cavity, and finish up with a sprinkling of roasted, chopped pecans.

Serve these perfect cookies immediately for tastiest results; you want those caramelized apples to feel amazing, so don't keep them waiting too long. You could also refrigerate the components individually, then assemble them when you're ready.

ROCKY ROAD COOKIES

Yield: 6 cookies
Mold: 3-inch (7½-cm) ring

Modern desserts are full of smooth textures and clean finishes, so when you actually get to bite into something super chunky, it shocks your system and wakes up your taste buds. It feels so raw and unexpected! That's exactly what happened when we dug into a tub of Rocky Road ice cream together and dreamed up this rugged cookie. There are so many options for how you could get a rocky texture, but in this recipe we've decided to go with a chunky chocolate cookie, cover it with unapologetic rough bits of streusel, and complement that with a rustic marshmallow topping.

Double Chocolate Cookie

¼ cup (45 g) 100% cocoa mass

½ cup + 1½ tsp (65 g) dark chocolate

3 tbsp + ½ tsp (45 g) butter

2 eggs

½ cup + 2 tbsp + 1 tsp (130 g) granulated sugar

1 tsp vanilla extract

3 tbsp + ½ tsp (25 g) all-purpose flour

⅛ tsp baking powder

Pinch of sea salt

⅜ cup (65 g) milk chocolate, roughly chopped

Caramel Toffee

2 tsp (10 g) butter, plus more for greasing the ring

½ cup + 1 tbsp (75 g) dark chocolate

½ cup + 1 tsp (125 g) heavy cream

¼ cup + 3 tbsp + ½ tsp (90 g) granulated sugar

⅓ cup + 1½ tsp (90 g) liquid glucose

1½ tsp (10 g) invert sugar

Chocolate Streusel

2 tbsp (30 g) butter, cold

2 tbsp + 1 tsp (30 g) granulated sugar

⅜ cup + 1 tsp (50 g) all-purpose flour

1 tbsp + 2½ tsp (10 g) cocoa powder

Vanilla Marshmallow

⅜ cup + 1 tbsp + 1 tsp (110 g) water, divided

1½ tbsp (10 g) gelatin

⅓ cup (40 g) dextrose

½ cup + 1 tbsp + 2 tsp (120 g) granulated sugar

1 tbsp (20 g) corn syrup

½ vanilla bean pod (see Quick Reference Notes, page 219)

For the Double Chocolate Cookie. In a double-boiler, heat the 100-percent cocoa mass, dark chocolate and butter until they're completely melted. Now in a stand mixer with a whisk attachment, let's whip the eggs, granulated sugar and vanilla extract on high for 3 minutes, so we get a fluffy, airy mixture. Gently fold in the melted chocolate mix. Next gently fold in the all-purpose flour, baking powder and salt until incorporated. Finish by dropping in the milk chocolate chunks; these are going to help put the "rock" in Rocky Road. Rest the dough in the refrigerator for 2 hours before we get to baking.

For the Caramel Toffee. Grease a 7-inch (17¾-cm) cake ring with extra butter and place it on a tray lined with baking paper. Place the butter and dark chocolate in a heatproof bowl and set it aside. In a saucepan, whisk together the cream, granulated sugar, liquid glucose and invert sugar and cook until it reaches 239°F (115°C). Pour the cream mixture into the bowl containing the butter and dark chocolate, stirring quickly to make sure it's well blended. Pour that out immediately into the greased cake ring and put it aside to set for 1½ hours. Once it's turned slightly firmer, cut it up into small cubes that we can use them during assembly.

For the Chocolate Streusel. In a bowl, rub together the butter, granulated sugar, all-purpose flour and cocoa powder between your fingers until it starts to form a breadcrumb consistency. Keep going until you notice they're forming those larger chunks of streusel crumble that will add a stunning texture to this cookie.

(continued)

Time for assembly. Preheat the oven to 320°F (160°C). Grease the rings with extra butter. Portion out 70 grams of dough, or one heaping ice-cream scoop, into each of the greased rings, pressing down gently to form a nice base. Place small chunks of caramel toffee over the base and cover the tops of each cookie with a generous amount of streusel. Pop these into the oven for 15 minutes, until the edges are firm to the touch. Allow them to cool, and remove them from the molds with care.

For the Vanilla Marshmallow. Add ¼ cup (60 g) of cold water to a small bowl. Next, add the gelatin and let it bloom for 5 minutes, until it absorbs the water and swells. Once it's finished, add it to a stand mixer bowl along with the dextrose. In a saucepan, add the granulated sugar, 3 tablespoons + 1 teaspoon (50 g) of water, the corn syrup and the vanilla, and cook them until the mix reaches 250°F (121°C). Transfer the hot mixture to the bowl containing the bloomed gelatin and dextrose. Use a spatula to stir well, ensuring that the gelatin is fully melted, then use a whisk attachment to mix until it's a light, airy marshmallow texture. We want a fluffy, delicious cloud. Use a spoon or palette knife to apply the marshmallow over the top of the cookies, and use a blowtorch to lightly brûlée them for an exquisite, artistic look. If you have some extra marshmallow left over, set it in a greased frame and chop it up as a side snack.

These rocky, chewy cookies are ready to eat. You can store them at room temperature for up to 1 day.

LET'S JAM LINZER

Yield: 8 cookies
Mold: 3-inch (7½-cm) cookie cutter and 1-inch (2.5-cm) cookie cutter

The Austrian classic linzer is one of the first cookies Andrés ever learned to make in pastry school. All the way across the world, Vinesh had already spent his youth at South Indian bakeries stuffing himself with a local version of the linzer: a cookie sandwich with a delightful sticky jam inside. So once we discovered our common admiration for this jammy classic, the only sensible thing to do was to create our own next-level version: pairing the depth of a chocolate cookie and ganache with the tangy brightness of raspberry jam!

Chocolate Linzer Dough

½ cup (110 g) butter

¼ cup + 2 tbsp + 1 tsp (80 g) granulated sugar

1 egg yolk

1 tsp milk

¾ cup (75 g) hazelnut flour

⅔ cup (85 g) all-purpose flour

¼ cup + 1 tbsp (28 g) cocoa powder

½ tsp baking powder

Pinch of ground cinnamon

Pinch of sea salt

Cocoa Nib Sugar

2 tbsp (30 g) brown sugar

¼ cup (30 g) cocoa nibs

Ganache Linzer

¾ cup (100 g) dark chocolate, chopped

¼ cup (55 g) heavy cream

2¾ tsp (15 g) invert sugar

1 tbsp + 1 tsp (20 g) butter, softened

Raspberry Jam

⅔ cup (85 g) raspberries, fresh or frozen

2 tbsp + 2½ tsp (35 g) granulated sugar, divided

½ tsp pectin

½ tsp lemon juice

For the Chocolate Linzer Dough. In a stand mixer with a paddle attachment, cream the butter and granulated sugar. Then add in the egg yolk and milk gradually, making sure to mix them in well. Next add in the hazelnut flour, all-purpose flour, cocoa powder, baking powder, cinnamon and salt, mixing them in gently to form a nice, even dough. Place this dough between two sheets of baking paper and use a rolling pin to flatten it out to ⅛ inch (3 mm). Freeze for 1 hour. While the dough is in the freezer, preheat the oven to 320°F (160°C). After an hour, use a cookie cutter to cut small discs of dough. Then from half of the discs, cut out a smaller hole in the center to make them look like donut discs.

For the Cocoa Nib Sugar. In a bowl, grind together the brown sugar and cocoa nibs, and sprinkle it generously on top of the discs. Save the extra sugar for garnishing the cookies later. Bake the cookies for 20 to 25 minutes, until the edges are firm to the touch.

For the Ganache Linzer. Place the dark chocolate in a heatproof bowl. In a saucepan, heat the cream along with the invert sugar and bring it to a simmer. Then pour it into the bowl containing the dark chocolate, allowing the chocolate to melt before using a hand blender to get a smooth chocolate cream. Let it cool to 113°F (45°C) before mixing in the soft butter as well, then store the ganache in the fridge for later.

For the Raspberry Jam. In a saucepan, combine the raspberries and 1 tablespoon + 1¼ teaspoons (17.5 g) of granulated sugar. Bring it to a boil. Combine the remaining 1 tablespoon + 1¼ teaspoons (17.5 g) of granulated sugar with the pectin, and add it to the heated raspberries, continuing to cook for about 2 minutes, until it thickens. Finally, turn off the heat, add the lemon juice and allow the jam to set as it cools.

Time for assembly. First, pipe the linzer ganache along the sides of the cookie discs, leaving space in the center. These will act as the base of the cookie. Then place the donut discs on top of the ganache, lining them up with the base to form perfect cookie sandwiches. Finally, coat the sides of each cookie with cocoa nib sugar, and spoon a bit of the raspberry jam right in the center as a highlight for both the look and the flavor. These crumbly cookie sandwiches are best eaten fresh. You can store them in an airtight container for up to 3 days.

THE BIG BOUNTY®

Yield: 5 cookies
Mold: 3-inch (7½-cm) ring

When was the first time you tried chocolate and coconut paired together? Like a lot of Indian kids, Vinesh had the fateful experience of a distant relative visiting from Dubai and bringing a load of Bounty chocolates with them. As travel became more frequent, the supply of Bounty became more and more steady as well. All grown-up now as pastry chefs, instead of sneaking into our kitchens and stealing chocolates from the fridge, we can just make our own! This recipe came around when one of our friends was complaining that they couldn't find any delicious vegan cookies on the market. We decided it was time to bring this classic chocolate-coconut pairing back in a new and exciting cookie-shaped way.

Coco-choco Cookie

½ cup (110 g) coconut oil

¼ cup + 3 tbsp + ½ tsp (90 g) granulated sugar

½ cup (100 g) brown sugar

¼ cup (50 g) almond milk

¾ tsp sea salt

½ tsp baking soda

1 cup + 1 tbsp + 1 tsp (135 g) all-purpose flour

½ cup + 1 tsp (45 g) cocoa powder

⅔ cup + 2 tsp (60 g) desiccated coconut

1 cup + 2 tbsp (150 g) dark chocolate, chopped

Bounty Filling

⅞ cup (200 g) coconut milk

⅓ cup + 2 tsp (75 g) granulated sugar

½ cup + 1 tbsp (50 g) desiccated coconut

Cocoa Crumble

¼ cup (30 g) oat flour

2 tbsp (15 g) cornstarch

2½ tbsp (15 g) cocoa powder

¼ cup (25 g) hazelnut flour

⅜ cup + 2 tsp (25 g) almond flour

⅛ cup + 1 tbsp + 2 tsp (50 g) brown sugar

1⅓ tbsp (10 g) cocoa nibs

⅛ + 2 tsp (35 g) coconut oil

1 tsp water

Coconut oil, for greasing rings
Icing sugar, for garnish
Cocoa powder, for garnish

For the Coco-choco Cookie. In a stand mixer with a paddle attachment, mix the coconut oil, granulated sugar and brown sugar for 5 minutes on low speed. Add in the almond milk, and continue to mix. Once those are combined, toss in the salt, baking soda, all-purpose flour, cocoa powder, desiccated coconut and dark chocolate, and mix well to form an even dough. Place the dough between two sheets of baking paper, and use a rolling pin to flatten it out into a ¼-inch (6-mm) sheet that we can rest in the fridge for 2 hours.

For the Bounty Filling. In a saucepan over low heat, heat the coconut milk and granulated sugar until it starts to reduce and thicken into a syrup consistency similar to condensed milk. This may take 1 to 2 hours, and you'll have to stir it every 10 minutes. Once it's reached the right consistency, add in the desiccated coconut and continue to cook until the mixture thickens further. Allow the pudding to cool and keep it aside for assembly.

For the Cocoa Crumble. In a large bowl, add the oat flour, cornstarch, cocoa powder, hazelnut flour, almond flour, brown sugar and cocoa nibs. Mix until everything is well combined. Then slowly add in the coconut oil so it starts to take on a more sandlike texture. Finally, pour in the water and mix until you get those larger, rough chunks that we can use as our topping.

Time for assembly. Preheat the oven to 320°F (160°C). Grease the rings with coconut oil and place on a tray lined with baking paper. Take the dough out of the fridge and use a 3-inch (7.5-cm) cookie cutter to make clean discs. Put a generous teaspoon of coconut filling onto one cookie, then place another cookie on top to form a cookie sandwich. Place these into the prepared rings, cover the tops with a generous helping of cocoa crumble, and bake for 15 to 20 minutes. Bring them out and dust some icing sugar and cocoa powder on top for a quick and simple finish. After all, it's what's on the inside that really counts.

These discs of pure joy are ready to be eaten fresh out of the oven. You can store them in an airtight container for up to 3 days.

MIDNIGHT
Layer Cakes

Whenever Vinesh thinks of his childhood birthday parties, of course there are all the happy memories of family and friends gathered in the evening, playing games and eating lots of snacks, but all of that other stuff is practically built around the most important tradition of all: cutting the cake. Invariably there would be huge leftover slices of this cake kept in the refrigerator, and after everyone had gone home, and Vinesh's parents were asleep, he'd sneak out of bed and get that one extra slice of cake. Somehow it was even more delicious and moist and creamy in the middle of the night when no one was watching!

We've decided to build this entire chapter around the magic of Midnight Cakes. They're built up with slabs of cake or brownie and layered with unbelievably tasty jams and ganache spreads. So slip out of bed to grab another bite of that Pandan Pumpkin Chiffon (page 119), or chat late into the night with a friend over a German Chocolate Stout Cake (page 107), or take a break from that all-nighter in your office to help yourself to the Japanese-Spiced Mango Brownie Cake (page 101). These spongy layer cakes make for tempting, sexy moonlit companions.

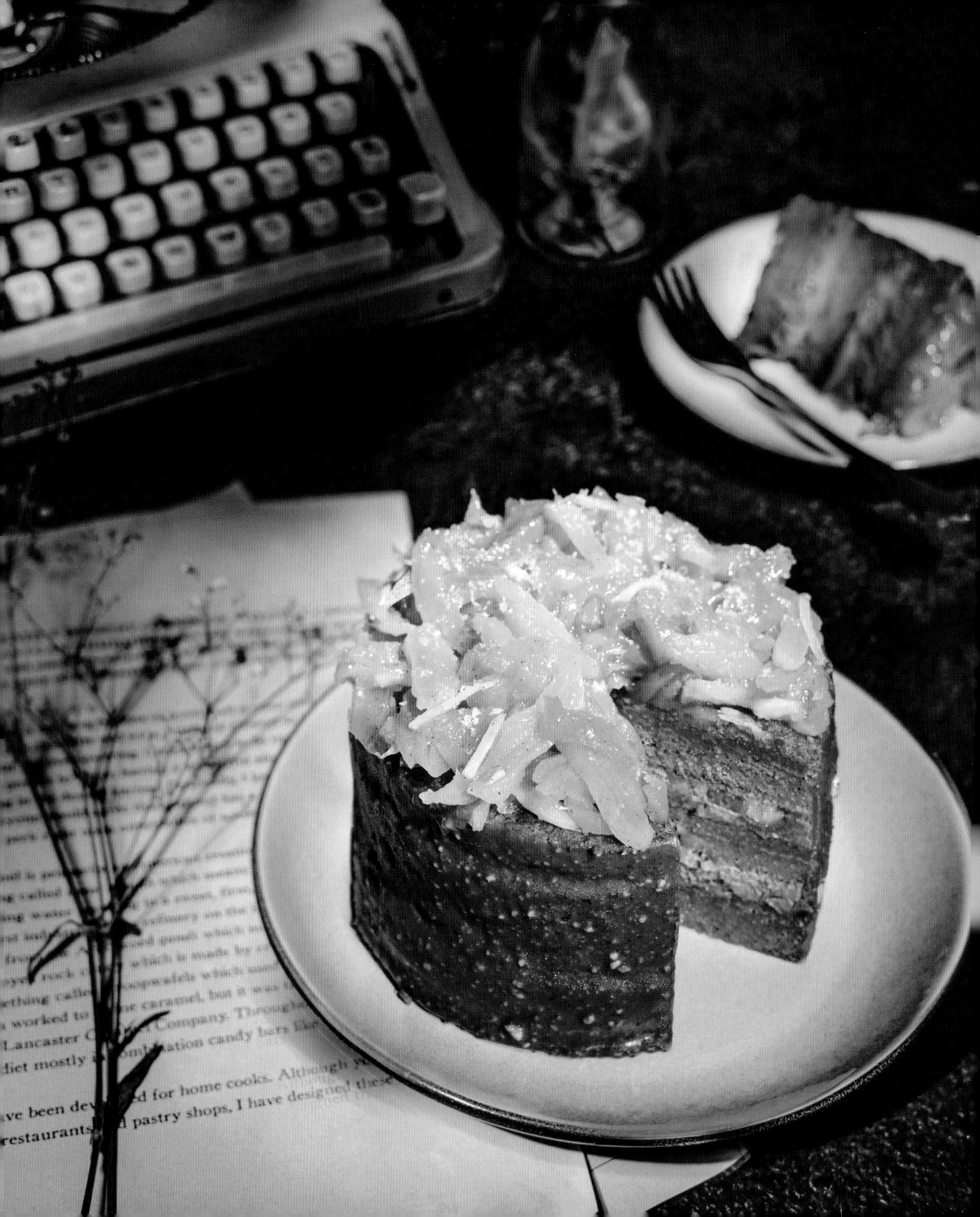

JAPANESE-SPICED MANGO BROWNIE CAKE

Yield: 1 cake
Mold: 6-inch (15¼-cm) ring

In India you often see carts outside every school selling mangoes that have been cut up and heavily spiced. Since his school days, Vinesh has always felt that mixing sweet and spicy flavors can bring out a delightfully unexpected experience. But it wasn't until Andrés visited Japan and discovered togarashi that things fell in place for this cake! Togarashi is a typical Japanese table condiment usually only seen at ramen shops, but we've decided to adapt it into this incredible layered chocolate brownie.

Banana Brownie

¾ cup + 1½ tsp (180 g) butter

½ cup (100 g) granulated sugar

½ cup (100 g) brown sugar

1½ cups (225 g) ripe bananas, mashed

3 eggs

⅞ cup + 1 tsp (150 g) milk chocolate, melted

¼ tsp sea salt

¾ cup (90 g) all-purpose flour

Apricot Ginger Confit

½ cup (100 g) granulated sugar

1 vanilla bean pod (see Quick Reference Notes, page 219)

1 cup + 2½ tsp (250 g) water

3⅛ cups (375 g) dried apricots, sliced

⅓ cup (100 g) candied ginger, chopped

3 tbsp (45 g) dark rum

Mango Togarashi Mousse

1 tsp gelatin

2½ tsp (12 g) cold water

⅓ cup (80 g) mango purée

Pinch of sea salt

½ tsp togarashi spice

Zest of 1 lemon

¾ cup + 1 tbsp + 1 tsp (140 g) milk chocolate, melted

⅔ cup + 1 tsp (165 g) heavy cream

Nutty Chocolate Coating

1 cup + 3 tbsp (200 g) milk chocolate, melted

⅜ cup + 1 tbsp + 1 tsp (100 g) cocoa butter, melted

⅞ cup (200 g) clarified butter, melted

1⅛ cup (150 g) hazelnuts, toasted and chopped

For the Banana Brownie. Preheat the oven to 320°F (160°C). In a stand mixer with a paddle attachment, cream together the butter, granulated sugar and brown sugar. Add the mashed bananas to the butter and mix. Gradually add the eggs, a little at a time, making sure they're fully incorporated. Add in the milk chocolate and salt, and finish by folding in the all-purpose flour until it's just combined. Divide the batter up between three 6-inch (15¼-cm) rings and bake 25 to 30 minutes. Use a cake tester to check if the baking is done, or use a probe thermometer to know when the cakes reach 203°F (95°C).

For the Apricot Ginger Confit. In a saucepan, let's bring a mixture of the granulated sugar, vanilla and water to a nice boil. Add in the apricots, candied ginger and rum, and let it all boil for 4 to 5 minutes, until the fruit softens and the sugar forms a thin, shiny glaze. Turn the heat off, and set the confit aside until we're ready for assembly.

For the Mango Togarashi Mousse. In a small bowl, combine the gelatin and cold water. Let the gelatin bloom for 5 minutes, until it swells. Now in a saucepan, begin warming the mango purée along with salt, togarashi and lemon zest. Bring the mixture to a boil, then turn off the heat and add in the bloomed gelatin, stirring to make sure it dissolves completely. To finish up, add in the milk chocolate and use a hand blender to get a smooth consistency. Once it's cooled, in a stand mixer with a whisk attachment, whip the cream for 2 minutes, until it develops soft peaks, then fold it into the chocolate mixture to make it soft and delicate.

(continued)

JAPANESE-SPICED MANGO BROWNIE CAKE *(continued)*

Time for assembly. Set aside two-thirds of the apricot confit as the final decoration, and mix the remaining one-third into the mango togarashi mousse for us to use as a filling. Take one of the brownie layers as the base, and spread a generous amount of the filling over it using a palette knife. Then repeat the process by placing a second layer of brownie gently on top, and spreading another layer of filling. Finally, place the third layer of brownie, and pop the cake into the freezer for 4 hours to harden.

For the Nutty Chocolate Coating. In a bowl that's large enough to fit the cake, mix together the milk chocolate and cocoa butter, then add in the clarified butter. Toss in the hazelnuts, and allow it to cool to 95°F (35°C).

Put a tray beneath a wire rack to catch excess glaze. Place baking paper on another tray. Bring the cake out from the freezer and place it on the wire rack. Pour the chocolate glaze so it evenly coats the top and side surfaces of the cake. Transfer that beautifully coated cake over to the prepared tray to set for about 10 minutes, then cover the top of the cake with apricot confit to form a fresh, fruity crown.

This magnificent layered brownie is ready to be sliced and served fresh. You can store it in the refrigerator for up to 2 days.

CRÊPE SUZETTE CAKE

Yield: 1
Mold: 6-inch (15¼-cm) ring

Whenever we travel to new places, the most important thing we make sure to do is visit the local bakeries for inspiration. On one of our trips through Southeast Asia, we came across these insane layered crêpe cakes flavored with matcha or tropical fruits and thought it would be fun to combine this concept with a classic French favorite, the suzette. This one is all about balance, not just physically because we're stacking a dozen crêpes on top of a cake, but also balance between all the bright and zesty flavors packed inside this delicious dessert.

Orange Chantilly

¾ cup (130 g) white chocolate, chopped

Zest of 2 oranges

2 tsp (15 g) corn syrup

1 cup + 2 tbsp (270 g) heavy cream, divided

Orange Cake

Butter, for greasing ring

1 egg

¼ cup + 2½ tsp (60 g) granulated sugar

2 tsp (15 g) honey

¼ cup + 2 tsp (60 g) vegetable oil

½ tsp vanilla extract

¼ cup (60 g) orange juice

½ cup + 1 tbsp + 2 tsp (75 g) all-purpose flour

¼ cup (15 g) almond flour

½ tsp baking powder

Zest of ½ lemon

Zest of ½ orange

Crêpes

2 cups + 1½ tsp (500 g) milk

2 tsp (10 g) vanilla extract

⅓ cup + 2 tsp (75 g) granulated sugar

4 eggs

1⅜ cups + 1 tbsp (180 g) all-purpose flour

2 tbsp (30 g) butter, melted, plus more for greasing the pan

Icing sugar, for dusting

Orange Marmalade

1 unpeeled orange

3 tbsp (45 g) orange juice

¾ cup + 2 tbsp (175 g) granulated sugar, divided

1 tsp pectin

Brandy Sauce

2 tbsp + 1 tsp (30 g) granulated sugar

1 tbsp + 2¼ tsp (25 g) butter

⅝ cup (150 g) orange juice

¼ cup (40 g) brandy

Caster sugar, for garnish

Fresh orange segments, for garnish

Icing sugar, for garnish

For the Orange Chantilly. Add the white chocolate to a heatproof bowl and set aside. In a saucepan over medium heat, warm the orange zest and corn syrup with ¼ cup + 1 tablespoon (70 g) of cream. Pour the mixture into the bowl containing the white chocolate and allow it to melt, then use a hand blender to emulsify the mixture to a perfectly smooth consistency. Use a spatula to fold in ¾ cup + 1 tablespoon (200 g) of cream until it feels light and rich, then refrigerate overnight for best results.

For the Orange Cake. Preheat the oven to 320°F (160°C). Grease the ring with butter and place on a tray lined with baking paper. In a stand mixer with a whisk attachment, whip the egg, granulated sugar and honey until it turns light and airy. Then, with a spatula, gently fold in the oil, vanilla extract and orange juice, followed by the all-purpose flour, almond flour and baking powder. Finish by mixing in the lemon and orange zest to give it a beautiful citrus aroma.

Pour the batter into the prepared ring and bake for 30 to 35 minutes. Use a cake tester to check if the baking is done, or use a probe thermometer to know when the cake reaches 203°F (95°C). Once it's cooled and demolded, use a serrated knife to trim the top layer to get yourself a neat 1-inch (2.5-cm) slab of orange cake.

(continued)

CRÊPE SUZETTE CAKE *(continued)*

For the Crêpes. In a mixing bowl, combine the milk, vanilla extract, granulated sugar, eggs and all-purpose flour. You can use a hand blender to mix them in one at a time, and then mix in the butter to get a smooth batter and avoid any lumps. Rest this batter in the refrigerator for 1 hour before using. When it's ready, heat a flat skillet and grease it with butter to start making the crêpes. Pour a ladle of batter in and swirl the skillet to get a uniform round shape. Pour any excess batter back out into the batter bowl. When the edges start to brown, flip to cook the other side as well. Repeat this process to get 15 to 18 thin, crispy crêpes. If you're storing these on top of one another, dust each one with some icing sugar to prevent them from sticking together.

For the Orange Marmalade. In a large saucepan filled with water, take the whole orange and bring it to a boil for a good 2 hours, making sure to replace the water every 40 minutes to help get rid of the bitterness. Let the orange cool for a while before chopping it up into small, ½-inch (1.3-cm) pieces and removing all the seeds to get a nice mixture of pulp and rind. In a new saucepan, add the orange pieces, orange juice and ⅜ cup + 1 tablespoon (87.5 g) of the granulated sugar over a medium heat. Once the stewing oranges have reached 104°F (40°C), add in the pectin and the remaining ⅜ cup + 1 tablespoon (87.5 g) of granulated sugar. Continue heating and bring it to a boil until it reaches a thick, jam-like consistency, then reserve until after we're done baking.

For the Brandy Sauce. In a saucepan over medium heat, spread the granulated sugar evenly and mix until it caramelizes to a deep amber color. Then stir in the butter and add the orange juice to help deglaze the pan, continuing to cook for a few minutes. In a ladle, start heating the brandy, and use a blowtorch to ignite the surface for a few seconds before pouring it into the sauce. This will give our crêpe suzette a classic flambé touch.

Time for assembly. First take out the orange chantilly and whip it well, until it gets nice and fluffy. Use the orange cake as the base of your creation. Use a palette knife to apply a very thin layer of whipped chantilly, and drizzle a teaspoon of brandy sauce on top. Then place a crêpe, spread another thin layer of chantilly and another teaspoon of brandy sauce. Every five layers of crêpes, instead of using chantilly, spread a nice layer of orange marmalade over the crêpe, and then continue. Repeat this process until we have ourselves a grand stack of layered crêpes, layered with chantilly and marmalade. Freeze the stack for 2 hours. Now dust caster sugar over the top and lightly brûlée it using a blowtorch. Decorate with fresh orange segments, and sprinkle a little icing sugar on top to finish.

Your tower of layered crêpes is ready to devour. In case you don't finish it all up at once, you can store it in the refrigerator for 1 day.

GERMAN CHOCOLATE STOUT CAKE

Yield: 1 cake
Mold: 6-inch (15¼-cm) ring

Beer is one of those beverages that can change so drastically depending on where in the world you're drinking it. There seems to be an infinite amount of variations, different strengths and styles and flavors, some fruitier and more refreshing, and some deeper and more complex. We're using a stout in this recipe to give this classic layered German chocolate cake a rich and complex flavor. But that's not all—since beer is typically paired with lighter snacks, we've got candied puffed rice on top to give this cake a delightful and surprising texture.

Stout Cake

⅓ cup + 2½ tbsp (110 g) butter, plus more for greasing rings

1 cup + 1½ tbsp (140 g) all-purpose flour

½ tsp baking soda

⅜ cup + 1 tbsp + 1 tsp (40 g) cocoa powder

¼ tsp sea salt

⅓ cup + 2 tbsp (110 g) stout beer

¼ cup + 3½ tbsp (95 g) granulated sugar

⅜ cup + 1 tbsp (95 g) brown sugar

1 egg

¼ cup + ½ tsp (60 g) sour cream

Chewy Coconut Pecan Filling

1 cup (300 g) condensed milk

2 egg yolks

⅓ cup + 1 tbsp (90 g) butter

¾ cup + 1 tbsp (90 g) pecans, toasted and chopped

1 cup (100 g) coconut flakes

¾ tsp vanilla extract

Dark Chocolate Ganache

1½ cups (200 g) dark chocolate, chopped

¾ cup + 1 tbsp + 1 tsp (200 g) heavy cream

1½ tsp (10 g) invert sugar

3½ tbsp (50 g) butter, at room temperature

Candied Puffed Rice

¼ cup + 1 tsp (55 g) granulated sugar

1 tbsp (15 g) water

2 cups (30 g) puffed rice

For the Stout Cake. Preheat the oven to 320°F (160°C). Grease three rings with extra butter and set aside. In a heatproof bowl, add the all-purpose flour, baking soda, cocoa powder and salt and mix well. Set this aside. In a saucepan, let's warm the stout beer along with the butter, granulated sugar and brown sugar until the sugars have completely dissolved. Allow the mixture to cool before pouring it into the bowl containing the flour mixture. Once it's all come together, gradually incorporate the egg and sour cream using a whisk.

Portion the batter out between the prepared rings, and bake for 25 to 30 minutes. Use a cake tester to check if the baking is done, or use a probe thermometer to know when the cakes reach 203°F (95°C).

For the Chewy Coconut Pecan Filling. In a saucepan, cook the condensed milk, egg yolks and butter together over low heat until the mixture reaches 176°F (80°C). Toss in the pecans and coconut flakes and continue cooking for about a minute before adding in the vanilla extract. Reserve this delicious filling in the refrigerator until we're layering the cake.

For the Dark Chocolate Ganache. To a heatproof bowl, add the dark chocolate and then set it aside. In a saucepan, first warm the cream and invert sugar to a simmer, and then pour it into the bowl containing the dark chocolate, allowing it to melt. Mix and let it cool a bit. Then add in the butter and use a hand blender to emulsify it into a beautiful, creamy consistency. Pop it in the refrigerator for 2 hours to get a perfect chocolate ganache.

(continued)

GERMAN CHOCOLATE STOUT CAKE *(continued)*

For the Candied Puffed Rice. Line a tray with baking paper and set it aside. In a saucepan, heat the granulated sugar and water until it reaches 244°F (118°C) or a soft-ball stage. At that point, add in the puffed rice and stir continuously, allowing the sugar to crystallize and coat the rice in sugary goodness. Continue to cook over low heat and the rocky appearance of the sugar will slowly turn to an even caramel layer. Once it's taken on a golden brown color, spread the puffed rice out across the prepared tray and allow it to cool.

Time for assembly. Take one of the layers of cake as your base. Use a palette knife to spread a layer of chewy pecan filling across the cake base, followed by a layer of chocolate ganache. Then repeat the process with another layer of cake, followed by pecan filling and ganache. Place the final layer of cake, spread some ganache across it, and carefully heap the candied puffed rice on top as a stunning, unique topping for this cake.

This decadent stout cake is best served at room temperature. You can wrap it well and store in the refrigerator for up to 3 days.

FIRST DATE CAKE

Yield: 1 cake
Mold: 6-inch (15¼-cm) ring

As pastry chefs, not only do we create cakes for our own shops and classes, but we get called out to do trials and create interesting menus for other restaurants across the world. This one was created while testing desserts for a project in Saudi Arabia, and we were excited to use their famously sweet dates and spices. Unfortunately that project never took off, but fortunately that means we could include this rich and intimate Middle East–influenced date cake for you to try in your own kitchen. Even better, share it with someone special on a date!

Dark Chocolate Glaze

1¼ cups + 1 tbsp + ½ tsp (175 g) dark chocolate, chopped

2 tsp (10 g) cocoa butter

½ cup + 1 tsp (125 g) heavy cream

½ cup + 1 tsp (125 g) water

¾ cup (150 g) granulated sugar

¼ cup + 2 tsp (25 g) cocoa powder

Spiced Date Cake

⅓ cup + 2½ tbsp (110 g) butter, plus more for greasing rings

1⅔ cups (210 g) all-purpose flour

½ tsp sea salt

¼ tbsp ground cinnamon

⅓ tsp ground cloves

⅓ tsp ground cardamom

¼ tsp ground black pepper

⅓ tsp ground cumin

¼ tsp ground nutmeg

⅓ tsp paprika

⅞ cup + 1 tbsp + ½ tsp (225 g) water

1¼ tsp (6 g) baking soda

1⅔ cups (285 g) dates, pitted and chopped

½ cup + 1 tbsp (125 g) brown sugar

2 eggs

1 egg yolk

2 tsp (10 g) vanilla extract

Coffee Buttercream

¼ cup + 3 tbsp + ½ tsp (90 g) granulated sugar

3 tbsp + 1 tsp (50 g) water, divided

3 egg yolks

¾ cup + 1½ tsp (180 g) butter, at room temperature

2½ tbsp (7.5 g) instant coffee

Hazelnut Spread

2 tbsp (25 g) hazelnut praline paste (see Quick Reference Notes, page 219)

⅛ cup (35 g) hazelnut paste (see Quick Reference Notes, page 219)

⅔ cup + 1 tsp (115 g) milk chocolate, chopped

⅓ cup (80 g) heavy cream

¼ cup + ½ tsp (65 g) milk

Milk Chocolate Ganache

⅞ cup + tbsp + ½ tsp (160 g) milk chocolate, chopped

⅓ cup (80 g) heavy cream

1 tsp invert sugar

½ tsp sea salt

2 tbsp (30 g) butter

Dark Chocolate Crumble

¼ cup + 1½ tsp (35 g) all-purpose flour

2½ tbsp (15 g) cocoa powder

3½ tbsp (50 g) butter, cold

¼ cup (50 g) granulated sugar

¾ cup + 1 tbsp + 1 tsp (50 g) almond flour

For the Dark Chocolate Glaze. In a heatproof bowl, combine the dark chocolate and cocoa butter. In a saucepan, combine the cream, water, granulated sugar and cocoa powder, and bring the mixture to a boil for 2 minutes. Pour this into the bowl containing the chocolate and cocoa butter, allowing them to melt with the heat. Use a hand blender to get the mixture to a smooth consistency, then cover and keep this at room temperature overnight to set.

For the Spiced Date Cake. Preheat the oven to 320°F (160°C). Grease three rings with extra butter and set aside. In a large bowl, sift together the all-purpose flour, salt, cinnamon, cloves, cardamom, black pepper, cumin, nutmeg and paprika. Set it aside. In a saucepan, add the water and baking soda and bring it to a boil. Pop in the dates and allow them to soak, cooking the mixture until it forms a lovely, thick purée, about 10 minutes. Now in a stand mixer with a paddle attachment, cream the butter and brown sugar. Gradually add in the eggs, egg yolk and vanilla extract, and combine well.

(continued)

FIRST DATE CAKE *(continued)*

Add half of the sifted flour and spices mix into the batter. Now mix in half of the date purée. Add the remaining flour and spices, and the remaining purée, and mix until it all comes together evenly to form a chunky dough. Portion the batter between the prepared rings, and bake for 25 to 30 minutes. Use a cake tester to check if the baking is done, or use a probe thermometer to know when the cakes reach 203°F (95°C).

For the Coffee Buttercream. In a saucepan, heat the granulated sugar and ⅛ cup (30 g) of water until it forms a hot sugar syrup. In a stand mixer with a whisk attachment, start whipping the egg yolks on a slow speed. When the sugar syrup reaches 244°F (118°C) or a soft-ball stage, pour it over the egg yolks and continue whipping until it builds in volume and the temperature cools. Add in the butter, a small portion at a time, until the butter is fully incorporated. In a separate bowl, mix the instant coffee with 1 tablespoon + 1 teaspoon (20 g) of water to make a paste, and add that into the buttercream to bring in some strong coffee flavors.

For the Hazelnut Spread. In a heatproof bowl, add the hazelnut praline paste, hazelnut paste and milk chocolate and set aside. In a saucepan over medium heat, bring the cream and milk to a simmer. Pour the hot cream into the bowl containing the milk chocolate mixture and allow it to melt. Then use a hand blender to create a perfect, creamy emulsion, and keep the spread in the refrigerator to set for 2 hours.

For the Milk Chocolate Ganache. In a heatproof bowl, add the milk chocolate and set it aside. In a saucepan, warm the cream and invert sugar to a simmer, and then pour it into the bowl containing the milk chocolate, allowing it to melt. Then add in the salt and butter and use a hand blender to emulsify the mix to a beautiful, creamy consistency. Pop this in the refrigerator for 2 hours to get a perfect chocolate ganache.

For the Dark Chocolate Crumble. Preheat the oven to 320°F (160°C). In a food processor add the all-purpose flour, cocoa powder, butter, granulated sugar and almond flour, and blend to get a crumble texture. You can stop once larger chunks of crumble begin to form, then lay them out on a tray and freeze for 30 minutes to get them firm. Bake for 20 minutes. It should turn firmer and crispier when it cools completely.

Time for assembly. Take one of the layers of cake as your base. Use a palette knife to apply a layer of hazelnut spread, followed by a layer of coffee buttercream. Repeat the process with the next layer of cake, hazelnut spread and buttercream. Place the final layer of cake on top and finish it with a neat layer of milk chocolate ganache, starting at the top and then going all around the sides to form a smooth coating. Leave this in the freezer for 4 hours. Let's warm the glaze in the microwave until it's half melted, and use a hand blender to emulsify it until it reaches the perfect temperature for glazing, 86°F (30°C). With the cake placed on a wire rack, pour the glaze over to coat it evenly. Then lift it, scrape any excess glaze from the bottom, and place it on a cake board or serving tray for a few minutes to let it set. To wrap things up, sprinkle that dark chocolate crumble over the top to finish the look.

This scrumptious layered date cake is ready to slice and serve. You can store it in the refrigerator for up to 2 days.

NINETIES BLACK FOREST CAKE

Yield: 1 cake
Mold: 6-inch (15¼-cm) round cake tin

The Black Forest cake might be a German creation, but once it was introduced to India in the '90s it quickly became the undisputed champion of cakes for an entire generation of kids. We're not exaggerating when we say Vinesh grew up eating this cherry-chocolate cake at literally every birthday party, anniversary and family function he attended as a kid. Social events were practically incomplete without a Black Forest cake. It took a while for people to remember that any other cakes even existed. But to pay tribute to this obsessive period in Indian cake history, we've decided to make our own insane version of this cherry-chocolate fan favorite.

Vanilla Whipped Ganache

¾ cup + 2 tsp (135 g) white chocolate, chopped

1 cup + 1 tbsp + 2 tsp (265 g) heavy cream, divided

2 tsp (15 g) corn syrup

1 vanilla bean pod (see Quick Reference Notes, page 219)

Flourless Chocolate Sponge

½ cup + 1½ tbsp (135 g) butter, plus more for greasing tins

½ cup + 1 tsp (45 g) cocoa powder, sifted

2 cups (120 g) almond flour

¾ cup + 1 tsp (185 g) heavy cream

1 cup + 2 tbsp (150 g) dark chocolate

4 egg yolks

½ cup + 2 tbsp + 1 tsp (130 g) granulated sugar, divided

1 tsp vanilla extract

5 egg whites

Cherry Confit

1¾ cups (250 g) cherries, frozen

½ cup (100 g) granulated sugar, divided

1¾ tsp (5 g) pectin

1 tsp lemon juice

Dark Chocolate Ganache

¾ cup + 1 tbsp (110 g) dark chocolate, chopped

¼ cup + 1 tsp (50 g) milk chocolate, chopped

⅔ cup (160 g) heavy cream

1 tsp invert sugar

1 tbsp + ¼ tsp (15 g) butter, at room temperature

Tempered dark chocolate, for garnish (see Quick Reference Notes, page 219)

Fresh cherries, for garnish

For the Vanilla Whipped Ganache. In a heatproof bowl, add the white chocolate and set it aside. In a saucepan, heat ¼ cup + 1 teaspoon (65 g) of cream along with the corn syrup and vanilla. Bring the mixture to a simmer, then pour it into the bowl containing the white chocolate, allowing it to melt with the heat. Use a hand blender to get it feeling silky smooth. Fold in ¾ cup + 1 tablespoon + 1 teaspoon (200 g) of cream to get it nice and light, then leave it in the refrigerator overnight.

For the Flourless Chocolate Sponge. Preheat the oven to 338°F (170°C). Grease four cake tins with extra butter and set aside. In a bowl, add the cocoa powder and almond flour. In a saucepan, heat the cream, butter and dark chocolate until it comes together nicely, then turn off the heat and allow it to cool. In a stand mixer with a whisk attachment, whip the egg yolks, ¼ cup + 1 tablespoon + ½ teaspoon (65 g) of the granulated sugar and vanilla extract until they're light and airy. Add in the creamy chocolate mixture we made, followed by the cocoa powder and almond flour, and combine well.

(continued)

Next we're going to make a meringue using the stand mixer, so we'll need a fresh bowl and whisk. Whip the egg whites on medium speed, adding in ¼ cup + 1 tablespoon + ½ teaspoon (65 g) of granulated sugar a little at a time. Then turn it up to high speed until you reach a perfect glossy meringue with medium peaks, and use a spatula to gently fold it into the chocolate batter. Portion the batter out between the four prepared cake tins. Bake for 25 to 30 minutes. Use a cake tester to check if the baking is done, or use a probe thermometer to know when the cakes reach 203°F (95°C). Allow the cakes to cool before carefully demolding.

For the Cherry Confit. In a saucepan, add the cherries and ¼ cup (50 g) of granulated sugar, and leave it over a medium heat until the mixture turns warm, about 140°F (60°C). Stir in the pectin and ¼ cup (50 g) of granulated sugar, and boil until the mixture starts to thicken. Then turn off the heat, and add in the lemon juice for some lovely citrus notes.

For the Dark Chocolate Ganache. In a heatproof bowl, add the dark and milk chocolates and set aside. In a saucepan, heat the cream and invert sugar to a simmer, then pour it into the bowl containing the chocolate and allow it all to melt. Once it's cooled a little, add in the butter, and use a hand blender to bring it to a luscious, creamy consistency. Keep it in the refrigerator for 2 hours to get a perfect ganache.

Time for assembly. First, whip the vanilla ganache. Next, take one of the discs of cake to be your base, and use a palette knife to spread a layer of vanilla whipped ganache over it right to the edges. Fill a heaped tablespoon with cherry confit and form a nice, delicious layer on top. Now repeat the process by adding layers of cake, vanilla whipped ganache and cherry confit, in that order, ending with the fourth and final cake disc. Leave this in the freezer for 2 hours.

For the finishing. Spread a thin, even layer of tempered dark chocolate over a marble slab, and leave it to set. Touch to check it feels almost set, but not hard. If the chocolate sets completely, you might notice it cracking instead of curling smoothly when making cigars, so we're aiming for a soft pliable stage of chocolate. Use a chocolate scraper at a 30-degree angle to curl the chocolate away from you into tubular cigar shapes. We're going to need a lot of cigars to cover this cake, so be patient and keep scraping them out. Think of all the compliments you'll get once it's done!

Bring that four-layer cake back out of the freezer, and use a palette knife to spread a layer of chocolate ganache all over it—starting at the top and making your way all around the sides to get a nice even coating. Now it's time to place the dark chocolate cigars. There's no wrong way to do this, so get creative. Completely cover the sides of the cake with cigars to get that stunning look, and finish by placing some fresh cherries on top.

This insane chocolate tower is finally ready to be sliced, served, and complimented. You can store it in the refrigerator for up to 2 days.

A CHOCOLATE CAKE

Yield: 1
Mold: 6-inch (15¼-cm) round cake tin

Let's be real, when you think cake, you think chocolate cake. It's rare for an ingredient to become so overwhelmingly famous that it dominates the entire industry, but these days it would be surprising to find a pastry shop in any corner of the world that doesn't sell a chocolate cake. The chocolate cake is essential, and we take it seriously. Ready or not, here's a sultry, moist cake layered with a deeply satisfying ganache that's smooth as silk. We're going to be finishing it using a couple of smart tricks, like using an acetate sheet as a mask to create a beautiful, shaped-chocolate coating, and lining it with silver foil to get an aptly iconic look for this truly iconic product.

Rich Chocolate Sponge

Butter, for greasing tins

1½ cups (300 g) granulated sugar

2 eggs

2 egg yolks

⅔ cup + 1 tbsp (180 g) milk

¾ cup (180 g) water

3 tbsp (10 g) coffee powder

1½ cups + 1 tbsp + 2 tsp (200 g) all-purpose flour

⅞ cup + 2½ tsp (80 g) cocoa powder

1 tsp baking powder

½ tsp baking soda

½ tsp salt

⅜ cup + 1 tbsp (90 g) vegetable oil

Chocolate Filling

⅔ cup (90 g) dark chocolate, chopped

2½ tbsp (30 g) milk chocolate, chopped

¾ cup + 2 tbsp (210 g) heavy cream, divided

¾ tsp corn syrup

1 tbsp + ¼ tsp (15 g) butter, at room temperature

Chocolate Coating

1 cup + 2 tbsp (150 g) dark chocolate, chopped

2 tsp (10 g) cocoa butter, finely chopped

¼ cup (60 g) milk

⅓ cup + 1 tbsp + 1 tsp (100 g) heavy cream

Velvet Spray (optional)

⅓ cup + 2 tsp (50 g) dark chocolate

1½ tbsp (25 g) cocoa butter

Edible silver leaf, for garnish

For the Rich Chocolate Sponge. Preheat the oven to 320°F (160°C). Grease three cake tins with butter and set them aside. In a stand mixer with a whisk attachment, add the granulated sugar, eggs and additional egg yolks and whip until it's light and fluffy. Then in a saucepan, heat the milk, water and coffee powder together until it's warm and fully dissolved. Gradually add this heated coffee mixture into the eggs, followed by the all-purpose flour, cocoa powder, baking powder, baking soda and salt. Mix gently until just combined, then add in the oil as well. Portion the batter equally between the three prepared tins. Let's bake these for 25 to 30 minutes. Use a cake tester to check if the baking is done, or use a probe thermometer to know when the cakes reach 203°F (95°C). Then allow it to cool and set it aside until assembly.

For the Chocolate Filling. To a heatproof bowl, add the dark and milk chocolates. In a saucepan, heat ½ cup (120 g) of the cream along with the corn syrup, and bring it to a simmer. Then pour the mixture into the bowl containing the chocolate, and allow it to melt. Once that's cooled slightly, add in the butter and use a hand blender to bring it all to a luscious, creamy consistency. Let it set in the refrigerator for 1 hour. Once the chocolate ganache is set, whip ⅜ cup (90 g) of cream in a stand mixer with a whisk attachment, and fold it into the chocolate ganache.

For the Chocolate Coating. In a heatproof bowl, add the dark chocolate and cocoa butter. In a saucepan, add the milk and cream and heat it to a simmer. Then pour it into the bowl containing the chocolate mix, allowing it to melt. Use a hand blender to get a perfectly smooth emulsion, and pop it in the refrigerator for 2 hours to set.

(continued)

A CHOCOLATE CAKE *(continued)*

Time for assembly. Take the first slab of cake to use as your base. Pipe a generous layer of chocolate filling onto it. Repeat the process by placing another slab of cake on top and piping the ganache on top. Place the final cake slab in line with the others, and use a palette knife to even out any ganache spilling out on the sides. Now take a 5-inch (13-cm) tall strip of acetate and cut a wavy pattern out from one side, so it wraps around the base of the cake with the waves pointing upward. This is going to act as a mask during the finishing process. Use a palette knife to start spreading the chocolate coating evenly over the top and sides of the cake, covering the edge of the acetate. Place the cake in the freezer for about 2 hours before spraying.

For the Velvet Spray. This step requires a spray gun; you can skip it if you don't have one. Your dessert will still look amazing, it just won't have the exact same matte finish. Melt the dark chocolate and the cocoa butter, then mix them together and allow it to cool to 86°F (30°C). Use a spray gun to spray this mixture evenly over the top and sides of the cake to give it that incredible velvet finish. Now carefully peel open the acetate to reveal that perfect wave pattern.

Last up, use a tweezer to line the edge of the wave with silver leaf, giving your cake the most stunning decorative accent.

This layered chocolate beauty can be sliced and served cold or at room temperature. You can store it in the refrigerator for up to 2 days.

PANDAN PUMPKIN CHIFFON

Yield: 1 cake
Mold: 7-inch (17½-cm) round cake tin

This incredibly light, delicious cake brings delicate, aromatic Asian flavors into your baking repertoire: a sweet and popular coconut jam (kaya), a fragrant tropical leaf (pandan) and an unprocessed form of cane sugar (jaggery). The idea came about when Vinesh visited his wife's side of the family in a little town in Malaysia called Teluk Intan. The resident pastry expert Aunty Sayee made this unforgettable, delicious sponge cake using all these subtle and aromatic ingredients. Vinesh was so enamored that he came right back to India and started growing his own crop of pandan leaves while Andrés ended up naming one of his dogs Kaya.

Pumpkin Spice Kaya

⅞ cup + 2 tsp (225 g) pumpkin purée

¾ cup (150 g) jaggery

⅞ cup (200 g) coconut milk

1 tbsp (7 g) pumpkin spice mix

Pinch of sea salt

Pandan Chiffon Cake

6 egg yolks

1 egg

3 tbsp (40 g) grapeseed oil

1 tbsp (15 g) pandan juice

⅓ cup + 1 tsp (80 g) coconut milk

⅔ cup (85 g) all-purpose flour, sifted

6 egg whites

Pinch of cream of tartar

¼ cup + 2 tbsp + 2 tsp (85 g) granulated sugar

Coconut Ganache

½ cup + 1 tsp (90 g) white chocolate, chopped

¾ tsp cocoa butter, finely chopped

⅜ cup + 1 tbsp (100 g) coconut cream, divided

2 tsp (15 g) corn syrup

2 tsp (10 g) coconut rum (We recommend Malibu)

½ cup + 2 tsp (130 g) heavy cream

Pinch of sea salt

Coconut flakes, for garnish
Pumpkin seeds, for garnish

For the Pumpkin Spice Kaya. In a saucepan, add the pumpkin purée and jaggery and cook over low heat. If you can't find jaggery, a good replacement would be brown sugar. Add in the coconut milk and continue to cook, thickening the jam for about 40 minutes, until it turns nice and creamy. Season with the pumpkin spice mix and salt, then use a hand blender to bring it all together in a smooth emulsion. Let's set this aside for us to use during the layering process.

Note from the Chefs:

If you're using fresh pumpkin for the purée, cut the pumpkin into small chunks and coat with some brown sugar, butter and pumpkin spice mix. Roast at 356°F (180°C) until it's soft and tender, then grind it into a paste, adding water if necessary.

For the Pandan Chiffon Cake. Preheat the oven to 320°F (160°C). In a mixing bowl, mix together the egg yolks, whole egg, oil, pandan juice and coconut milk. Then use a whisk to mix in the all-purpose flour, and keep this mix aside for a bit. Make a meringue by whipping up the egg whites with the cream of tartar to get them frothy, and add in the granulated sugar a little at a time. Keep whipping until your meringue reaches a perfect medium peak stage, then gently fold it into the egg-flour mixture. Divide the batter up between two ungreased rings and bake the cakes for 35 to 40 minutes, until they're golden brown on top.

(continued)

For the Coconut Ganache. In a heatproof bowl, add the white chocolate and cocoa butter and set it aside. In a saucepan, heat 3½ tablespoons (50 g) of coconut cream and the corn syrup until it reaches 140°F (60°C). Pour the hot coconut mixture into the bowl containing the chocolate mixture, and allow it to melt. Then add 3½ tablespoons (50 g) of coconut cream, followed by the coconut rum, cream and salt. To help set the ganache faster, let's spread it out onto a large tray and refrigerate for 2 hours.

Time for assembly. Bring out that coconut ganache and whip it in a stand mixer with a whisk attachment so it's nice and light. Place the base layer of cake onto a cake board, and start piping the pumpkin spice kaya in concentric circles starting from the middle and making your way to the edge. Follow that by piping a layer of the whipped coconut ganache. Then place the second layer of cake and press down gently so the filling reaches the edges of the cakes. Repeat the process of piping another layer of kaya and ganache the same way. Finish with a generous amount of toasted coconut flakes and pumpkin seeds over the entire top surface to give it an incredible textural look.

This delightful cake is best served chilled to fully appreciate its light and refreshing flavors. You can store it in the refrigerator for up to 2 days.

LEMON MERINGUE CAKE

Yield: 1 cake
Mold: 6-inch (15¼-cm) round cake tin

The lemon meringue pie is arguably one of the most popular lemon desserts ever, finding its roots all the way back in Ancient Greece. Of course a lot has changed since then, and this citrus pie has evolved to become lighter and sweeter, with the meringue adding that dreamy layer we all love. We wanted to bring the legacy of lemon meringue one step further with this exciting layer cake. Depending on where you are, you might be able to get many different varieties of lemons to give these components a distinct flavor, but the combination of cakes and creams and meringues are always going to work their magic.

Lemon Whipped Ganache

¾ cup + 2 tsp (135 g) white chocolate, chopped

1 cup + 1 tbsp + 2 tsp (265 g) heavy cream, divided

2 tsp (15 g) corn syrup

Zest of 1 lemon

Crumble

¼ cup + 1 tbsp + ¾ tsp (75 g) butter, cold, plus more for greasing tins

½ cup + 1 tbsp + 2 tsp (75 g) all-purpose flour

1¼ cup (75 g) almond flour

⅓ cup + 2 tsp (75 g) granulated sugar

Zest of 1 lemon

Lemon Sponge

1¼ cups + 1½ tsp (160 g) all-purpose flour

¾ tsp baking powder

3 eggs

Zest of 1 lemon

1 cup (200 g) granulated sugar

¼ cup + 2 tbsp (90 g) heavy cream

¼ cup + ¾ tsp (60 g) butter, melted

Lemon Curd

1½ tsp (3 g) gelatin

1 tbsp + ½ tsp (18 g) cold water

3 tbsp (45 g) lemon juice

1 egg

¼ cup + 2½ tsp (60 g) granulated sugar

⅓ cup + 1 tbsp (90 g) butter

French Meringue

2 egg whites

¼ cup + 1 tsp (55 g) granulated sugar

⅜ cup + 1 tbsp + 1 tsp (55 g) icing sugar, sifted

Italian Meringue

¾ cup (150 g) granulated sugar

2 tbsp (30 g) water

3 egg whites

For the Lemon Whipped Ganache. In a heatproof bowl, add the white chocolate and then set it aside. In a saucepan, heat ¼ cup + 1 teaspoon (65 g) of cream along with the corn syrup and lemon zest. Bring the mixture to a simmer, then pour it into the bowl containing the white chocolate, allowing it to melt with the heat. Use a hand blender to get it feeling silky smooth. Fold in ¾ cup + 1 tablespoon + 1 teaspoon (200 g) of cream to get it nice and light, then leave it in the refrigerator overnight.

For the Crumble. Preheat the oven to 320°F (160°C). Grease three tins with extra butter and set aside. In a food processor, add the all-purpose flour, almond flour, butter, granulated sugar and lemon zest. Blend to get a crumble texture. Keep going until larger chunks of crumble begin to form, then lay them out on a tray and freeze for 30 minutes to get them firm.

Once the crumble is firm, sprinkle a layer of crumble into each prepared tin to form a chunky base. Bake these for 20 minutes, until the crumble turns golden brown.

For the Lemon Sponge. Leave the oven at 320°F (160°C). In a bowl, sift together the all-purpose flour and baking powder and set aside. In a stand mixer with a whisk attachment, add the eggs, lemon zest and granulated sugar and whip it until it starts to form ribbon shapes falling from the whisk. Add in the cream and fully incorporate, then fold in the sifted flour mix using a spatula. Finish by gently mixing in the melted butter to complete the batter.

(continued)

Portion this batter out into the cake tins, over the crumble, and bake the cakes for 25 to 30 minutes. Use a cake tester to check if the baking is done, or use a probe thermometer to know when the cakes reach 203°F (95°C). Allow the cakes to cool, then carefully demold and trim the top of the sponge off with a small knife.

For the Lemon Curd. In a bowl, add the gelatin and water and let the gelatin bloom for 5 minutes, until it swells. Now, in a saucepan, start boiling the lemon juice. In a bowl, mix the egg and granulated sugar. Pour one-third of the heated lemon juice into the sugar mix to help temper the egg. Then pour that egg mixture back into the saucepan with the rest of the lemon juice, and continue to cook. Once it's reached 185°F (85°C), turn off the heat and stir in the bloomed gelatin, making sure it's fully dissolved. Leave it to cool a little, then add in the butter and use a hand blender to bring it all to a smooth consistency. Store this in the refrigerator until we're ready to assemble.

For the French Meringue. Preheat the oven to 167°F (75°C). Line a tray with baking paper and set it aside. In a stand mixer with a whisk attachment, start whipping the egg whites on a low speed until they're white and foamy. Add in the granulated sugar gradually, one spoon at a time, to ensure that it dissolves properly. Continue whipping until it turns glossy and the meringue forms stiff peaks. Finish by gently folding in the icing sugar with a spatula. Spread the meringue in a thin layer onto the prepared tray, and let it dehydrate for 2 hours in the oven, until it's dry and crispy. Once cooled, break it into elegant shards that are each about 1 inch (2.5 cm) tall to use at the very end.

For the Italian Meringue. In a saucepan, heat the granulated sugar and water. When the syrup reaches 221°F (105°C), start foaming the egg whites in a stand mixer with a whisk attachment. Once the sugar syrup is at 250°F (121°C), pour the hot syrup into the egg whites slowly in a steady stream, and continue whipping until the meringue turns stiff and glossy, then keep it aside to cool.

Time for assembly. In a stand mixer with a whisk attachment, whip the lemon ganache until it's nice and light. Take one of the layers of cake as your base, with the crumble side at the bottom. Spread a nice layer of lemon ganache onto the cake with a palette knife, then use a piping bag to pipe the lemon curd in concentric circles starting from the center and progressing outward. Now place the next disc of cake, again with the crumble side down, and add another layer of ganache and lemon curd. Place the final slab of cake, aligning the edges perfectly, and keep it in the freezer for 2 hours. Finish the cake by using a palette knife to spread a nice even layer of Italian meringue all around the sides, and contrast it by forming rough peaks of meringue on the top surface. Use a blowtorch or heat gun to lightly brûlée that top layer, then press the French meringue shards at angles against one side of the cake for an artistic look.

This reimagining of the lemon-meringue classic is going to be amazing served chilled. You can store it for up to 3 days in the refrigerator.

PINEAPPLE INSIDE-OUT CAKE

Yield: 1 cake
Mold: 6-inch (15¼-cm) round cake tin

Sure, you've probably heard of a pineapple upside-down cake, a simple cake that captures the essence of this beloved tropical fruit. But what if there was a brand new way? Introducing the Pineapple Inside-Out: a majestic layered sponge with yogurt chantilly and pineapple compote on the inside, and a glistening caramelized pineapple crown on the outside. As with a lot of our desserts, we're always looking to existing classics for inspiration, or taking recipes people take for granted and finding ways to bring that extra level of excitement and flavor into it.

Yogurt Chantilly

⅔ cup + 2 tsp (120 g) white chocolate, chopped

¾ cup + 2 tbsp (210 g) heavy cream

2 tsp (15 g) corn syrup

2¾ tsp (15 g) invert sugar

1 vanilla bean pod (see Quick Reference Notes, page 219)

⅓ tsp sea salt

⅔ cup (150 g) Greek yogurt

Vanilla Sponge Cake

Butter, for greasing tins

2 cups (250 g) all-purpose flour

1½ tsp (8 g) baking powder

1½ tsp (8 g) baking soda

2 eggs

1¾ cups + 2 tbsp + 1 tsp (380 g) granulated sugar

1⅛ cups (280 g) milk

⅝ cup (140 g) vegetable oil

1 vanilla bean pod (see Quick Reference Notes, page 219)

1⅛ cups + 1½ tsp (280 g) boiling water

1¼ cups (180 g) fresh blueberries

Pineapple Compote

1¼ cups (210 g) fresh pineapple, diced

2 tbsp (30 g) butter

3 tbsp (40 g) brown sugar, divided

½ cup (120 g) pineapple purée

1 tsp sea salt

1½ tsp (4 g) pectin NH

1 tbsp (15 g) lime juice

Zest of 1 lime

Pineapple Crown

3½ tbsp (50 g) butter, plus more for greasing ring, at room temperature

2 lbs + 2 oz (approximately 3¼ cups) (964 g) pineapple, cut into thin slices

2 cups (400 g) granulated sugar

Apricot jam, for garnish

Blueberries, for garnish

For the Yogurt Chantilly. In a heatproof bowl, add the white chocolate and set it aside. In a saucepan, heat the cream, corn syrup, invert sugar and vanilla to a boil. Pour the hot mixture into the bowl containing the white chocolate, allowing it to melt, then add in the salt and use a hand blender to get a beautiful, smooth consistency. To finish, gently fold in the Greek yogurt and mix until incorporated. Keep this in the refrigerator overnight. Right before using it in the cake, make sure to whip the chantilly in a stand mixer to get it nice and fluffy.

For the Vanilla Sponge Cake. Preheat the oven to 320°F (160°C). Grease three tins with butter and set them aside. Sift together into a bowl the all-purpose flour, baking powder and baking soda and then mix them together. In a stand mixer with a whisk attachment, combine the eggs, sugar, milk, oil and vanilla until it's light and airy. Then fold in the mixed dry ingredients a little at a time, making sure they're fully incorporated. Add the boiling water as you continue to mix, and you should end up with a nice smooth batter.

Portion the batter between the three prepared tins a little at a time, stopping at intervals to sprinkle in some fresh blueberries. This is to help get the fruit evenly distributed into the cakes. Pop them in the oven for 25 to 30 minutes. Use a cake tester to check if the baking is done, or use a probe thermometer to know when the cakes reach 203°F (95°C). Allow the cakes to cool, then carefully demold and keep them aside until assembly.

(continued)

For the Pineapple Compote. In a saucepan, add the fresh pineapple, butter and 1½ tablespoons (20 g) of brown sugar. Sauté the pineapple until the sugar caramelizes and the fruit starts to brown. In another saucepan, heat the pineapple purée along with the salt, until it's nice and warm, then pour it into the sautéed pineapples to help deglaze the pan. Follow this by adding a combination of pectin and the remaining 1½ tablespoons (20 g) of brown sugar, and cook until it starts to thicken. Turn off the heat, and finish by adding in the lime juice and zest, for those lovely citrus notes.

For the Pineapple Crown. Line the bottom of a ring with aluminum foil, and use butter to generously grease all the inner surfaces. Line a tray with baking paper and set it aside. Preheat the oven to 320°F (160°C). Cut the pineapple slices in half so we get lovely, thin semi-circles of pineapple to use for our cake crown. Arrange the slices into the prepared ring, starting from the outer edge and working your way to the center. Let the slices overlap and form concentric circles like a lovely, large rose pattern.

In a saucepan, heat the granulated sugar until it caramelizes to a deep amber, then mix in the butter to help stop the cooking. Pour it out onto the prepared tray and allow it to cool and harden. Break the caramel sheet into smaller chunks, and chuck them in your food processor for a minute to form a powder. Now sift this caramel powder over your floral arrangement of pineapples, until it's completely covered, and bake for 20 minutes, until the pineapple looks tender and is a beautiful, golden color. You'll notice that the caramel powder melts, and the pineapple cooks in that golden sugary goodness. After baking, allow the crown to cool in the refrigerator for 2 hours.

Time for assembly. Let's whip the yogurt chantilly before using it. Take one of the discs of cake to be your base, and use a palette knife to spread some yogurt chantilly over it, right up to the edges. Fill a heaped tablespoon (15 g) with pineapple confit and form a nice delicious layer on top. Now repeat the process with another layer of cake, more yogurt chantilly and confit. Neatly place the third cake disc on top as the final layer, and pop it in the freezer for 2 hours.

For the finishing. Once the cake is nice and cold, use a palette knife to spread a layer of yogurt chantilly all over it, starting at the top and making your way all around the sides to get a nice even coating. Bring the pineapple crown out from the refrigerator as well, and carefully remove it from the ring. Melt some apricot jam, and brush it over the crown to form a beautiful glistening glaze. Then carefully place it on top of the cake, perfectly lining up the edges, and finish with a handful of fresh blueberries.

This elegant, creamy cake is ready to eat. Serve it chilled or at room temperature. You can store it in the refrigerator for up to 2 days.

MASCARPONE COMFORT CAKE

Yield: 1 cake
Mold: 6-inch (15¼-cm) round cake tin

Smoothie bowls are all the rage these days, and we totally approve. They're full of fruit so they feel healthy, but they're also full of creamy sweetness to soothe your palate, and with such a massive variety, everyone seems to have their own favorite. Our favorite smoothie bowl involves chopped up strawberries and a spoonful of mascarpone to give it some extra richness, but it wasn't long until we realized this would also make for a stunning dessert recipe. This elegant creation takes the best parts of a creamy smoothie bowl and combines it with the best parts of a moist and delicious cake. It's both refreshing and soothing; we definitely approve.

Mascarpone Chantilly

1 tbsp (6 g) gelatin

2 tbsp + 1 tsp (36 g) cold water

1¼ cups (300 g) heavy cream

¼ cup (50 g) granulated sugar

1 vanilla bean pod (see Quick Reference Notes, page 219)

1⅓ cups (300 g) mascarpone cheese

Vanilla Sponge

Butter, for greasing tins

6 eggs

¾ cup + 1 tbsp + 1 tsp (165 g) granulated sugar

1 vanilla bean pod (see Quick Reference Notes, page 219)

1½ cups (195 g) all-purpose flour, sifted

⅔ tsp sea salt

2 tbsp (30 g) vegetable oil

Soaking Syrup

½ cup (100 g) granulated sugar

⅔ cup + 1 tbsp + ½ tsp (175 g) water

1 tbsp + ½ tsp (25 g) honey

Zest of ½ a lemon

Strawberry Confit

¾ cup (125 g) strawberries, sliced

¼ cup (50 g) granulated sugar, divided

1¾ tsp (5 g) pectin

½ tsp lemon juice

Fresh strawberries, sliced, for garnish

For the Mascarpone Chantilly. In a small bowl, add the gelatin and water, letting the gelatin bloom for 5 minutes, until it absorbs the water and swells. Next up, in a saucepan heat the cream with the granulated sugar and vanilla over medium heat and bring to a simmer. Stir in the bloomed gelatin and allow it to fully dissolve. Pour the mascarpone cheese in as well, and use a hand blender to whip everything up to a smooth, creamy texture. Keep it in the refrigerator overnight before using.

For the Vanilla Sponge. Preheat the oven to 320°F (160°C). Grease three tins with butter and set them aside. In a stand mixer with a whisk attachment, add the eggs, granulated sugar and vanilla. Whip until the mix doubles in volume and you notice it forms ribbons falling from the whisk. At that point, gently fold in the all-purpose flour and salt, taking care to avoid any lumps. Add the oil gradually in a thin stream, and mix until fully incorporated. Portion the batter between the three tins so each is about halfway full. Bake immediately for 30 to 35 minutes, until the cakes are golden brown. Use a cake tester to check if the baking is done, or use a probe thermometer to know when the cakes reach 203°F (95°C). After baking, let the cakes cool and demold them carefully.

For the Soaking Syrup. In a saucepan over medium heat, add the granulated sugar, water, honey and lemon zest until the sugar is completely dissolved. Turn off the heat, and allow the syrup to cool to room temperature before brushing it across the surface of all three cakes to get them a little more moist.

(continued)

MASCARPONE COMFORT CAKE (continued)

For the Strawberry Confit. In a saucepan, add the strawberries and ⅛ cup (25 g) of granulated sugar. Once it's warm, add in the pectin mixed with the remaining ⅛ cup (25 g) of granulated sugar, and continue to boil until it starts to thicken. Turn off the heat, and add the lemon juice for those lovely citrus notes. Set aside to cool while we get the last component ready.

Time for assembly. Take one of the soaked discs of cake to use as your base. Spread a nice layer of mascarpone chantilly onto the cake with a palette knife, then use a piping bag to pipe the strawberry confit in concentric circles, starting from the center and progressing outward. Place the next disc of cake and press gently so the confit lines up with the edge. Now repeat the process by adding a layer of chantilly, piping more confit, placing the final disc of cake, and topping it with a generous amount of chantilly. Leave this in the freezer for 2 hours. Now take the remaining amount of mascarpone chantilly in a piping bag with a grass nozzle, and pipe down the sides of the cake, starting from the top and making your way to the bottom. Once you've formed neat lines all around the cake, finish things off by decorating it with the fresh strawberry slices.

This fruity, creamy cake is best enjoyed cold and fresh. You can store it in the refrigerator for a day.

TRES LECHES MOUSSE CAKE

Yield: 1 cake
Mold: 6-inch (15¼-cm) ring

Andrés used to make this version of tres leches whenever he visited Vinesh in Bangalore. Loaded with a dulce de leche mousse and hazelnuts, this quickly became a secret favorite among the staff at Lavonne—but we couldn't keep that secret to ourselves forever!

Vanilla Sponge

½ cup + 1 tbsp + 1 tsp (115 g) granulated sugar

1 egg

2 egg yolks

¾ tsp vanilla extract

¼ cup + 1¾ tsp (65 g) butter, melted

2 tsp (10 g) rum

⅝ cup + ¾ tsp (80 g) all-purpose flour

1 tsp baking powder

¼ tsp sea salt

Soaking Syrup

⅓ cup + 1 tbsp (100 g) evaporated milk

⅓ cup (100 g) condensed milk

⅜ cup + 1½ tsp (100 g) milk

Dulce de Leche

⅔ cup (200 g) condensed milk

Dulce de Leche Mousse

1¾ tsp (3.5 g) gelatin

1 tbsp + 1 tsp (20 g) cold water

1 cup + 1 tbsp (255 g) heavy cream, divided

½ cup (150 g) dulce de leche

1 egg yolk

Candied Hazelnuts

½ cup (100 g) granulated sugar

2 tbsp (30 g) water

¾ cup (100 g) hazelnuts, toasted and halved

1 tbsp + ¼ tsp (15 g) butter

For the Vanilla Sponge. Preheat the oven to 320°F (160°C). In a large mixing bowl, whisk the granulated sugar, whole egg, egg yolks, and vanilla extract until it's light and foamy. Slowly add in the butter, followed by the rum, while continuing to whisk. Then fold in the all-purpose flour, baking powder and salt, and mix until fully combined. Pour the batter into the cake ring, and bake for 25 to 30 minutes, until it turns a perfect golden brown. Use a cake tester to check if the baking is done. Once it's cooled, use a knife to trim the top so we get a nice, neat 2-inch (5-cm) slab of cake.

For the Soaking Syrup. In a saucepan, combine the evaporated milk, condensed milk and milk and heat them to 158°F (70°C). Pour this over the cake to let it soak up the syrup.

For the Dulce de Leche. Drop the whole tin of condensed milk into a saucepan full of water, and boil it for 3 hours straight. Then let it cool, open the tin, and you should find a beautiful, thick toffee inside. Spoon out ½ cup (150 g) of this dulce de leche for us to use in the next step.

For the Dulce de Leche Mousse. In a small bowl, add the gelatin and water, letting the gelatin bloom for 5 minutes, until it swells. In a saucepan over medium-low heat, cook ⅜ cup (90 g) of cream, the dulce de leche, and the egg yolk, stirring continuously. Once it's reached 180°F (82°C), turn off the heat, mix in the gelatin completely, and allow it to cool. In a stand mixer with a whisk attachment, whip ⅝ cup + 1 tablespoon (165 g) of cream and once the mousse reaches 86°F (30°C), fold it into the mousse to make it soft and delicate.

For the Candied Hazelnuts. Line a tray with baking paper. In a saucepan, heat the granulated sugar and water until it reaches 244°F (118°C). Toss in the hazelnuts and stir continuously, allowing the sugar to crystallize and coat the nuts. Continue to cook over a low heat, and the rocky appearance of the sugar will slowly turn to an even caramel layer. Finally, add in the butter—this helps to keep the caramelized nuts separated. Lay them out on the prepared tray and allow it to cool.

Time for assembly. Line the inside of the cake ring with a 4-inch (10-cm) tall strip of acetate, then place the soaked cake inside to serve as the base. Pour that incredible dulce de leche mousse in, filling it up until it reaches ½ inch (1.3 cm) from the top of the acetate. Let's leave this in the freezer for 3 hours to set. Finally, demold the cake and remove the acetate sheet, then refrigerate it for 2 hours to reach the perfect temperature. Slice this cake up and serve it cold. You can store it in the refrigerator for up to a day.

SCRUMPTIOUS
Snacks

There are a lot of recipes throughout this book to create large, elaborate, layered desserts, or even sharing-style portions of cookies or tea cakes that have to be carefully sliced and served out for all the hungry folks around you. But sometimes you just need a quick snack all to yourself; something sweet to lift your spirits with just a bite or two, something to keep you company on the couch when relaxing after a long day, and that's where this chapter comes in.

Savory snacks are delicious, but they're also a dime a dozen. Everywhere you go snacks seem to be salted and fried. To remedy this under-representation of sweet snacks, we've put together this set of innovative little bite-size dessert recipes—they're super easy to pick up straight with your fingers and eat literally any time of day. Brighten up your afternoon with the crunchy, sticky textures of the Pumpkin Seed Nougat (page 153), relive your childhood memories with the playful mix of jelly and marshmallow in the Gourmet SnoBalls (page 150) or set up the most impressive high tea with the alluring Truffle Madeleines (page 156) and Sacherons (page 139). As always, the goal is to take things a step further than the usual recipes; let's try and add some more interesting components and combinations and make sure that the one bite we take really hits the spot!

JAGGERY BLONDIE

Yield: 8 blondies
Mold: 3-inch (7½-cm) fluted tart shell

We love brownies of all kinds, whether they're chewy or crumbly or dark or light. Blondies are the blonde cousins of the ever-popular brownie—they use white chocolate so the color tends to be lighter, and the caramelized flavor goes perfectly with an assortment of fruits and nuts. To bring a fresh, earthy sweetness into this snack, we've decided to use jaggery—a natural, unprocessed form of cane sugar that's super popular in South Asia. It's available powdered or in the form of these massive rocks that you can break up and use in recipes, but we won't be surprised if you decide to eat bits of it plain. Yep, it's just that tasty.

Blondie Batter

½ cup + 1 tsp (120 g) butter, plus more for greasing molds

½ cup + 2 tsp (120 g) brown sugar

2½ tbsp (30 g) jaggery, powdered

1 egg

½ tsp vanilla extract

⅜ cup + 1 tbsp (75 g) white chocolate, melted

⅜ cup (45 g) dried cranberries, chopped

¼ cup + 1½ tsp (40 g) almonds, toasted and chopped

¾ cup (95 g) all-purpose flour

¼ tsp baking powder

Pinch of sea salt

Desiccated coconut, for garnish

For the Blondie Batter. In a stand mixer with a paddle attachment, cream the butter, brown sugar and jaggery together on medium speed. Gradually add in the egg and vanilla extract a little at a time until they're fully incorporated. Bring the mixer speed down to low, and add in the white chocolate. Add the cranberries and almonds; these will bring some interesting textures to every bite.

Then at the very end, use a spatula to gently fold in the all-purpose flour, baking powder and salt to form a thick, even batter. Wrap this with cling film and rest it in the refrigerator for 2 hours.

> *Note from the Chefs:*
>
> This is by far one of the quickest recipes in the book; you can whip it up on super short notice, in any emergency snack situation. If you don't have the time to rest the batter for a full 2 hours, skip over that step and head straight into baking, and more importantly, eating!

Time for baking. Preheat the oven to 320°F (160°C). Grease eight molds with extra butter. Portion the batter out into the prepared molds and bake for 20 to 25 minutes, until they turn a lovely brown. Allow them to cool, then demold—they're often quite soft and crumbly, so be gentle. To finish up, cover the top and bottom of each snack with a coating of desiccated coconut to complete the look.

These simple, delicious blondies are ready to be feasted upon. You can store them in an airtight container in the refrigerator for up to 3 days.

CHOCOLATE BANANA CARAMEL SNACK

Yield: 6 pastries
Mold: 3-inch (7½-cm) ring

So many times as teenagers we found ourselves suddenly hungry in the middle of the night. We'd go into the kitchen and gather all the tasty ingredients we could find, and roll it all up into one crazy package of flavors. Now we get to do that professionally! Imagine this: a crumbled-up tart shell, a decadent ganache, pieces of banana fruit candy and sticky, chewy caramel, all tossed together and layered into one blissfully messy bite.

Cocoa Nib Crumble

½ cup (115 g) butter, cold

½ cup + 1 tbsp + 2 tsp (120 g) granulated sugar

1 cup (100 g) hazelnut flour

¼ cup + 2 tsp (25 g) cocoa powder

1 tbsp (3 g) ground coffee

Pinch of sea salt

½ cup (75 g) almonds, sliced

⅔ cup (80 g) cocoa nibs

Ganache

2¼ cups (300 g) dark chocolate, chopped

1½ cups (360 g) heavy cream

3 tbsp (60 g) invert sugar

6 tbsp + 1 tsp (90 g) clarified butter

Chewy Caramel Toffee

1 tbsp + 1 tsp (20 g) butter, plus more for greasing a frame

1 cup + 2 tbsp (150 g) dark chocolate, chopped

1 cup + 2 tsp (250 g) heavy cream

¾ cup + 2 tbsp (175 g) granulated sugar

½ cup + 1½ tsp (175 g) corn syrup

1⅓ tbsp (25 g) invert sugar

Banana Pâte de Fruit

2 tbsp + 1 tsp (35 g) butter, plus more for greasing a frame

1 cup + 1 tbsp (250 g) banana purée

1½ tsp (2.5 g) ginger, grated

1 cup + 2 tbsp (225 g) granulated sugar, divided

2 tsp (6 g) pectin

⅛ cup + 1½ tbsp (75 g) corn syrup

¼ cup + 2 tbsp (90 g) heavy cream

1⅓ tbsp (25 g) invert sugar

1¼ tsp (5 g) citric acid

1 tsp hot water

Chocolate Coating

1¼ cups + 1 tbsp + ½ tsp (175 g) dark chocolate

¼ cup (50 g) grapeseed oil

Salt, for garnish

For the Cocoa Nib Crumble. Line a tray with baking paper and set it aside. In a stand mixer with a paddle attachment, add the butter along with the granulated sugar, hazelnut flour, cocoa powder, ground coffee and salt. Mix until they combine into a nice crumble. Fold in the almonds along with the cocoa nibs, to add some great texture. Lay this crumble out on the prepared tray, wrap it in cling film, and keep it in the refrigerator for 2 hours. While it's chilling, preheat the oven to 320°F (160°C). Bake the chilled crumble for 15 to 20 minutes, then set this aside until the assembly.

For the Ganache. In a heatproof bowl, add the dark chocolate and set it aside. In a saucepan, heat the cream and invert sugar until it simmers. Pour the hot cream into the bowl with the chocolate, allowing the chocolate to melt. Add in the butter and use a hand blender to emulsify all these ingredients into a smooth, luscious ganache. Wrap it in cling film and leave to set in the refrigerator for 2 hours.

(continued)

For the Chewy Caramel Toffee. Grease a 9 x 9–inch (23 x 23–cm) frame and line it with baking paper. In a heatproof bowl, add the butter and dark chocolate, then set it aside. In a saucepan, whisk together the cream, granulated sugar, corn syrup and invert sugar, and cook the mixture to 237°F (114°C). Pour it into the bowl containing the butter and chocolate, allowing the chocolate to melt, then mix well until you get a smooth consistency. Pour this onto the prepared frame to get a ½-inch (1.3-cm)-thick layer, then allow it to set at room temperature for 2 hours. Use a knife to dice the set caramel toffee into tiny cubes; these are going to add some incredible bursts of sweetness.

For the Banana Pâte de Fruit. Grease a frame with extra butter and line it with baking paper. In a saucepan, add the banana purée, ginger and ½ cup + 1 tablespoon (112.5 g) of granulated sugar, and heat the mixture until it's nice and warm. Combine the pectin with the remaining ½ cup + 1 tablespoon (112.5 g) of granulated sugar, and toss that in as well, while bringing the mixture to a boil. Now mix in the corn syrup, cream, invert sugar and butter, and cook until it reaches 216°F (102°C), then turn off the heat. In a small bowl, dissolve the citric acid in the water, then add that into this mixture as well.

We'll need to cast this immediately into the prepared frame to get a ½-inch (1.3-cm) thick layer, then allow it to set at room temperature for 2 hours. Cut it up into tiny cubes, just like we did with the caramel toffee, and keep it aside for a bit longer.

For the Chocolate Coating. In a large bowl, temper the dark chocolate (see Quick Reference Notes, page 219) and mix it with the oil. We're going to dip the snacks into this at the very end.

Time for assembly. Line six tart rings with 1-inch (2.5-cm) tall acetate strips, and lay them out on a tray lined with baking paper. Now pipe a small layer of ganache into each ring, and cover it with pieces of crumble, caramel toffee, and banana pâte de fruit. Cover that up by piping another layer of ganache, and add even more chunks of the crumble, caramel and pâte de fruit, so each snack starts looking super decadent.

Add a sprinkling of salt on top, and put the tray in the freezer for 2 hours to help them harden. Once the snacks are back out and demolded, let's coat them in chocolate. First, line a tray with baking paper. Next, heat the chocolate coating to 77°F (25°C) before using. Use a small knife inserted into the top of the snack to dip it into the bowl of tempered chocolate coating, until just the top is exposed. Scrape the excess chocolate off from the bottom, and leave it on the prepared tray to set.

These incredible banana-caramel chocolate snacks look like a million bucks. Eat them immediately, or store them in the refrigerator for up to 3 days.

THE SACHERON

Yield: 16 macarons

Macarons are one of those products that never go out of fashion. The little French classics are just the right balance of crumbly and chewy, and capable of taking on so many flavors and fillings, it's no wonder the world can't get enough! Reminiscent of the famous Sacher torte, a legendary Viennese chocolate dessert with apricot jam filling, the Sacheron is destined to become one of your favorite macaron variants of all time. They're perfect chocolate shells with a beautiful combination of apricot confit and dark chocolate ganache.

Macaron Shells

1⅔ cups (100 g) almond flour

2½ tbsp (15 g) cocoa powder

¾ cup + 1 tbsp + 1 tsp (100 g) icing sugar

2 egg whites, divided

1½ tbsp (26.5 g) water

½ cup (100 g) caster sugar

Cacao nibs, for topping

Apricot Confit

⅓ cup (90 g) apricot purée

¼ vanilla bean pod (see Quick Reference Notes, page 219)

¼ tsp salt

2½ tbsp (50 g) invert sugar

¾ cup + 1 tbsp + 1 tsp (100 g) dried apricots, finely chopped

¼ cup (50 g) granulated sugar

2 tsp (6 g) pectin NH

2 tsp (10 g) lemon juice

Dark Chocolate Ganache

¾ cup + 2½ tbsp (120 g) dark chocolate, finely chopped

⅓ cup + 1 tbsp + 1 tsp (100 g) heavy cream

¼ tsp salt

1 tbsp (20 g) invert sugar

1½ tsp (10 g) corn syrup

1 tbsp + 1 tsp (20 g) butter

For the Macaron Shells. Preheat the oven to 284°F (140°C). In a food processor, add the almond flour, cocoa powder and icing sugar, blending it to a fine powder then sieving to get it an even finer base. Add in one egg white and mix to get a paste consistency.

Now we're going to begin making a meringue. In a saucepan, mix the water and caster sugar over medium heat, and use a thermometer to keep an eye on the temperature. In a stand mixer with a whisk attachment add an egg white. Once the sugar syrup reaches 230°F (110°C), start whipping the egg white. Then in about a minute, once the sugar syrup reaches 244°F (118°C), pour the sugar syrup in a thin stream into the foaming egg white, while continuing to whip until you get a nice Italian meringue with stiff peaks.

Use a spatula to gently fold the meringue into the almond paste we made earlier; do this in three parts, adding one-third at a time while continuing to fold. You'll know the batter consistency is perfect when it falls from your spatula in ribbons, and blends easily back into the remaining batter.

Let's use a stencil when piping our macarons so they all come out the same size. Turn a baking tray upside down, place a macaron stencil, and cover it with baking paper or a silicon mat. Use a piping bag fitted with a ½-inch (1.3-cm) round nozzle to pipe out 1½-inch (3.8-cm) macaron shells. Sprinkle some cacao nibs over the top of each macaron to add to the texture and flavor. Once you're done, gently knock the bottom of the tray against the table to get rid of any air bubbles in the mix. Rest them at room temperature for an hour, allowing the macarons to form a skin that feels dry to the touch. Bake these for 15 minutes, until the macarons rise and form their signature "feet."

(continued)

THE SACHERON *(continued)*

For the Apricot Confit. In a saucepan over medium heat, add the apricot purée, vanilla, salt, invert sugar and dried apricots. Once it's nice and warm, mix in the granulated sugar and pectin, and cook to a nice boil. Turn off the heat, add the lemon juice for those lovely citrus notes, and allow the confit to cool in the refrigerator until we're ready for assembly.

For the Dark Chocolate Ganache. In a heatproof bowl add the dark chocolate. In a saucepan, warm the cream, salt, invert sugar and corn syrup to a simmer. Pour the heated mixture into the bowl containing the chocolate and use a hand blender to bring it all together as a nice emulsion. Add the butter and continue to emulsify the mixture until you get a shiny, smooth ganache.

Time for assembly. Grab a freshly baked macaron shell and pipe in a generous amount of ganache in a circular form, leaving the center empty. Spoon a little apricot confit into that central space so it's neatly surrounded by the ganache, then place another shell over it and press lightly to form a beautiful looking macaron. Continue assembling until you have a tray full of macarons, then pop them in the refrigerator for a few hours to bring them to the perfect temperature.

Arrange these delicate treats on the fanciest tray you can find and serve them chilled. You can store them in an airtight container in the refrigerator for up to 3 days.

MISO-MAPLE SANDWICH

Yield: 12 pastries
Mold: 2½-inch (6-cm) oval cookie cutter

If you're like us, you've had the fortune of visiting different countries and being exposed to different cultures, and you'll know Japan is in its own category when it comes to food. As a chef, it's impossible to not be inspired by the sheer variety and impeccable quality of the food they put out at every street corner. One night in Kyoto we discovered a savory dish with the unexpected combination of miso and hazelnuts—it was absolutely mind blowing! So when it came time to think up this unique dessert sandwich, the umami of miso seemed to be the perfect match for the deep sweetness of our maple caramel. Put it between two sablés, with a sprinkling of matcha for good measure, and you're immediately transported right back to the streets of Japan.

Pâté Sablé

½ cup + 1 tsp (120 g) butter, at room temperature

Pinch of sea salt

¾ cup (90 g) icing sugar

½ cup (30 g) almond flour

1 egg

1¾ cups + 1 tbsp + 1 tsp (230 g) all-purpose flour

Maple Miso Jam

⅓ cup + 2 tbsp (110 g) heavy cream

⅓ cup (105 g) maple syrup

2 tbsp + 1 tsp (35 g) butter

Zest of 1 lemon

3 tbsp (40 g) white miso

Desiccated coconut, for garnish

Matcha powder, for garnish

For the Pâté Sablé. Preheat the oven to 320°F (160°C). Line a tray with baking paper and set it aside. In a stand mixer with a paddle attachment, mix the butter with the salt, icing sugar and almond flour. Then gradually add in the egg and mix until the ingredients feel well combined. Proceed to mix in the all-purpose flour as well and form a nice, even dough. Place the dough between two sheets of baking paper and flatten it a little before resting it in the refrigerator for 2 hours. Once it's well rested, use a rolling pin to roll the dough out into a sheet ⅛ inch (3 mm) thick. Use an oval 2½-inch (6-cm) cookie cutter to cut out discs of sablé dough. Lay them out on the prepared tray and bake for 20 minutes or until they turn a perfect golden brown.

For the Maple Miso Jam. In a saucepan, cook the cream and maple syrup until it reaches 225°F (107°C). Allow it to cool down to 140°F (60°C) before adding in the butter and mixing vigorously. Wrap it up by adding in the lemon zest and miso to give the jam a gorgeous and unforgettable flavor. Rest this in the refrigerator for 2 hours to set, then once it's back out, paddle the jam in a bowl to get it feeling soft again before using.

Time for assembly. Pipe a layer of maple miso jam onto a sablé, cover it with another sablé, and gently coat the sides with desiccated coconut. Repeat this process until we have a tray of neat little miso sandwiches. Finally, grab the cutest little stencil you have, and dust matcha powder over each snack to finish the look.

These exotic snacks are now ready to comfort your taste buds. Serve them immediately or store in an airtight container in the refrigerator for up to 3 days.

POACHED BERRY PISTACHIO FINANCIER

Yield: 8 pastries
Mold: 4 x 2-inch (10 x 5-cm) bar mold

Brown butter has one of the most distinct, memorable aromas in all of baking and pastry. Once you've had the experience of making it in the kitchen, there's no going back. It'll become one of your most-used ingredients! Beurre noisette is formed when we heat butter enough for the milk components to start browning, releasing an aroma that can only be described as life-changing. Similar to how you can have a range of caramels, brown butter also takes on darker colors and more complex flavors the further you heat it. This financier uses the gentle, earthy aromas of brown butter and pistachio, along with a poached strawberry filling, to create a light and fluffy all-day snack!

Pistachio Cake

½ cup + 1 tsp (120 g) butter

2 cups (190 g) pistachio flour

1½ cups + 1 tbsp + 1 tsp (190 g) icing sugar

3 tbsp + ½ tsp (25 g) all-purpose flour

3 tbsp (25 g) cornstarch

8 egg whites

Poached Strawberries

⅞ cup (125 g) strawberries, halved

⅜ cup + 2 tsp (50 g) icing sugar

Pistachio powder, for garnish

Apricot jam, warmed, for garnish

Snow sugar, for garnish

For the Pistachio Cake. We'll need to start by browning our butter before using it. In a saucepan over medium heat, cook the butter until it begins to boil and turn brown, releasing that gorgeous, nutty aroma. Allow it to cool before using in the recipe.

In a large bowl, use a whisk to combine the pistachio flour, icing sugar, all-purpose flour and cornstarch. Then gradually add in the egg whites, and mix until fully incorporated. Finish the batter by adding in that brown butter and mixing it to a smooth consistency.

For the Poached Strawberries. To a bowl, add the strawberries and icing sugar and allow the mixture to rest for about an hour. You'll notice how they naturally release some of their own juices. In a saucepan, add the strawberry mix and proceed to cook this mixture over medium heat for 5 minutes, until it starts to thicken and forms a nice compote. Remove it from the heat and allow it to cool before using.

Time for assembly. Preheat the oven to 320°F (160°C). Place the mold on a weighing scale, and pipe out 3 tablespoons (40 g) of the financier batter as a base. Then add 2 teaspoons (12 g) of strawberry compote in a straight line down the center, and cover it by piping another 3 tablespoons (40 g) of batter on top. Sprinkle pistachio powder over the tops, and pop them in the oven for 25 minutes. Use a cake tester to know if the baking is done, or a probe thermometer to check when the cakes reach 203°F (95°C). Bring them out of the oven and allow them to cool. Let's lightly brush warm apricot jam over the top surface, and sprinkle over some more pistachio powder. Finish off by dusting some fine snow sugar along the edges of the financier for a delicate look.

This dreamy pistachio financier is best served chilled so that fruit filling feels super refreshing. You can store it in an airtight container in the refrigerator for up to 3 days.

LARA'S GAINZ BARS

Yield: 16 bars
Mold: 8 x 8 x 2-inch (20⅓ x 5 x 5-cm) frame

For a pastry chef who is constantly around pastries, Andrés hardly eats any sweets on a regular basis. But even if you're obsessed with fitness, working out in the gym or wandering around the great outdoors, certain snacks can give you that boost of energy when you need it most. Unfortunately, a lot of the store-bought energy bars can be overly saccharine, so we recommend making your own that has a nice balance of healthy nutty goodness and enough sweetness to still feel like a treat. These yummy bars are packed with natural ingredients and have some added protein for good measure—so whip them up, pack some in your gym bag or take them on your next adventure!

For the Protein Bar. Before we begin, let's soak the dates in hot water for about 20 minutes to get them nice and soft. Grease the frame with butter and set it aside. Now transfer the soaked dates over to a food processor along with the cashews and peanut butter, and blend it all to a paste. Use a spatula to mix in the cocoa powder, protein powder and salt into the mixture. Finally, fold in the dark chocolate and almonds, mixing so they're evenly distributed. Transfer the mixture into the prepared frame to form a layer about 1 inch (2.5 cm) thick, and leave it in the refrigerator to set for 2 hours.

Once it feels firmly set, demold carefully, and cut out neat little bar shapes of 4 x 1–inch (10 x 2.5–cm) each. You could finish them up any way you like—coat them with ground coconut or roll them in crushed nuts.

These quick and easy protein bars are the perfect guilt-free snack, literally any time of day or night. You can store them in an airtight container in the refrigerator for up to 7 days.

Protein Bar

1 cup (170 g) dates

Butter, for greasing the frame

1 cup (160 g) cashews

½ cup (130 g) peanut butter

⅛ cup + 1 tbsp + 2 tsp (20 g) cocoa powder

⅓ cup + ½ tbsp (35 g) protein powder

½ tsp sea salt

⅓ cup + 2 tsp (50 g) dark chocolate, chopped

⅜ cup + 2 tsp (60 g) whole almonds, roasted

Ground coconut, crushed nuts or your preferred garnish

GRAND SCONES

Yield: 6 scones
Mold: 2-inch (5-cm) cookie cutter

Scones are an integral part of the English tea-time tradition; unfortunately over the years they've garnered a reputation of being overly dry, and always needing a cream or jam to compensate. We wanted to bring some excitement back to these fancy snacks. Adding some caramelized white chocolate to the dough, and topping with beautifully roasted pine nuts, apricots and cranberries will give this old-school treat a mouthwatering upgrade.

Scones

¼ cup + 1 tbsp + ¾ tsp (75 g) butter, cold

3 cups + 3 tbsp (400 g) all-purpose flour

1 tbsp (14 g) baking powder

1½ tsp (8 g) sea salt

⅓ cup + 2 tsp (75 g) granulated sugar

Zest of 1 orange

⅓ cup + 1 tsp (90 g) buttermilk

1 egg

¼ cup + 2 tbsp (90 g) heavy cream

¼ cup (30 g) dried cranberries

¼ cup (30 g) dried apricot

⅔ cup (115 g) caramelized white chocolate, chopped (see Quick Reference Notes, page 218)

Egg Wash

3 egg yolks

1 tbsp (15 g) heavy cream

Pinch of sea salt

⅓ cup + 1 tsp (50 g) pine nuts, whole, for garnish

2 tbsp (40 g) pearl sugar, for garnish

For the Scones. In a stand mixer with a paddle attachment, add the butter, all-purpose flour, baking powder, salt, granulated sugar and orange zest. Mix it into a sandy, crumble consistency. Gradually add the buttermilk and egg, followed by the cream, and continue to combine. Once the ingredients have formed an even dough, start gently folding in the dried fruit and white chocolate to make each bite more exciting. Place the dough between two sheets of baking paper and flatten it to 1 inch (2.5 cm) thick. Leave it in the freezer to rest for 2 hours to help it harden slightly.

For the Egg Wash. Make a quick and easy egg wash in a bowl by combining the egg yolks, cream and sea salt.

Time for assembly. Preheat the oven to 356°F (180°C). Line a tray with baking paper. Bring the dough back out of the freezer, and let's use a 2-inch (5-cm) cookie cutter to cut out thick discs of dough. Place them on the prepared tray, then brush an even layer of egg wash over the entire surface of your scones. Sprinkle a generous amount of pine nuts and pearl sugar on top, and pop them in the oven for 15 to 20 minutes, until they turn a delicious golden brown.

Serve these scones fresh out of the oven for best effect, or pair them with honey or your favorite jam. You can also store them in an airtight container in the refrigerator for up to 3 days.

GOURMET SNOBALLS

Yield: 10 SnoBalls
Mold: 2-inch (5-cm) dome shape

This incredibly unique and fancy dessert was ironically inspired by a cheap confection found at an American convenience store. It had sponge on the outside and jelly on the inside—one of those industrial-made, artificial sweets that you immediately regret eating. But clearly, beauty is waiting to be found in the rarest of places! Our goal was to use some pastry arts trickery to transform that simple product into a beautiful, layered dome of gourmet flavors and textures, while still retaining the immensely fun experience of eating something so unpredictably soft and jiggly.

Orange Marmalade

1 unpeeled orange, large

2 tbsp (30 g) orange juice

½ cup + 2 tbsp (125 g) granulated sugar, divided

½ tsp pectin

Dark Chocolate Orange Cake

⅔ cup (85 g) all-purpose flour

¼ cup + 2 tsp (25 g) cocoa powder

Pinch of sea salt

1 tsp baking powder

⅓ cup + 1⅔ tbsp (100 g) butter, at room temperature

¼ cup + 2 tbsp + 1 tsp (80 g) granulated sugar

2½ tbsp (15 g) trehalose

2 eggs

3 tbsp (25 g) dark chocolate, melted

2 tsp (15 g) candied orange peel

1½ tbsp (30 g) orange marmalade

Soaking Syrup

¼ cup + 1 tsp (55 g) granulated sugar

3 tbsp + 1 tsp (50 g) water

2 tsp (10 g) dark rum

Milk Chocolate Ganache

½ cup + 1½ tsp (90 g) milk chocolate, chopped

¼ cup + 2 tbsp (95 g) heavy cream

¼ vanilla bean pod, split lengthwise (see Quick Reference Notes, page 219)

Zest of ½ orange

1 tbsp + ¼ tsp (15 g) butter, at room temperature

Sablé Cacao

¼ cup + 1¾ tsp (65 g) butter

¼ cup + 2 tsp (35 g) icing sugar

¼ tsp sea salt

1 tbsp + 2 tsp (25 g) milk

⅞ cup + 1 tbsp + 1 tsp (120 g) all-purpose flour

1 tbsp + 2½ tsp (10 g) cocoa powder

Raspberry Marshmallow

2 tbsp (12 g) gelatin

¼ cup + 2½ tsp (72 g) cold water

⅔ cup (80 g) dextrose

½ cup + 1 tsp (125 g) raspberry purée

¼ cup + 3½ tbsp (95 g) granulated sugar

⅞ cup + 5½ tsp (95 g) trehalose

3 tbsp (60 g) corn syrup

¾ tsp citric acid powder

Baking spray, for greasing domes

Desiccated coconut, for garnish

For the Orange Marmalade. In a large saucepan filled with water, take the whole orange and bring it to a boil for a good 2 hours, making sure to replace the water every 40 minutes to help get rid of the bitterness. Let the orange cool for a while before chopping it up into small ½-inch (1.3-cm) pieces and removing all the seeds to get a nice mixture of pulp and rind. Place the orange pieces in a new saucepan and add in the orange juice and ¼ cup + 1 tablespoon (62.5 g) of granulated sugar over medium heat. In a separate bowl, mix the pectin with ¼ cup + 1 tablespoon (62.5 g) of granulated sugar, and once the stewing oranges have reached 104°F (40°C), add in the pectin-sugar mixture. Continue heating to bring it to a boil until it reaches a thick, jam-like consistency.

(continued)

For the Dark Chocolate Orange Cake. Preheat the oven to 320°F (160°C). Line a 10-inch (25-cm) square frame with baking paper. In a large bowl, sift together the all-purpose flour, cocoa powder, salt and baking powder. Set the mix aside. In a stand mixer with a paddle attachment, mix the butter, granulated sugar and trehalose for about a minute. Gradually add in the eggs a little at a time until they're fully incorporated. Then mix in the dark chocolate, followed by the sifted ingredients. Gently fold in the candied orange peel and measured orange marmalade. Pour the batter into the prepared frame and bake for 15 to 20 minutes. You'll know it's done when the edges start to release from the tray.

> *Note from the Chefs:*
>
> The advantage of using trehalose sugar is the extremely low sweetness when compared to other forms of sugar. If you can't find it, no worries, just switch it out for granulated sugar.

For the Soaking Syrup. In a saucepan, bring the granulated sugar and water to a boil, then allow it to cool before mixing in the dark rum. Once the cake is out of the oven, brush the syrup evenly over it to add some heady flavors. Then use a 1½-inch (3.8-cm) cookie cutter to cut out small discs of cake, and reserve them for assembly.

For the Milk Chocolate Ganache. In a heatproof bowl, add the milk chocolate and set it aside. In a saucepan over medium heat, bring the cream, vanilla and orange zest to a boil. Then turn off the heat, cover with a lid, and allow it to infuse for about 10 minutes. Strain the mixture, and reheat to a simmer. Then pour it into the bowl containing the milk chocolate, allowing the chocolate to melt. Use a hand blender to get a smooth, creamy consistency, and allow it to cool. Add in the butter, and use a hand blender to bring it all together into an emulsion. Allow it to set in the refrigerator for 2 hours.

For the Sablé Cacao. Preheat the oven to 320°F (160°C). In a stand mixer with a paddle attachment, mix together the butter, icing sugar and salt. Then slowly add in the milk before gently mixing in the all-purpose flour and cocoa powder. Once it's all come together, place the dough between two sheets of baking paper, flatten and rest it in the refrigerator for 2 hours. After resting, roll the dough out into a very thin 5/64-inch (2-mm) sheet, and use a 2-inch (5-cm) cookie cutter to form sablé discs. Now we're ready to bake them for 15 to 20 minutes, until they're firm to the touch.

For the Raspberry Marshmallow. In a medium bowl, add the gelatin and water, and allow the gelatin to bloom for 5 minutes, until it swells. Then add in the dextrose sugar, and set it aside for a moment. Now in a saucepan, take the raspberry purée, granulated sugar, trehalose and corn syrup, and heat them to 230°F (110°C). Pour the mixture over the gelatin and dextrose, and stir well until it's completely dissolved. Transfer it all into a stand mixer with a whisk attachment and whip the mixture until it doubles in volume. You'll know it's the right consistency when the mixture falls in thick ribbons from the whisk. Finally, add the citric acid to give our marshmallow some extra punch.

Time for assembly. Lightly grease the dome-shaped molds with baking spray. Use a piping bag to pipe out a layer of ganache onto each of the sablé discs. Pipe marshmallow into the dome molds until they're almost full, then insert the dark chocolate orange cake discs and press gently until they're halfway through the marshmallow. Place a sablé, with the ganache-side touching the cake discs, into the marshmallow to form the base. Put these in the refrigerator for 4 hours, then leave them at room temperature overnight to fully set. Once they're ready, grease your hands lightly with baking spray, and pull the sides of the mold away from each snack before popping them out carefully. Immediately roll them in desiccated coconut to coat the marshmallows.

These heavenly soft SnoBalls are ready to be picked up and eaten with unbridled joy. You can store them at room temperature for up to 5 days.

PUMPKIN SEED NOUGAT

Yield: 16 bars
Mold: 8-inch (20⅓-cm) square frame

This ultra-popular confection has literally been around for centuries, and seems to have found its way to every corner of the world, gaining lots of interesting variations along the way. We're fans of the classic-style nougat with its subtle caramel flavors and crunchy inclusions like these healthy pumpkin seeds. As simple and lovely as this treat is to eat, making nougat requires a careful balance of ingredients and temperatures. We're here to walk you through it step by step. So sharpen up your senses and keep your probe thermometer nearby—let's dive into this delicious trail-mix nougat.

Nougat

Oil, for greasing frame

Rice or wafer paper, for lining frame

3 cups (400 g) pumpkin seeds

⅝ cup (150 g) water

5 tbsp (60 g) isomalt

¼ cup + 1 tsp (90 g) corn syrup

2 cups (400 g) granulated sugar, divided

1 cup + 1½ tsp (350 g) honey

3 egg whites

1 tsp sea salt

Pinch of cream of tartar

½ cup + 2½ tsp (120 g) cocoa butter, melted

For the Nougat. Preheat the oven to 320°F (160°C). Oil the sides of the square frame and line the base with a sheet of rice paper and keep another sheet nearby for later. Toast the pumpkin seeds for 10 minutes.

A probe thermometer is going to be essential for this recipe so keep that handy. In a saucepan over medium-high heat add the water, isomalt, corn syrup and 1⅞ cups (380 g) of granulated sugar. Avoid stirring because the sugar might get lumpy.

Place the honey in another saucepan. When the sugar syrup reaches 239°F (115°C), start cooking the honey over high heat. Meanwhile, in a stand mixer with a whisk attachment, let's drop in the egg whites, remaining ⅛ cup (20 g) of granulated sugar, salt and the cream of tartar, and start whipping them on a low speed. Notice the mixture doubles in volume and becomes light and fluffy. Check on the sugar syrup at this point, to make sure it's approaching 311°F (155°C), because we'll need that soon.

Just before we add the honey, turn the mixer up to medium speed. When the honey reaches 250°F (121°C), pour it over the egg whites slowly and continuously as they're being whipped. If the sugar syrup has reached 311°F (155°C), add that in as well in the same way—slowly but continuously. Then turn the mixer up to maximum speed for about 8 minutes so that the overall temperature drops to around 158°F (70°C), then drop the mixer back down to medium speed.

Now we can add the cocoa butter to the mixture. Don't worry if the mixture starts to separate, it'll come back together with a few more minutes in the mixer. Once it's all come back together, switch to a paddle attachment and mix in the toasted pumpkin seeds gradually.

Transfer the nougat into the prepared frame, using a spatula to form a 1-inch (2.5-cm) thick layer. Then cover the top with the extra sheet of rice paper and flatten gently. Leave it at room temperature overnight to make sure it's completely set. Use a small knife to cut the nougat up into small bars of 1 x ½ inch (2.6 x 1.3 cm), and wrap them individually with cellophane or candy wrappers so they can be easily stored without melting.

Pick one of these treats up at any time during the day, and get your hit of chewy, sugary, nougat goodness. You can store these in a cool, dry place for up to 2 weeks.

*See photo on page 133.

BUTTERY PINEAPPLE TART

Yield: 6 tarts
Mold: 3-inch (7½-cm) round tart shell

Pineapple is one of the most underrated fruits in pastry, offering a sharp, tangy sweetness hidden in every juicy, satisfying bite. While the Western world uses it in classics like the pineapple upside-down cake, the Eastern equivalent is the mighty pineapple tart, a fruity stuffed pastry. JohnyLara's take on this street-style dessert combines a zesty pineapple filling that packs an undeniably powerful punch, wrapped in a gorgeous buttery tart shell that instantly melts in the mouth.

Tart Dough

⅓ cup + 2 tbsp (105 g) butter, at room temperature

⅓ cup + 2 tsp (75 g) granulated sugar

Pinch of sea salt

Zest of 1 lemon

¾ cup + 1 tbsp + 1 tsp (50 g) almond flour

1 egg yolk

2 tsp (10 g) milk

1 cup + 1 tbsp + 1 tsp (135 g) all-purpose flour

Pinch of baking powder

Pineapple Confit

1⅓ cups (220 g) pineapple, fresh

1 tbsp + 2 tsp (25 g) water

½ cup (125 g) pineapple juice

⅓ cup + 2 tsp (75 g) granulated sugar

1½ tsp (4 g) pectin

2 tsp (10 g) lemon juice

Zest of 2 lemons

⅓ tsp sea salt

Butter, for greasing tart shells

Egg Wash

3 egg yolks

1 tbsp (15 g) heavy cream

Pinch of sea salt

For the Tart Dough. In a stand mixer with a paddle attachment, start by creaming the butter with the granulated sugar and salt. Run it at medium speed until the butter looks light and fluffy. Next, add the lemon zest, then mix in the almond flour, egg yolk and milk, followed by the all-purpose flour and baking powder, to get a uniform soft dough. Place the dough between two sheets of baking paper, and roll it down to a thickness of ¼ inch (6 mm). Leave it to rest in the refrigerator overnight for best results.

For the Pineapple Confit. Cut the fresh pineapple down into tiny cubes, then combine it with the water and pineapple juice in a heavy-bottomed pan. Using fresh pineapple juice here would be perfect. Heat the mix to 104°F (40°C), then add in a combination of granulated sugar and pectin. Continue to cook over medium heat until the mixture reaches a steady boil. Once it thickens, add the lemon juice, then allow the confit to cool. Finally, season it with some lemon zest and sea salt to round out the flavors.

Time for assembly. Preheat the oven to 320°F (160°C). Lightly grease the tart shells with butter, then cut out 6 (4-inch [10-cm]) discs of dough as the tart base. To line the mold, place a disc in the center and press gently starting from the base and working your way up the sides. If the edges are above the rim, carefully trim them with a small knife. Fill the pineapple confit almost to the top of each tart. Then cut out discs of dough large enough to cover the tops, and place them over the pineapple filling, gently pressing to seal the edges together and neatly trimming any excess.

For the Egg Wash. In a bowl, mix the egg yolks, cream and salt together, and gently brush it over the top of the tarts. Make some decorative slashes with a knife to get a really stunning look, and pop them in the oven for 20 to 25 minutes, until the tarts turn a delicious golden brown.

These refreshing, tangy tarts can be eaten straight out of the oven or at room temperature. You can store them in an airtight container for up to 3 days.

TRUFFLE
MADELEINE

Yield: 10 pastries
Mold: Madeleine mold

The traditional madeleine is a lovely European cake known for its soft sponge and signature bump, often baked with a shell-shaped design. With a few twists in the ingredient list, we've turned this classic cake into a luxurious dream. The truffle oil in this recipe helps make the cake unbelievably moist and adds a distinct aroma to the product that is recognizable long before you take that first bite. A chocolate-coated delight that is simultaneously light and impressive, we find this madeleine makes any high tea instantly feel more majestic.

Madeleine

2 eggs

⅓ cup + 1½ tsp (80 g) brown sugar

2½ tbsp (20 g) dextrose

1 tbsp + ½ tsp (25 g) truffle honey

Zest of ½ lemon

1 tbsp + 2 tsp (25 g) milk

1 cup + 1 tbsp + 1 tsp (135 g) all-purpose flour

1 tsp baking powder

⅓ cup + 1 tsp (75 g) white truffle oil

Manié butter, for greasing mold (see Quick Reference Notes, page 218)

Glaze

⅔ cup + 2 tsp (120 g) milk chocolate

1½ tbsp (20 g) cocoa butter

2 tbsp (30 g) hazelnut oil

Pinch of sea salt

Edible gold flake, for garnish

For the Madeleine. In a stand mixer with a whisk attachment, whip the eggs, brown sugar, dextrose, truffle honey and lemon zest until it reaches a soft ribbon consistency. Gradually mix in the milk and combine well. Then fold in the all-purpose flour and baking powder, followed by the truffle oil. This batter needs some time to rest, so let's leave it in the refrigerator overnight so it's properly hydrated.

Preheat the oven to 338°F (170°C). Grease the madeleine molds with manié butter. Pipe the batter into the molds, filling them right to the top. Use a palette knife to flatten the surface of the batter in each of the molds, then bake for 12 to 15 minutes, until they turn a gorgeous golden brown. Once they're baked, pop them in the freezer for 2 hours.

For the Glaze. First melt the milk chocolate and cocoa butter. Allow it to cool, then mix in the hazelnut oil and the salt. Store this in a bowl at 77 to 82°F (25 to 28°C) for us to dip the madeleines.

Time for assembly. These madeleines are going to have a gorgeous trademark bump on top, and a coated chocolate bottom. Line a tray with baking paper, then use a small knife inserted into the top surface of each madeleine to dip it halfway into the tempered chocolate glaze. Add a sprinkling of gold flakes to this coated side, and lay it down on the prepared tray to completely set.

These sumptuous madeleines are ready to be adored, photographed and eaten with the utmost attention. You can store them in an airtight container at room temperature for up to 2 days.

GLORIOUS Breakfast Bakes

They say breakfast is the most important meal of the day. We say it's the most delicious. Who can resist a basket of freshly baked breads lit by the glorious golden morning sunlight? With so much traveling, we end up staying in a lot of hotels, and when we're heading to bed at night the only thing we can think of is all those fresh breads and sugary pastries waiting for us in the breakfast buffet.

It's possible to make a cake without getting your hands dirty, but breads are so much more involved. There's something raw and physical about working with dough, kneading it down and knocking it back, stretching it out or rolling it up. You sort of become one with the product.

Unlike the other chapters, here we're going to be using bread flour, which has a higher amount of gluten than the all-purpose flour we've been using so far. The extra protein helps give these bread doughs that distinctive, stretchy texture we all love. If you're using instant dry yeast, simply use half the portion. So whether it's the sweet and chunky Pass-It-Here Gibassier (page 168), the adorable sugar-coated cubes of our Saffron Milk Brioche (page 171) or all the varieties of laminated pastries like the coconut-filled South Indian Coconut Croissant (page 183), you're going to love these morning delights.

CARAMEL BABKA

Yield: 2 loaves
Mold: 6½ x 3-inch (16½ x 7½-cm) loaf tin

As much as we enjoy modern cuisine, sometimes tradition just tastes too damn good. That seems to be the case with this sweet braided bread invented by the Jewish communities in Poland. It was originally made with fruity or spiced filling, but the version we're making here is going to be layered with chocolate and caramel so each bite feels rich and decadent. And if you're wondering why the name sounds so cute to say out loud, Babka literally translates to "grandmother" in Polish. We told you it was traditional!

Dough

1¾ cups + 1 tbsp (250 g) bread flour, plus more for dusting

2 tbsp (25 g) granulated sugar

1 tbsp + 1¾ tsp (13.5 g) fresh yeast

2 tbsp (30 g) butter

1 egg

½ cup + 2 tsp (130 g) water

1 tsp salt

Milk Chocolate Caramel

⅓ cup + 1 tbsp (60 g) milk chocolate, chopped

1½ tsp (10 g) honey

⅓ cup + 1 tbsp + 1 tsp (100 g) heavy cream

¼ cup + 1 tsp (55 g) granulated sugar

2 tbsp (30 g) butter, at room temperature

½ tsp sea salt

Dark Chocolate Ganache

⅔ cup (90 g) dark chocolate, chopped

¾ tsp corn syrup

¼ cup + 2 tbsp (90 g) heavy cream

2 tsp (10 g) butter, plus more for greasing the loaf tin

⅓ cup (30 g) almond flakes, for garnish

Milk, for brushing

For the Dough. Let's start off with a stand mixer with a hook attachment. Add the bread flour, granulated sugar, yeast, butter, egg, water and salt. Knead the dough for 8 minutes at medium speed until it comes together well and no longer sticks to the sides of the bowl. Perform a window-pane test on the dough by taking a small, flattened piece and gently spreading it apart with your fingers: if the dough forms a thin, even, translucent membrane without tearing, then the gluten is perfectly developed. If a clear "window" isn't forming yet, keep kneading and checking until the dough is ready. We also want to make sure that the dough temperature always stays between 68 and 75°F (20 and 24°C) so our bread has the best flavor and an even rise.

Dust a bowl with flour, take the dough out of the mixer and shape it into a nice smooth mound. Place it in the bowl, then cover with cling film and rest it at room temperature for an hour. Once the dough has risen, you'll need to knock it back. Do this by firmly pressing or punching down the dough to properly distribute the air bubbles. Then place the dough on a surface dusted with flour, and roll it into a rectangle of 8 x 6 inches (20⅓ x 15¼ cm) that's ½ inch (1.3 cm) thick. Transfer the dough to a tray, wrap it with cling film and keep it in the refrigerator for later.

For the Milk Chocolate Caramel. In a heatproof bowl, add the milk chocolate and set it aside. In a saucepan, warm the honey and cream. In another saucepan, start heating the granulated sugar, stirring continuously, until it caramelizes to a deep amber color. Add the butter to the sugar to help deglaze the pan. Add in the warmed honey-cream mixture, stirring until it all comes together. Pour the mixture into the bowl containing the milk chocolate, allowing it to melt. Toss in the salt, and use a hand blender to bring it to a smooth emulsion, then refrigerate for 2 hours to get it to the right consistency.

For the Dark Chocolate Ganache. In a heatproof bowl, add the dark chocolate and set it aside. In a saucepan, add the corn syrup and cream, and heat it to a simmer. Then pour the heated mixture into the bowl containing the dark chocolate, and allow it to melt. Mix well, and let it cool to room temperature. Add in the butter at the end, and use a hand blender to get a nice smooth ganache.

(continued)

CARAMEL BABKA *(continued)*

Time for assembly. Grease the loaf tin with butter. Spread a layer of chocolate ganache on the dough within ½ inch (1.3 cm) of the edges. Then use a piping bag to drizzle milk chocolate caramel all over the ganache, and roll the dough along the longer side into a log. Wrap this in cling film and freeze for an hour to get the dough a little firmer. Now use a small sharp knife to cut along the center of the log lengthwise, so we get two long halves with the layers exposed. Twist the halves together to form a braid, and place it into the prepared loaf tin. Leave it to proof in a bread fermentation box at 79°F (26°C) and 60 percent humidity, or place it in a switched-off oven with a bowl of hot water. Proofing usually takes about 2 hours; you'll know it's just right when the dough has doubled in size.

While the dough is proofing, soak some almond flakes in a bowl of water to get them ready for baking. Once the bread is proofed, brush a layer of milk over the surface, and sprinkle the almond flakes on top. Also preheat the oven to 392°F (200°C). We're finally ready to bake this for 35 to 40 minutes, until it turns a perfect golden brown.

This beautiful layered babka is ready to serve up nice and warm. You can store it wrapped at room temperature for up to a day.

BRUNCH-STYLE KUGELHOF

Yield: 10 pastries
Mold: 4-inch (10-cm) kugelhof Bundt pan

If Andrés had to choose just one baked bread to eat for the rest of his life, this would be it. The kugelhof is an anytime treat with a super-recognizable shape—some historic accounts say it comes from the shape of a hat or a turban! This recipe kicks the classic Alsatian version up a notch; the olive oil helps make it super moist, while the raisins and oranges add those absolutely delightful bursts of flavor. Oh, did we mention that once this jumps out of the oven, it's soaked in sinful amounts of melted butter and orange liqueur-sugar syrup? It's a boozy, brunch-style upgrade to an already iconic bread.

Starter

1¼ cups + 1 tbsp (180 g) bread flour

⅜ cup + 2 tsp (100 g) water

⅓ tsp fresh yeast

Dough

1⅓ cups + 2 tsp (200 g) raisins, chopped

⅓ cup + 1½ tsp (90 g) milk

2 tbsp + 1 tsp (20 g) fresh yeast

1⅜ cups (190 g) bread flour

1½ cups (190 g) all-purpose flour, plus more for dusting

1 tbsp + 2½ tsp (25 g) brown sugar

2 tbsp (40 g) invert sugar

1½ tsp (10 g) sea salt

1⅓ cups (215 g) starter

3 eggs

¼ cup + 1 tsp (60 g) olive oil

⅓ cup + 1 tbsp (90 g) butter, plus more for greasing the pan

¼ tsp ground nutmeg

Zest of 1½ oranges

2 tbsp + ½ tsp (30 g) orange liqueur (We recommend Cointreau™)

1 cup + 2 tbsp (150 g) dark chocolate, chopped

Almond flakes, for garnish

Orange Liqueur Sugar Syrup

½ cup + 2½ tsp (110 g) granulated sugar

⅜ cup + 2 tsp (100 g) water

1 tbsp + 2½ tsp (25 g) orange liqueur (We recommend Cointreau™)

Pinch of saffron

35 oz (1 kg) clarified butter, melted, for dipping

For the Starter. In a large bowl, mix the bread flour, water and yeast. Knead until it forms a nice, smooth dough. Cover with cling film and leave it to ferment at room temperature for 12 hours.

For the Dough. Soak the raisins in hot water for about 30 minutes, until they're soft and tender. Add the milk to a bowl and stir in the yeast to dissolve it. Transfer this to a stand mixer with a hook attachment, and add in the bread flour, all-purpose flour, brown sugar, invert sugar, salt and measured starter. While continuing to mix, add in the eggs gradually, followed by the olive oil, and let it knead for 10 minutes at a medium speed until a dough comes together and no longer sticks to the sides of the bowl. That's when we add in the butter a little at a time and mix until fully incorporated.

> *Note from the Chefs:*
>
> Fats are an often underexplored part of many recipes. Here, instead of just using butter, we're opting to add in some olive oil to give extra moisture to this amazing sweet bread.

(continued)

Perform a window-pane test on the dough by taking a small, flattened piece and gently spreading it apart with your fingers: if the dough forms a thin, even, translucent membrane without tearing, then the gluten is perfectly developed. If a clear "window" isn't forming yet, keep kneading and checking until the dough is ready. We also want to make sure that the dough temperature always stays between 68 and 75°F (20 and 24°C) so our bread has the best flavor and an even rise. Toss in the nutmeg and orange zest for some lovely aromas, and finish up by mixing in the raisins, orange liqueur and dark chocolate to make every bite feel special.

Dust a bowl with flour. Now take the dough out of the mixer and shape it into a nice smooth mound. Place it in the bowl, cover with cling film, and leave it at room temperature to rest for 2 hours. Soak the almond flakes in a bowl of water for at least 10 minutes so they're ready for baking. Generously grease the Bundt pan with extra butter. Once the dough has risen, you'll need to knock it back. Do this by firmly pressing or punching down the dough to properly distribute the air bubbles. Sprinkle the soaked almond flakes into the prepared pan for a textural crunch. Shape the dough into a ball, and poke a hole through the center before fitting it into the mold. The center of the mold should come straight through the dough and be clearly visible. Leave it to proof in a bread fermentation box at 86°F (30°C) and 60 percent humidity, or place it in a switched-off oven with a bowl of hot water. Proofing usually takes about 2 hours; you'll know it's just right when the dough has doubled in size.

For the Orange Liqueur Sugar Syrup. In a saucepan over medium heat, add the sugar, water, orange liqueur and saffron. Allow the mixture to reach a gentle boil before turning off the heat and allowing it to cool.

Time for baking. Preheat the oven to 392°F (200°C). Bake the dough for 35 to 40 minutes to get a perfect golden brown. Once it's done baking, grab two bowls to use for dipping; fill one with the orange liqueur sugar syrup and the second with melted clarified butter. Make sure they're both nice and warm, at least 158°F (70°C) so they get perfectly absorbed by the bread, giving you a gorgeous, memorable flavor. Proceed to dip each kugelhof into the syrup first, then into the butter, and then set them onto a wire rack with a tray beneath to catch any dripping excess. Repeat till you have a full set of incredible, soaked treats, and allow them to cool before serving.

This stunning bread-cake is ready to grace your palate. You can store it wrapped at room temperature for up to a day.

LEMON-GLAZED BERLINER

Yield: 10 doughnuts
Mold: 3-inch (7½-cm) cookie cutter

We're going to be honest, as much as we love making desserts with a bunch of unique ingredients and complex components, there's nothing better than a quick, delicious recipe when you're craving something fun to eat. This might be the easiest recipe in the book, but we have no doubt it'll be one of your favorites; this doughnut is soft and sweet and tangy with just the right amount of bite.

Sponge Starter

⅞ cup + 2 tsp (125 g) bread flour

⅓ cup + 1 tsp (85 g) water

1½ tbsp (13 g) fresh yeast

Dough

⅞ cup + 2 tsp (125 g) bread flour

⅞ cup (110 g) all-purpose flour

3 eggs

¾ tsp salt

¼ cup + ½ tsp (60 g) granulated sugar

1⅓ cups (215 g) sponge starter

¼ cup + 1 tbsp + ¾ tsp (75 g) butter, plus more for greasing a tray, at room temperature

Lemon Glaze

⅓ cup (80 g) lemon juice

2½ cups (300 g) icing sugar

Oil, for frying
Lemon zest, for garnish

For the Sponge Starter. In a large bowl, mix the bread flour, water and yeast. Knead the mix until it forms a nice, smooth dough. Cover it with cling film and leave it to ferment at room temperature for 2 hours.

For the Dough. In a stand mixer with a dough hook, add the bread flour, all-purpose flour, eggs, salt, granulated sugar and the measured sponge starter, and run them at the lowest speed for 5 minutes, until a dough comes together and no longer sticks to the sides of the bowl. Incorporate the butter and mix until elastic. Perform a window-pane test on the dough by taking a small flattened piece and gently spreading it apart with your fingers: if the dough forms a thin, even, translucent membrane without tearing, then the gluten is perfectly developed. If a clear "window" isn't forming yet, keep kneading and checking until the dough is ready. We also want to make sure that the dough temperature always stays between 68 and 75°F (20 and 24°C) so our bread has the best flavor and an even rise.

Grease a tray with butter before taking the dough out of the mixer. Shape the dough into a nice smooth mound. Place it on the prepared tray, cover with cling film and leave it at room temperature to rest for 20 minutes. Once the dough has risen, you'll need to knock it back. Do this by firmly pressing or punching down the dough to properly distribute the air bubbles. Roll it out to ½-inch (1.3-cm) thick, then place it in a tray, cover it with cling film, and refrigerate for 2 hours. Once the sheet is back out, use a 3-inch (7.5-cm) cookie cutter to cut small discs of dough. Let's put these on small, individual pieces of baking paper. Leave these to proof in a bread fermentation box at 86°F (30°C) and 60 percent humidity, or place it in a switched-off oven with a bowl of hot water. Proofing usually takes about 2 hours; you'll know it's just right when the dough has doubled in size.

For the Lemon Glaze. In a bowl, mix together the lemon juice and icing sugar to form a thick glaze.

Time for finishing. Place a wire rack on top of a tray to hold the doughnuts and catch any excess glaze. Preheat the oven to 320°F (160°C). Now heat about 2 inches of oil in a pan to 338°F (170°C) so we can start frying the doughnuts. Use the baking paper at the bottom of each donut to help tip them gently into the oil, and fry until they're golden brown on both sides, with a white ring around the center. Leave them on a wire rack to cool, then pour the lemon glaze over the doughnuts. Pop them in the oven for a minute or two until the glaze is set, and grate some lemon zest over the tops.

PASS-IT-HERE GIBASSIER

Yield: 10 pastries

Whenever we see one of these delicious breads, we can't help but say "pass it here!" The gibassier is an often-overlooked recipe from the Southern French village of Provence. It's an enriched buttery dough that hides a long list of wonderfully aromatic ingredients inside. We get hints of orange blossom water, anise, olive oil and candied orange peels, not to mention the entire dough is dipped in clarified butter and rolled in fennel sugar, so if you're eating a gibassier and accidentally think you're in heaven, we completely understand.

Starter

⅓ cup + 1 tsp (85 g) whole milk

1 cup + 3 tbsp (165 g) bread flour

2 egg yolks

⅓ tsp fresh yeast

Gibassier Dough

1⅝ cups + 1 tsp (225 g) bread flour

1¾ cups + 1½ tsp (225 g) all-purpose flour, plus more for dusting

½ cup + 1 tbsp + 1 tsp (115 g) granulated sugar

3 tbsp + 2½ tsp (32 g) fresh yeast

1¼ cups +2 ¾ tsp (210 g) starter

3 eggs

2 tbsp + 2 tsp (40 g) water

2 tbsp (30 g) orange blossom water

1¾ tsp (8.5 g) sea salt

⅓ cup + 1 tsp (80 g) butter, firm and cubed

⅓ cup + 2 tsp (80 g) olive oil

1 tbsp (8 g) fennel seeds, plus more fennel seeds for garnish

¼ cup (85 g) candied orange peel

Zest of 1 orange

Fennel Seed Sugar

¼ cup + 1 tbsp (30 g) fennel seeds

35 oz (1 kg) granulated sugar

35 oz (1 kg) clarified butter, melted, for dipping

For the Starter. In a large bowl, mix the milk, bread flour, egg yoks and yeast. Knead until it forms a smooth dough. Then cover it with cling film, and leave to ferment at room temperature for 24 hours.

For the Gibassier Dough. In a stand mixer with a hook attachment, mix together the bread flour, all-purpose flour, granulated sugar, yeast, measured starter, eggs, water, orange blossom water and salt, for about 5 minutes at medium speed until a dough comes together well and no longer sticks to the sides of the bowl. Add in the butter a little at a time, followed by the olive oil, until they're fully incorporated. Perform a window-pane test on the dough by taking a small flattened piece and gently spreading it apart with your fingers: if the dough forms a thin, even, translucent membrane without tearing, then the gluten is perfectly developed. If a clear "window" isn't forming yet, keep kneading and checking until the dough is ready. Make sure that the dough temperature always stays between 68 and 75°F (20 and 24°C) so our bread has the best flavor and an even rise. Finish up by mixing in the fennel seeds, candied orange peel and orange zest.

Dust a bowl with flour. Take the dough out of the mixer and shape it into a nice smooth mound. Place it in the bowl, cover it with cling film, and leave it at room temperature to rest for 2 hours. You'll notice the dough has risen and you'll need to knock it back. Do this by firmly pressing or punching down the dough to properly distribute the air bubbles inside it. Portion out ¼-pound (112-g) balls, and roll them in crushed fennel seeds.

Make two slits near the top of each ball of dough, and place them in a tray with space between each. Leave them to proof in a bread fermentation box at 86°F (30°C) and 60 percent humidity, or place in a switched-off oven with a bowl of hot water. Proofing usually takes about 2 hours; you'll know it's just right when the dough has doubled in size.

For the Fennel Seed Sugar. Mix the fennel seeds and granulated sugar in a bowl and set aside.

Time for baking. Preheat the oven to 347°F (175°C). Bake these for 10 to 15 minutes, until they turn golden brown. Once they're done, dip them in the melted clarified butter, and roll them in fennel seed sugar to get that delicious aromatic coating. Serve warm and store wrapped at room temperature for up to a day.

SAFFRON MILK BRIOCHE

Yield: 5 pastries
Mold: 2½-inch (6-cm) cube tin

To say saffron is precious is an understatement. It's handpicked from thousands of tiny flowers in a process that's intensely laborious and produces only a few little stands of spice. And yet, India is all about that saffron. It's used in milk and rice and sweets, and lends this subtle distinct flavor to everything it touches, so we wanted to bring that subtlety to the French brioche. Shaped as unique little cubes, this incredibly soft bread blessed with saffron milk and dusted with sugar is going to feel like a warm hug on a winter day.

Starter

3 tbsp + 1 tsp (50 g) milk

2⅛ tsp (1.5 g) saffron

⅓ cup + 1½ tsp (50 g) bread flour

2 tsp (5 g) fresh yeast

Brioche Dough

¼ cup + ¾ tsp (60 g) butter, plus more for greasing tins, at room temperature

¾ cup (100 g) starter

1 cup (120 g) bread flour

2 tbsp + 1 tsp (30 g) granulated sugar

⅓ tsp salt

1 tbsp (8 g) fresh yeast

1 egg

2 tbsp + ¼ tsp (30 g) clarified butter

Saffron Sugar

1½ cups (300 g) granulated sugar

1 tsp saffron

Butter, for brushing

For the Starter. In a saucepan, heat the milk until it's warm, then turn off the heat before adding in that delicate saffron and allowing it to infuse for 2 hours. Then mix in the bread flour and yeast, and bring it all together to form a dough. Cover it with cling film, and leave it to ferment at room temperature for 3 hours.

For the Brioche Dough. Grease five cube tins with extra butter. In a stand mixer with a hook attachment, mix the measured starter along with the bread flour, granulated sugar, salt, yeast and egg. Mix it for 8 minutes at medium speed until a dough comes together that no longer sticks to the sides of the bowl. This is when we can start adding in the butter and clarified butter a little at a time and mix until it's fully incorporated.

Perform a window-pane test on the dough by taking a small, flattened piece and gently spreading it apart with your fingers: if the dough forms a thin, even, translucent membrane without tearing, then the gluten is perfectly developed. If a clear "window" isn't forming yet, keep kneading and checking until the dough is ready. We also want to make sure that the dough temperature always stays between 68 and 75°F (20 and 24°C) so our bread has the best flavor and an even rise. Portion out small spheres of 1½ ounces (42 g) each, and place them in the prepared cube tins. Leave them to proof in a bread fermentation box at 86°F (30°C) and 60 percent humidity, or place them in a switched-off oven with a bowl of hot water. Proofing usually takes about 2 hours; you'll know it's just right when the dough has doubled in size.

For the Saffron Sugar. In a bowl, add the sugar and saffron. Use your fingers to gently rub the saffron strands with the sugar until they're well mixed.

Time for baking. Preheat the oven to 392°F (200°C). Cover the bread tins with their lids, and bake for 10 to 12 minutes, until they turn golden brown. Once they're out of the oven, brush them with melted butter and toss them in saffron sugar for that perfect snowy coating.

These heavenly brioche cubes are calling your name; eat them warm out of the oven if possible. You can store them wrapped at room temperature for up to a day.

6AM STICKY BUNS

Yield: 1 large bun (serves 6 to 7)
Mold: 6-inch (15¼-cm) ring

Vinesh's first trip to the United States was in 2016. He flew into Boston, checked into his hotel and noticed right across the street was a practically never-ending line of eager faces waiting to enter this small bakery. And this was at 6 in the morning! So he did the only sensible thing: stood in line. And as soon as he got in he was confronted with rack upon rack of delicious baked goods! The pecan sticky bun left such an impression that not only did he eat it every single morning for the entire trip, but also he came back and insisted we make our own version of this nutty, caramel-covered beauty.

Starter

½ cup (60 g) bread flour

3 tbsp + 1 tsp (50 g) milk, warmed

2½ tsp (7 g) fresh yeast

Caramel Sauce

3 tbsp + ½ tsp (45 g) butter, plus more for greasing ring

1¾ cups (200 g) pecans, whole

⅓ cup + 2 tsp (75 g) granulated sugar

2 tbsp + 1 tsp (45 g) heavy cream

Cinnamon Sugar

½ cup (100 g) brown sugar

2 tsp (5 g) ground cinnamon

Dough

1 cup (175 g) starter

¾ cup (90 g) bread flour, plus more for dusting

1 tbsp + 2 tsp (25 g) heavy cream

3 tbsp + 2 tsp (45 g) granulated sugar

½ tsp (3 g) sea salt

2 tbsp + 2 tsp (40 g) butter

For the Starter. In a large bowl, mix the bread flour, milk and yeast. Knead it until it forms a nice, smooth dough. Cover it with cling film, and leave it to ferment at room temperature for 2 hours.

For the Caramel Sauce. First, grease the ring mold generously with extra butter, then line the bottom of the mold with a good amount of whole pecans. In a saucepan, heat the granulated sugar, stirring continuously until it caramelizes and takes on a deep amber color, then turn off the heat. In another saucepan, warm the cream before pouring it over the caramel to help deglaze the pan. Allow the cream-caramel mixture to cool for a couple of minutes before adding the butter in parts and mixing well to form a rich caramel sauce. Pour this into the mold, coating the pecans with this heavenly glaze, and leave it aside to set.

For the Cinnamon Sugar. In a bowl, combine the brown sugar and cinnamon. Set this aside for later.

For the Dough. In a stand mixer with a hook attachment, add the measured starter, bread flour, cream, granulated sugar and salt, and mix at a low speed for a few minutes to form a rough dough. Increase the speed to medium high, and knead for about 8 minutes, until a smooth dough comes together and no longer sticks to the sides of the bowl. That's when we can add in the butter a little at a time until fully incorporated.

Perform a window-pane test on the dough by taking a small, flattened piece and gently spreading it apart with your fingers: if the dough forms a thin, even, translucent membrane without tearing, then the gluten is perfectly developed. If a clear "window" isn't forming yet, keep kneading and checking until the dough is ready. We also want to make sure that the dough temperature always stays between 68 and 75°F (20 and 24°C) so our bread has the best flavor and an even rise.

(continued)

6AM STICKY BUNS *(continued)*

Dust a bowl with flour. Now take the dough out of the mixer and shape it into a nice smooth mound. Place it in the bowl, cover with cling film, and leave it at room temperature to rest for 1 hour. Once the dough has risen, you'll need to knock it back. Do this by firmly pressing or punching down the dough to properly distribute the air bubbles. Let's now roll this out into an 8 x 8–inch (20⅓ x 20⅓–cm) square, and sprinkle the cinnamon sugar over the entire surface. Roll it up from one of the edges to form a log, and place it in the freezer for about 15 minutes to get a little firmer.

Time for assembly. Once it's back out of the freezer, cut the log into six equal parts, and place them into the mold lined with those caramel-coated pecans. Start with one piece in the middle, with the layers facing upward, and then place the rest around that, making sure to leave ample space between them. Leave it to proof in a bread fermentation box at 86°F (30°C) and 60 percent humidity, or place it in a switched-off oven with a bowl of hot water. Proofing usually takes about 2 hours; you'll know it's ready to bake when the dough has expanded into the spaces we had left, and each of the pieces are now gently pressing against each other. After proofing, remove the dough and preheat the oven to 392°F (200°C). Bake for 25 minutes, until it turns golden brown. Once it's out of the oven, carefully demold that incredible bun onto a wire rack, and allow it to cool.

As soon as you're ready to eat, pull these sticky buns apart and feast on their nutty, fluffy goodness. You can store them wrapped at room temperature for up to a day.

STOLLEN MY HEART

Yield: 1 pastry

If you run a pastry or cake shop, December is undoubtedly the busiest time of year. Christmas seems to sharpen up everyone's sweet tooth, and for good reason. The season is known to make people crave plum puddings, Yule logs, and if you're like us, a good old-fashioned Dresden stollen. This rich, German bread-cake is filled with wintery fruits and spices and coated with a layer of sugar, but what makes it most special is the hidden surprise inside—a sweet and addictive marzipan that's too perfect to resist.

Starter

3 tbsp (25 g) bread flour

3 tbsp + ½ tsp (25 g) all-purpose flour

¼ cup (60 g) milk

1 tbsp + ¾ tsp (10.5 g) fresh yeast

Fruit Mixture

¾ cup + 1½ tbsp (125 g) golden raisins

⅓ cup (50 g) almonds, toasted and chopped

1 tbsp (20 g) candied orange peel, chopped

2 tbsp + ½ tsp (30 g) dark rum

Marzipan

⅓ cup + 1½ tbsp (60 g) raw almonds

2½ tbsp (20 g) icing sugar

2½ tsp (10 g) granulated sugar

1 tsp invert sugar

¾ tsp corn syrup

2 tsp (10 g) water

Spice Mix

⅓ tsp ground nutmeg

⅓ tsp ground cardamom

½ vanilla bean pod (see Quick Reference Notes, page 219)

Zest of 1 lemon

Stollen Dough

Starter mixture

⅓ cup + 1½ tsp (50 g) bread flour

⅜ cup + 1 tsp (50 g) all-purpose flour

1 tbsp + 2 tsp (20 g) granulated sugar

¼ tsp sea salt

Prepared spice mix

1 tsp Amaretto liqueur

⅓ cup + 1 tbsp (55 g) dark chocolate, cut into chunks

¼ cup + 1 tbsp + ¾ tsp (75 g) butter, cold and cubed

Fruit mixture

Clarified butter, melted, for dipping

Caster sugar, for garnish

Icing sugar, for garnish

For the Starter. In a large bowl, mix the flours, milk and yeast. Knead until it forms a nice smooth dough. Cover it with cling film and leave it to ferment at room temperature overnight.

For the Fruit Mixture. In a bowl, mix the raisins, almonds, candied orange peel and rum. Cover tightly with cling film and keep it in the refrigerator for 24 hours to give the fruits and nuts enough time to soak up some of that rum.

For the Marzipan. In a food processor, grind the almonds and icing sugar to a fine powder. Then in a saucepan, heat the granulated sugar, invert sugar and corn syrup along with the water and bring them to a boil. Add this heated syrup into the food processor and mix for it to all come together, forming a lovely marzipan dough.

> **Note from the Chefs:**
> Tonka beans are a rare but beautiful ingredient that release a spicy, fruity aroma when grated. If you manage to get your hands on some, then replace the Amaretto liqueur in this recipe with ⅛ tsp of grated tonka bean for a unique and flavorful twist.

(continued)

For the Spice Mix. In a bowl, mix together the nutmeg, cardamom, vanilla and lemon zest. Keep this mix close by for us to use while making the dough.

For the Stollen Dough. In a stand mixer with a hook attachment, add the starter, along with the bread flour, all-purpose flour, granulated sugar, salt, spice mix, Amaretto liqueur and dark chocolate. Mix it for about 5 minutes at low speed for a dough to form, then turn it up to high speed for another 5 minutes, until it all comes together and no longer sticks to the sides of the bowl. Add in the butter a little at a time until it's fully incorporated. We also want to make sure that the dough temperature always stays between 68 and 75°F (20 and 24°C) so that our bread has the best flavor and gets an even rise.

Once the dough feels nice and elastic, add in the fruit mixture and run it in the mixer for another 2 minutes so the fruit is evenly distributed. Remove the dough from the mixer and make a smooth mound, covering it with cling film and allowing it to rest at room temperature for 20 minutes. To shape the stollen, flatten the dough into a square, then roll the marzipan into a log shape and place it in the middle of the flattened dough. Fold the dough over the marzipan log and roll into place to get that classic stollen shape. Leave it to proof in a bread fermentation box at 79°F (26°C) and 60 percent humidity, or place it in a switched-off oven with a bowl of hot water. Proofing usually takes about 45 minutes; you'll know it's just right when the dough has doubled in size.

Time for baking. Preheat the oven to 356°F (180°C). Bake for 25 minutes, until golden brown. Once it's out of the oven, dip the stollen in the clarified butter and coat with sugar. As tempting as it is to eat right away, stollen needs to rest for at least 24 hours to let the flavors develop. When it's time, dust the entire surface with icing sugar to finish the look.

Slice this up and serve it slightly warmed, and we promise it'll be over before you know it. You can store this wrapped at room temperature for up to 7 days.

LAMINATED CROISSANT DOUGH

Yield: 2 lbs (1 kg)

The ultimate French classic, and contender for the food item that people mispronounce the most, the croissant is now made and beloved all across the world. What separates it from normal breads is a process called lamination, where the dough is folded into many thin layers, often in the hundreds, each separated by . . . you guessed it, butter. That's what makes it so deliciously comforting. A great croissant dough takes some time and love to make but once you've got that down, it opens up a world of new possibilities. In the following pages we'll make a range of incredible croissants and danishes using this dough, and you'll find even more ways to use it in unique variants of your own.

Dough

3⅔ cups (500 g) bread flour, plus more for dusting

1 tbsp + 2¼ tsp (25 g) butter

2 tbsp + ½ tsp (18 g) fresh yeast

¼ cup + 1 tsp (55 g) granulated sugar

1 egg

⅞ cup (210 g) water

1 tbsp (12 g) sea salt

Lamination

1 cup + 4 tsp (250 g) dry butter slab

For the Dough. In a stand mixer with a hook attachment, add the bread flour, butter, yeast, granulated sugar, egg, water and salt, and knead the mix at a slow speed for 10 minutes for the dough to begin forming. Then turn it up to a fast speed until it all comes together and no longer sticks to the sides of the bowl. We want to make sure that the dough temperature always stays between 68 and 75°F (20 and 24°C) so our bread has the best flavor and an even rise.

Dust a bowl with flour. Now take the dough out of the mixer and shape it into a nice smooth mound. Place it in the bowl, cover it with cling film, and leave it at room temperature to rest for 1 hour. Once the dough has risen, you'll need to knock it back. Do this by firmly pressing or punching down the dough to properly distribute the air bubbles. Roll the dough into a 19 x 9½–inch (48 x 24–cm) rectangle, and leave it on a tray wrapped with cling film in the refrigerator for 1 hour.

> ### Note from the Chefs:
> Dry butter has a higher amount of fat and a lower amount of moisture than regular butter, which makes it especially suitable for layering into doughs. In case you can't find it, replace it with 84 percent European-style cultured butter.

For the Lamination. Prepare a dry butter slab by rolling it into a 9 x 9–inch (23 x 23–cm) square and store in the refrigerator until you're ready to laminate the dough. Now take out the chilled dough and place the butter slab exactly in the center. There should be equal amounts of dough showing on both sides. Fold those extra wings of dough over the butter slab from the left and right sides to meet exactly in the middle, without any overlap. Seal the seam gently with your fingers, and press down in different areas of the dough using the bottom of your palm to help the layers fuse together. The butter should now be perfectly encased in dough.

With the center seam vertical in front of you, start rolling the dough lengthwise along the seam to create a long rectangular sheet about 5⁄16 inch (8 mm) thick. When folding we want to visually divide the length of the dough into three equal parts: first fold the top section perfectly over the middle, and then bring the bottom section over to cover them both—similar to folding a letter. Wrap this in a tray, and refrigerate for an hour. That counts as one single-fold, and gives us nine layers of alternating dough and butter, but for a really amazing croissant we'll need to multiply those layers.

Repeat that exact same process two more times: roll the dough into a tall, 5⁄16-inch (8-mm) thick rectangle, fold the upper third down, fold the lower third up, then wrap and refrigerate for an hour. By the end, you should have successfully done the single-fold cycle a total of three times, and created dozens of layers of buttery dough.

Leave the dough wrapped in the refrigerator while you decide which of these amazing croissant variations you're most tempted to create next!

*Used in photos on recipes between page 181–182.

CHOCOLATE RASPBERRY CROISSANT

Yield: 14 croissants

The classic croissant is perennial; by now everyone has tried it and everyone loves it. But as the years go by and these products that started in one country have become more and more common across the world, customers at our shops are eager to have new experiences with their food. This chocolate-raspberry croissant takes on a contemporary look and sparks some exciting flavors in your mouth, while still retaining the comforting familiarity of that flaky, buttery croissant you know and love.

Dough

1 recipe (1 kg) Laminated Croissant Dough, page 178

Raspberry Gellan

⅔ cup (150 g) raspberry purée

3 tbsp + 1 tsp (40 g) granulated sugar

2 tbsp (30 g) water

⅔ tsp gellan

Additions

Croissant chocolate sticks

Egg Wash

3 egg yolks

1 tbsp (15 g) heavy cream

1 tbsp (15 g) milk

Pinch of salt

Tempered dark chocolate, for garnish (see Quick Reference Notes, page 219)

Freeze-dried raspberries, for garnish

Icing sugar, for garnish

For the Raspberry Gellan. In a large bowl, add the raspberry purée, granulated sugar, water and gellan and mix well, making sure to get rid of any lumps. Transfer that over to a saucepan over medium heat, and let this mixture boil for about a minute so it thickens slightly. Pour the raspberry gellan into a 6 x 3-inch (15¼ x 7½-cm) frame and leave it to set at room temperature for an hour. Then cut thin ½-inch (1.3-cm)-thick strips of gellan that we can fold into the croissant.

Time for assembly. Line a tray with baking paper. Bring out the laminated dough and roll it into a thin, even ⁵⁄₃₂-inch (4-mm) sheet. Cut out tall triangles that are 12 inches (30.5 cm) high and 3½ inches (9 cm) at the base. Place a chocolate stick as well as a strip of raspberry gellan together at the base. Fold the sides of the dough over the ends of the chocolate and raspberry strip, and start rolling the dough up along the triangle to form a perfect croissant shape. Now place these rolled croissants onto the prepared tray, making sure to leave space between them. Leave it to proof in a bread fermentation box at 79°F (26°C) and 60 percent humidity, or place it in a switched-off oven with a bowl of hot water. Proofing usually takes about 2 hours; you'll know it's just right when the dough has doubled in size.

For the Egg Wash. In a small bowl, mix the egg yolks, cream, milk and salt, and then strain the mixture. Use a brush to coat the surface of the dough with a thin layer of egg wash, to help bring out that beautiful brown color when baking.

Time for baking and finishing. Preheat the oven to 356°F (180°C). Let's bake the croissants for 12 to 14 minutes, until they are golden brown. Make chocolate shards by spreading tempered dark chocolate over an acetate sheet and leaving it to set. Then break it into shards that we can use as a garnish. You can dab a bit of melted chocolate on the croissant and then stick the shard on, forming an artistic decoration. At the very end, let's sprinkle freeze dried raspberries and dust a bit of icing sugar over the tops for a finished look.

As with most baked goods, these stunning raspberry croissants are best eaten straight out of the oven, so don't keep them waiting.

SOUTH INDIAN COCONUT CROISSANT

Yield: 14 croissants

A staple of South India, the ever-popular dil-kush is eaten by anyone and everyone that can get themselves to a local bakery. "Dil-kush" literally translates from Hindi to mean "happy heart," and once you taste it we're sure you'll agree how apt that name is. It's a street-style, rustic, flaky pastry filled with coconut pudding and candied fruit, except this time we've wrapped it all up in a crispy, buttery croissant. Come on, let's make your heart happy.

Dough

1 recipe (1 kg) Laminated Croissant Dough, page 178

Coconut Filling

1⅓ cups (125 g) unsweetened dry coconut

2 tbsp (15 g) dried apricot, chopped

2 tbsp (15 g) dried cranberries, chopped

1 tbsp + 2 tsp (15 g) raisins, chopped

2 tbsp (15 g) candied cherries

¼ tsp ground cardamom

¼ cup (75 g) condensed milk

1 tbsp + ¼ tsp (15 g) butter

1 tbsp (15 g) heavy cream

Egg Wash

3 egg yolks

1 tbsp (15 g) heavy cream

1 tbsp (15 g) milk

Pinch of salt

Glaze

½ cup (100 g) liquid glucose

2 tbsp + 2 tsp (40 g) water

Desiccated coconut, for garnish

For the Coconut Filling. First things first. In a bowl, add the coconut, apricot, cranberries, raisins, candied cherries and cardamom, and start tossing it to form a lovely spiced fruit mix. Add in the condensed milk, butter and cream, and mix until it all comes together as an evenly distributed mass. Portion out 1½-tablespoon (20-g) pieces, and roll them into log shapes that we can use in our croissants.

Time for assembly. Line a tray with baking paper. Bring out the laminated dough, and roll it into a thin, even ⁵⁄₃₂-inch (4-mm) sheet. Cut out tall triangles that are 12 inches (30½ cm) high and 3½ inches (9 cm) at the base. Also cut a 2-inch (5-cm) slit down from the tip of each triangle, and separate the two prongs. Place a log of coconut filling at the base, fold the left and right corners of the dough over the ends of the log, and start rolling the dough up along the triangle to form a perfect croissant shape. Now place these rolled croissants onto the prepared tray, making sure to leave space between them. Leave it to proof in a bread fermentation box at 79°F (26°C) and 60 percent humidity, or place it in a switched-off oven with a bowl of hot water. Proofing usually takes about 2 hours; you'll know it's just right when the dough has doubled in size.

For the Egg Wash. In a small bowl, mix the egg yolks, cream, milk and salt, then strain the mixture. Use a brush to coat the surface of the doughs with a thin layer of egg wash, to help bring out that beautiful brown color when baking.

For the Glaze. Make the glaze in a saucepan by mixing the liquid glucose and water and bringing the mixture to a boil. Turn off the heat and allow it to cool.

Time for baking. Preheat the oven to 356°F (180°C). Let's bake the croissants for 12 to 14 minutes, until they're golden brown. Wrap this recipe up by brushing the croissants with a thin layer of glaze for a sugary shine, and sprinkling desiccated coconut all over them as a rustic finish.

As with most baked goods, these incredible coconut croissants are best eaten fresh out of the oven, so don't keep them waiting.

CINNAMON ROLL CRÈME BRÛLÉE

Yield: 14 pastries
Mold: 3-inch (7½-cm) ring

If dessert didn't affect his waistline, this would be Vinesh's breakfast every single day. The last thing anyone would think of doing with a rich, beautiful cream is burning it, and yet somehow the French decided to do exactly that and created a dessert that's lasted through the ages as a perpetual favorite. We're glad they did, because now we get to use it as a component in this magnificent upgrade to the cinnamon roll. Our goal here is to create a splendid textural contrast between the delicately supple burnt cream and the crispy, flaky, spiced pastry.

Dough

1 recipe (1 kg) Laminated Croissant Dough, page 178

Almond Cream

¼ cup + 1 tbsp + ¾ tsp (75 g) butter

⅝ cup (75 g) icing sugar

1 egg

1 tsp vanilla extract

1¼ cups (75 g) almond flour

3 tbsp + ½ tsp (25 g) all-purpose flour

Cinnamon Sugar

½ cup (110 g) brown sugar

1¼ tbsp (10 g) ground cinnamon

Crème Brûlée

15 egg yolks

1¾ cups + 2 tbsp (450 g) heavy cream

½ vanilla bean pod (see Quick Reference Notes, page 219)

½ cup + 1 tbsp + 1 tsp (115 g) granulated sugar

½ cup + 1 tbsp + 2 tsp (150 g) milk

Egg Wash

3 egg yolks

1 tbsp (15 g) heavy cream

1 tbsp (15 g) milk

Pinch of salt

Butter, for greasing rings
Caster sugar, for garnish

For the Almond Cream. In a stand mixer with a paddle attachment, cream the butter together with the icing sugar. Gradually add in the egg a little at a time until it's fully incorporated, then add in the vanilla extract. Finish up by gently folding in the almond flour and all-purpose flour, mixing to get a smooth cream.

For the Cinnamon Sugar. In a bowl, combine the brown sugar and cinnamon, and set it aside for use at the very end.

For the Crème Brûlée. Preheat the oven to 320°F (160°C). Have a tray and hot water ready to make a water bath. In a large bowl, add the egg yolks. In a saucepan, heat the cream, vanilla, granulated sugar and milk in a saucepan, mixing until the sugar dissolves, then turn off the heat. Pour one-third of it into the bowl containing the yolks to help temper them, then strain the yolk mixture back into the saucepan containing the hot cream, and mix well. Let's now pour it into 14 (2½-inch [6-cm]) flat disc molds (if you don't have 14 molds, you can bake in batches), and bake with a water bath for 30 to 40 minutes. To make a water bath, place the mold in a tray filled with hot water and put the tray into the oven to bake. To check if it's done, give it a light shake, and just the center—about the size of a coin—should wobble. When they're finished, freeze them for about 2 hours so it's easier to remove the discs from the molds.

Time for assembly. Bring out the laminated dough and roll it into a ⅕-inch (5-mm)-thick sheet. Use a palette knife to spread a thin layer of almond cream on the entire surface, and sprinkle cinnamon sugar over it. Carefully roll the dough from either end so it meets in the middle.

For the Egg Wash. Cover a tray with cling film. In a small bowl, mix the egg yolks, cream, milk and salt, then strain it. Brush a little egg wash in the middle of the two rolled sides of dough to help them stick together. Keep the remaining egg wash to use right before baking. Place the dough on the prepared tray and freeze for 2 hours.

(continued)

Time for baking. Grease the rings with butter and place on a tray lined with baking paper. Once the dough is out of the freezer, brush a thin layer of egg wash over all the dough surfaces to help bring out that beautiful brown color when baking. Now roll this dough in caster sugar and start cutting out 1½-inch (3.8-cm) wide pieces from it. Place them each with the cut-side up into the prepared rings. Leave them to proof in a bread fermentation box at 79°F (26°C) and 60 percent humidity, or place them in a switched-off oven with a bowl of hot water. Proofing usually takes about 2 hours; you'll know it's just right when the dough has doubled in size. After proofing, remove the dough and preheat the oven to 392°F (200°C).

We'll want to bake these cinnamon rolls for 10 to 12 minutes, until they turn golden brown. Once they're out of the oven, remove them from the rings and allow them to cool. Use a small knife to trim the top of each cinnamon roll to make it flatter, and place the discs of crème brûlée on top. To wrap things up, sprinkle some caster sugar on top of the rolls and use a blowtorch to give the creme brûlée an incredible caramelized finish.

As with most baked goods, these loaded cinnamon rolls are best eaten fresh out of the oven, so don't keep them waiting.

OLIVE OIL DARK CHOCOLATE *TRESS*

Yield: 14 pastries
Mold: 3-inch (7½-cm) ring

It's often surprising when ingredients from the kitchens of culinary chefs find their way into a dessert. But dessert isn't just about sweetness; as pastry chefs we're always looking to balance out the sugary flavors with something fragrant or mature. Once you taste the mesmerizing combination of flavors in this olive oil dark chocolate danish, it'll open up a whole new world for you. And we'll finish it with a coating of cocoa nibs, which are a crushed and roasted form of cocoa beans that add a glorious, bittersweet texture to the bread.

Dough
1 recipe (1 kg) Laminated Croissant Dough, page 178

White Chocolate Caramel
⅓ cup + 1 tsp (60 g) white chocolate, chopped

1½ tsp (10 g) honey

⅓ cup + 1 tbsp + 1 tsp (100 g) heavy cream

¼ cup + 1 tsp (55 g) granulated sugar

2 tbsp (30 g) butter, at room temperature

½ tsp sea salt

Olive Oil Sea Salt Ganache
¾ cup (100 g) dark chocolate, chopped

⅓ cup (80 g) heavy cream

1 tsp invert sugar

2 tbsp + 1 tsp (30 g) olive oil

½ tsp sea salt

Cacao Nib Sugar
¼ cup (55 g) cacao nibs

¼ cup (55 g) brown sugar

Egg Wash
3 egg yolks

1 tbsp (15 g) heavy cream

1 tbsp (15 g) milk

Pinch of salt

Cacao nibs, for garnish

Toasted and chopped nuts, for garnish

Edible gold leaf, for garnish

For the White Chocolate Caramel. In a heatproof bowl add the white chocolate. In a saucepan, warm the honey and cream. In another saucepan, add the granulated sugar and heat, stirring continuously, until it caramelizes to a deep amber color. Add the butter into the caramel to help deglaze the pan. Add in the warmed honey-cream mixture, stirring until it all comes together. Pour the mixture into the bowl containing the white chocolate, allowing it to melt. Toss in the salt, and use a hand blender to bring it to a smooth emulsion, then refrigerate for 2 hours to get it to the right consistency.

For the Olive Oil Sea Salt Ganache. In a heatproof bowl, add the dark chocolate. In a saucepan, first warm the cream and invert sugar to a simmer, and pour it into the bowl containing the dark chocolate, allowing it to melt. Mix and let it cool a bit. Then add in the olive oil and salt and use a hand blender to emulsify into a beautiful creamy consistency. Pop this in the refrigerator for 2 hours to get a perfect chocolate ganache.

For the Cacao Nib Sugar. In a food processor, let's make a quick and tasty cacao-sugar by grinding together the cacao nibs and brown sugar to get a rough powder.

Time for assembly. Bring out the laminated dough and roll it down into a thin, even 5⁄32-inch (4-mm) sheet. Sprinkle the cacao nib sugar evenly across the top surface, then fold the dough in half so the sugar is in the middle, and cut out 1-inch (2.5-cm)-wide strips. To create the shape of this danish, twist a strip of dough and coil it around to resemble a rose. Leave the shaped doughs to proof in a bread fermentation box at 79°F (26°C) and 60 percent humidity, or place in a switched-off oven with a bowl of hot water. Proofing usually takes about 2 hours; you'll know it's just right when the dough has doubled in size.

(continued)

OLIVE OIL DARK CHOCOLATE TRESS *(continued)*

For the Egg Wash. In a small bowl, mix the egg yolks, cream, milk and salt, then strain the mixture. Use a brush to coat the surface of the doughs with a thin layer of egg wash, to help bring out that beautiful brown color when baking.

Time for baking. Preheat the oven to 356°F (180°C). Let's sprinkle some cocoa nibs over the tops to give them some crunch, then bake these for 12 minutes, until golden brown. Once they're out of the oven, push the nozzle of a piping bag into the back of each danish, and fill them with a good amount of white chocolate caramel. Finish off by piping a neat dollop of olive oil sea salt ganache in the center, followed by a sprinkling of toasted chopped nuts for texture and a touch of gold leaf.

As with most baked goods, these dark chocolate treats are best eaten fresh out of the oven, so don't keep them waiting.

PEAR-FECT WALNUT DANISH

Yield: 12 danish

Danishes are truly an artistic dream. Bakers have found every possible way to fold them and cut them and twist them and pinch them into astounding pieces of edible art. Not to mention the toppings: all forms of fruit and jam and cream have been historically layered atop these crunchy tasty breads. We're going to take up that responsibility today and create a folded Danish, filled with walnut cream, with a semi-circle extension to hold adorable little discs of apple-pear confit.

Dough

1 recipe (1 kg) Laminated Croissant Dough, page 178

Walnut Cream

¼ cup + 1 tbsp + ¾ tsp (75 g) butter

⅝ cup (75 g) icing sugar

1 egg

1 tsp vanilla extract

¾ cup + 1½ tsp (75 g) walnut powder

3 tbsp + ½ tsp (25 g) all-purpose flour

¼ tsp salt

Apple-pear Confit

1 tsp gelatin

2 tbsp + 1 tsp (36 g) cold water

⅔ cup (100 g) apples

½ cup (80 g) pears

¼ cup + ¾ tsp (60 g) butter

¼ cup + 1 tsp (60 g) brown sugar

¼ tsp ground cinnamon

¾ cup + 2 tbsp + 1 tsp (180 g) granulated sugar

⅓ cup + 1 tsp (85 g) heavy cream

Egg Wash

3 egg yolks

1 tbsp (15 g) heavy cream

1 tbsp (15 g) milk

Pinch of salt

For the Walnut Cream. In a stand mixer with a paddle attachment, cream the butter together with the icing sugar. Gradually add in the egg a little at a time until it's fully incorporated, then add in the vanilla extract. Finish up by gently folding in the walnut powder, all-purpose flour and salt, mixing to get a nice, smooth cream.

For the Apple-pear Confit. Place a 9 x 9–inch (23 x 23–cm) frame on a tray lined with baking paper. In a small bowl, add the gelatin and water, and let the gelatin bloom for 5 minutes, until it absorbs the water and swells. Dice up the apples and pears into small, $\frac{3}{16}$-inch (5-mm) cubes, and toss them into a saucepan over medium heat along with the butter, brown sugar and cinnamon. Cook until the fruits turn tender and are evenly coated with a thin caramel layer, then leave the mixture aside to cool.

In a saucepan over medium heat, add the granulated sugar. Heat until it caramelizes to a deep amber, then add in the cream to help deglaze the pan. Notice how the fruit mixture we just made has collected some excess liquid at the bottom—we'll need to pour that excess liquid into the caramel-cream, and continue to cook for a minute. Once it's reached a nice consistency, turn off the heat and add in the fruit mixture and bloomed gelatin, stirring well to make sure it's fully dissolved. Pour this into the prepared frame. There should be a ½-inch (1.3-cm) layer of confit. Allow it to set in the freezer for 2 hours. When it comes back out it should feel like a nice firm gel. Use a 1½-inch (3.8-cm) cookie cutter to get little discs of fruit confit to use during assembly.

Time for assembly. Bring out the laminated dough and roll it into an even $\frac{5}{32}$-inch (4-mm) sheet. Use a palette knife to spread a layer of walnut cream over the entire surface, then wrap this with cling film on a tray and put it in the freezer for 1 hour to set. Once it's back out, cut the sheeted dough up into 12 (5-inch [13-cm]) squares that we can turn into individual Danishes.

(continued)

Line a tray with baking paper before creating the Danishes. To create the unique shape of this Danish, rotate one of the dough squares so it looks like a diamond on the countertop in front of you. Position the diamond such that the bottom half of the shape is hanging off the edge of the counter. Press a 2-inch (5-cm) cookie cutter into the center of the dough that's still on the counter, making a semicircular slit. Now shift the dough back up onto the counter and fold the top corner downward to meet the opposite corner at the bottom. When done right, this should leave a triangular shape facing you, and a cut-out semicircular shape facing away. Repeat this process for each Danish, placing them on the prepared tray as you finish. Leave them to proof in a bread fermentation box at 79°F (26°C) and 60 percent humidity, or place them in a switched-off oven with a bowl of hot water. Proofing usually takes about 2 hours; you'll know it's just right when the dough has doubled in size. After proofing, remove the dough and preheat the oven to 356°F (180°C).

For the Egg Wash. In a small bowl, mix the egg yolks, cream, milk and salt, then strain the mixture. Use a brush to coat all the surfaces with a thin layer of egg wash, and bake them for 12 minutes, until golden brown. Allow your baked Danishes to cool, and place a disc of apple-pear confit into each of those circular protrusions in the dough, then carefully add gold leaf in the center of the confit for an exquisite finish.

As with most baked goods, these fruity walnut Danishes are best eaten fresh out of the oven, so don't keep them waiting.

STRAWBERRY CHEESECAKE DANISH

Yield: 14 danish
Mold: 2½-inch (6-cm) flat disc mold

Cheesecake has been a go-to favorite for a long time. A really, really long time. It was fed to athletes in Ancient Greece almost three millennia ago! And yet, somehow even today it retains its place as one of the most soothing desserts you can eat. That signature soft creaminess is often paired with a topping of fresh fruit to great effect. And you already know how much we love Danishes. The idea here was to bring the worlds of cheesecakes and Danishes together to create a thoroughly stimulating highlight to your breakfast.

Dough

1 recipe (1 kg) Laminated Croissant Dough, page 178

Baked Cheesecake

1 vanilla bean pod (see Quick Reference Notes, page 219)

3 tbsp + ½ tsp (45 g) butter

3 tbsp + 2 tsp (45 g) granulated sugar

2 eggs

2 tbsp + 1 tsp (45 g) heavy cream

1 tbsp (8 g) cornstarch

1 ⅜ cups (330 g) cream cheese

Strawberry Gellan

⅔ cup (150 g) strawberry purée

3 tbsp + 1 tsp (40 g) granulated sugar

2 tbsp (30 g) water

⅔ tsp gellan

Egg Wash

3 egg yolks

1 tbsp (15 g) heavy cream

1 tbsp (15 g) milk

Pinch of salt

Strawberries, sliced, for garnish

Microgreens, for garnish

For the Baked Cheesecake. Preheat the oven to 320°F (160)°C. Have a tray and hot water ready for the water bath. In a food processor, add the vanilla, butter, granulated sugar, eggs, cream, cornstarch and cream cheese. Blend until a smooth cheesecake mix begins to form. Pour the mix into 2½-inch (6-cm) flat disc molds, and bake in a water bath for 35 to 40 minutes. To make a water bath, place the mold in a tray filled with hot water and put the tray into the oven to bake. You'll know it's done when the cheesecake looks set on the top, but still has a nice wobble to it.

For the Strawberry Gellan. In a large bowl, add the strawberry purée, granulated sugar, water and gellan. Mix them well, making sure to get rid of any lumps. Transfer that over to a saucepan over medium heat, and let this mixture boil for about a minute so it thickens slightly. Pour the strawberry gellan into 2½-inch (6-cm) flat disc molds, and leave these to set at room -temperature for an hour.

Time for assembly. Bring out the laminated dough, and roll it into a thin, even 5⁄32-inch (4-mm) sheet. Use a 3-inch (7.5-cm) cookie cutter to get little discs of dough to be the base of each of our Danishes. Then use a 2½-inch (6-cm) cookie cutter to cut halfway through each base, leaving a ring-like mark, and place the discs of strawberry gellan in the center within these marks. Leave them to proof in a bread fermentation box at 79°F (26°C) and 60 percent humidity, or place them in a switched-off oven with a bowl of hot water. Proofing usually takes about 2 hours; you'll know it's just right when the dough has expanded and risen all around the discs of gellan.

For the Egg Wash. In a small bowl, mix the egg yolks, cream, milk and salt, then strain the mixture. Use a brush to coat all the dough surfaces with a thin layer of egg wash.

Time for baking. Preheat the oven to 356°F (180°C). Bake these for 12 minutes, until they turn a delicious golden brown. Once they're back out, slot the cheesecake discs in the center of each Danish, right over the strawberry gellan. Finish up by garnishing the cheesecake with some fresh sliced strawberries and microgreens for a dash of color.

As with most baked goods, these grand Danishes are best eaten fresh out of the oven.

*See photo on page 159.

SHOP-STYLE
Desserts

Pastry shops are our happy place. We've been fascinated by them from way before taking this up professionally; there's just something so reassuring about a space that's entirely dedicated to making your face happy. But just as food and cuisine changes, even the establishments that create and serve them evolve with the times. It's still super charming to see a family-run bakery with all these rustic products that are no doubt delicious in every way, but as you travel around you start finding these sleek and minimalist shops with counters full of strikingly artistic products.

We always try to imagine what the ideal pastry shop would be like. What fascinating creations would line the counters of a shop that effectively harmonized the past and future of dessert? This chapter is our answer to that question. We're going to go with an assortment of wild creations like the Cranberry Matcha Cakelet (page 215) or Beach-Side Pavlova (page 204), while still recognizing our pastry heritage with the likes of the wonderful Bertica's Strawberry Flan (page 203) and the arresting Red Velvet Profiterole (page 209). They're portioned perfectly for dining in and they're easy to pack and take away, so when a customer finally gets to eat them, they still look and taste as perfect as ever. Needless to say, even if you aren't running a business, these recipes work their magic around the kitchen table at home just as well.

BLACKBERRY TARRAGON SLICE

Yield: 12 slices
Mold: 6-inch (15¼-cm) cake ring

You don't need a fancy recipe book to know that chocolate is one of the most widely used flavors in the world of pastry. But what you may not know is how flexible it is, how it can be elevated with any number of fruits and herbs and spices, each giving it a completely new personality. This cake features a beautifully indulgent chocolate cremeux infused with the distinctive bittersweet aromas of tarragon—you gotta try it to believe it.

Chocolate Sablé

¼ cup + ¾ tsp (60 g) butter

¼ cup (30 g) icing sugar

⅓ tsp sea salt

1 tbsp (15 g) milk

¾ cup + 2½ tsp (100 g) all-purpose flour

¼ cup (15 g) almond flour

1 tbsp + 2½ tsp (10 g) cocoa powder

Chocolate Sponge

2½ tbsp (35 g) clarified butter, plus more for greasing rings

⅜ cup + 1 tsp (50 g) all-purpose flour

¼ cup (15 g) almond flour

2½ tbsp (15 g) cocoa powder

½ tsp baking soda

¼ tsp salt

2 tbsp + 1 tsp (30 g) granulated sugar

2½ tbsp (35 g) brown sugar

1 egg

2½ tbsp (35 g) mascarpone

1 tbsp (15 g) hazelnut praline paste

2 tbsp (30 g) hot espresso

Chocolate Tarragon Cremeux

½ tsp gelatin

1 tsp cold water

1½ cups + 3 tbsp + 1 tsp (225 g) dark chocolate, chopped

½ cup + 1 tbsp + 2 tsp (150 g) milk

½ cup + 2 tbsp (150 g) heavy cream

1 tsp fresh tarragon

3 egg yolks

1 tbsp + 1 tsp (15 g) granulated sugar

¼ tsp sea salt

Blackberries, for garnish

For the Chocolate Sablé. In a stand mixer with a paddle attachment, cream the butter, icing sugar and salt. Gradually add in the milk and mix until it's fully incorporated. Use a spatula to gently fold in the all-purpose flour, almond flour and cocoa powder to form a nice, even dough. Then place the dough between two sheets of baking paper and flatten into a ⅛-inch (3-mm)-thick sheet.

Now let's use a cookie cutter to cut out two 6-inch (15¼-cm) discs of dough, and divide them into six equal triangular slices. Rest these in the freezer for 1 hour. While they're resting, preheat the oven to 320°F (160°C) and line a tray with baking paper. After an hour, carefully transfer each slice onto the prepared tray and bake for 20 to 25 minutes, or until they're firm to the touch, to get our perfect sablé bases.

For the Chocolate Sponge. Preheat the oven to 320°F (160°C). Grease two cake rings with extra butter and line the base with foil. In a large bowl, sift together the all-purpose flour, almond flour, cocoa powder, baking soda and salt. In a large bowl, whisk together the granulated sugar, brown sugar, clarified butter and egg, until the sugar is fully dissolved. Now in a separate bowl, mix together the mascarpone and hazelnut praline paste, then start to add in the egg mixture a little at a time, mixing until it's fully incorporated. Fold the sifted ingredients into the batter, making sure there are no lumps. Now mix in the hot espresso.

(continued)

Divide the batter between the prepared cake rings, forming a ½-inch (1.3-cm)-thick layer in each. Bake for 25 to 30 minutes. Use a cake tester to check if the baking is done, or use a probe thermometer to know when the cakes reach 203°F (95°C). Allow them to cool, then use a knife to trim the top layer of the sponge. Line the inside of the cake ring with a 4-inch (10-cm) tall strip of acetate, then place the sponge back inside it to serve as the base during assembly.

For the Chocolate Tarragon Cremeux. In a small bowl, add the gelatin and water, allowing the gelatin to bloom for 5 minutes, until it swells. Add the dark chocolate to a bowl and set it aside. In a saucepan, warm the milk and cream together, and mix in the tarragon. Let it infuse for 2 hours, then strain, and start heating it again. In a heatproof bowl, add the egg yolks and granulated sugar. Add one-third of the milk mixture into the bowl containing the egg yolks, stirring continuously to help temper the eggs. Then pour that back into the saucepan containing the milk mixture and continue to cook it to 180°F (82°C). That's when we need to stir in the bloomed gelatin, making sure it's completely dissolved. Pour this into the bowl containing the dark chocolate, allowing it to melt, then add the salt and use a hand blender to emulsify to a smooth consistency.

Time for assembly. Pour the cremeux over the chocolate sponge to form a ½-inch (1.3-cm) layer, and allow it to set in the freezer for 2 hours until it's starting to turn firm. Then take it back out and cut it into six equal triangular slices, exactly like we did with the sablé. To finish up, place each of these cakes onto a sablé base, and cover the tops with sliced, fresh blackberries.

This fresh, indulgent dessert can now be served up as convenient little slices. You can store it in the refrigerator for up to 2 days.

PB PASSION FRUIT CREAMPUFF

Yield: 20 pastries

We love choux; it's the perfect vessel to hold a variety of delicate creams and fillings. But let's get away from the fancy French words for a minute and just call it a creampuff. This puff puts one of our favorite buddy-combos of peanut butter and banana into a thin, crumbly crust, but what really packs that extra punch is the passion fruit cream, adding a subtle acidity and sharpness to this creamy, sinful dessert.

Peanut Butter Cream

1 tsp gelatin

2½ tsp (12 g) cold water

¼ cup + 2 tsp (50 g) caramelized white chocolate, chopped (see Quick Reference Notes, page 218)

1 cup + 2 tbsp (250 g) heavy cream

2 tbsp + 2 tsp (45 g) peanut butter

Zest of ½ lemon

Craquelin

2 tbsp + 1 tsp (35 g) butter, cold

¼ cup + 1 tbsp (40 g) all-purpose flour

3 tbsp (40 g) brown sugar

Choux Paste

½ cup + 1 tbsp + 1 tsp (140 g) water

3 tbsp (45 g) milk

¼ tsp sea salt

1 tsp granulated sugar

¼ cup + 1 tbsp + ¾ tsp (75 g) butter

⅞ cup (110 g) all-purpose flour, sifted

3 eggs

Passion Fruit Cream

2 egg yolks

¼ cup + 1 tsp (55 g) granulated sugar

1½ tbsp (12 g) cornstarch

½ cup + 1 tsp (125 g) passion fruit purée

3 tbsp (45 g) milk

¼ cup + 2¾ tsp (70 g) butter

¾ cup + 1 tbsp + 1 tsp (200 g) heavy cream, lightly whipped

Caramelized Bananas

1 cup (150 g) bananas, chopped

1 tbsp + 1 tsp (20 g) butter

1½ tbsp (20 g) brown sugar

4 tsp (20 g) rum

Peanut Praline Paste

¾ cup + 1 tbsp (120 g) peanuts

¼ cup + 2 tbsp + 1 tsp (80 g) granulated sugar

Praline Chocolate Glaze

2 tbsp + 1 tsp (20 g) dark chocolate, melted

1½ tbsp (15 g) milk chocolate, melted

1 tbsp (15 g) cocoa butter, melted

½ cup (125 g) peanut praline paste

Peanuts, toasted and chopped, for garnish

Icing sugar, for garnish

For the Peanut Butter Cream. In a small bowl, add the gelatin and water, letting the gelatin bloom for 5 minutes, until it absorbs the water and swells. In a heatproof bowl, place the white chocolate. In a saucepan, heat the cream to a simmer, then add in the bloomed gelatin and stir until it's well dissolved. Pour this into the bowl containing the white chocolate, allowing it to melt, and use a hand blender to bring it to a smooth consistency. Toss in the peanut butter and lemon zest, and continue to blend. Keep this in the refrigerator overnight so the fats can properly crystallize.

For the Craquelin. In a mixing bowl, paddle together the butter, all-purpose flour and brown sugar to get a dough. Place that between two sheets of baking paper, and roll it out to a super-thin ½₂-inch (1-mm) sheet, then freeze for 2 hours. Cut out 20 (2½-inch [6-cm]) discs, a little larger than the choux we're planning, so they will fit over nicely.

> **Note from the Chefs:**
> Craquelin is that crunchy topping you often see on the top of a choux pastry; it's amazing how adding such a simple layer can bring out all those heavenly textures and flavors after baking.

(continued)

PB PASSION FRUIT CREAMPUFF *(continued)*

For the Choux Paste. Preheat the oven to 356°F (180°C). Line a tray with baking paper. In a saucepan, boil the water, milk, salt, granulated sugar and butter. Bring the pan off the heat just to add in the flour and mix, making sure there are no lumps. Then, resume cooking the mix until you get a thick dough that pulls easily away from the sides of the pan, leaving a thin skin at the bottom. Transfer this over to a stand mixer with a paddle attachment and start to slowly incorporate the eggs, a little at a time. Now, on the prepared tray, it's time to start piping mounds of choux, each about 1½-inch (3.8-cm) in diameter, and covering the tops with discs of craquelin. Pop the tray into the oven, leaving it to bake for 30 to 40 minutes, until the choux rises and the craquelin forms a lovely crust on top.

For the Passion Fruit Cream. In a heatproof bowl, add the egg yolks, granulated sugar and cornstarch. In a saucepan, boil the passion fruit purée for a minute. In another saucepan, start heating the milk until it's nice and warm. Add one-third of the hot milk into the bowl containing the egg yolk mixture while stirring continuously to help temper the eggs. Then pour the egg yolk mixture back into the dish containing the milk, and add in the heated passion fruit purée as well, so we have everything coming together. Continue to cook until it starts to thicken, then turn off the heat and allow it to cool. Add in the butter and use a hand blender to get a smooth, creamy consistency. Finally, add the lightly whipped cream and fold it into the mix to give it a rich, light texture.

For the Caramelized Bananas. Dice the bananas up into small ½-inch (1.3-cm) cubes, and add them to a saucepan over low heat. Add in the butter and brown sugar. Now add the rum and cook for 2 minutes, coating the bananas in a lovely caramel, then set it aside to use as filling.

For the Peanut Praline Paste. Preheat the oven to 320°F (160°C). Line a tray with baking paper. Toast the peanuts for 10 minutes, and spread them out on the prepared tray. In a saucepan, heat the granulated sugar and stir continuously until it caramelizes to a light golden brown, then pour it over the toasted peanuts. Allow this to cool and harden, then break it into pieces and toss those in the food processor to make a nutty, praline paste.

For the Praline Chocolate Glaze. In a bowl, add the dark chocolate, milk chocolate and cocoa butter, then mix in the measured peanut praline paste and allow it to cool to room temperature before using.

Time for assembly. Before using the peanut butter cream, we'll need to put it in a bowl and paddle it until it turns nice and light, about 3 minutes. Bring out a piping bag, and fill one side of the bag with the peanut butter cream and the other side with the passion fruit cream so we can pipe them both simultaneously. Now from the back of each choux, pipe them full of that delicious combination of creams.

It's time for coating! Line a tray with baking paper. Dip these choux buns almost halfway into the praline chocolate glaze, removing any dripping excess before placing them on the prepared tray. Sprinkle some toasted and chopped peanuts over the glaze before it sets, to add some crunch. Finally, using a sheet of paper as a stencil, dust icing sugar over the other side of the choux to get that incredible striped look.

These perfect puffs are decadent enough to satisfy you, but light enough to have you reaching for another. Once the choux are assembled, make sure to finish them off within a day while they're at their tastiest.

BERTICA'S STRAWBERRY FLAN

Yield: 1 flan
Mold: 6-inch (15¼-cm) ring

What's your earliest memory of strawberries? If you lived near a hilly farm, you could have picked them straight off the bush. If you were in Japan you might have eaten them with condensed milk. Or dipped them in chocolate. Like a lot of kids in South America, Andrés grew up making flan with his Grandma Bertica. We tried to keep this recipe as old-school as possible—flan encased in a butter pie shell and topped with berries and condensed milk—so no matter where you're from you can feel nostalgia in every bite.

Flan Mix

¼ cup (30 g) cornstarch

2 tsp (5 g) all-purpose flour

1 cup + 3½ tbsp (300 g) milk

1¼ cups (300 g) heavy cream

2 vanilla bean pods (see Quick Reference Notes, page 219)

½ cup + 2½ tsp (110 g) granulated sugar

Pie Dough

½ cup (120 g) butter, plus more for greasing, at room temperature

¼ tsp sea salt

¾ cup (90 g) icing sugar

½ cup (30 g) almond flour

1 egg

1⅞ cups (235 g) all-purpose flour

Condensed Milk Gel

½ cup + 2 tbsp + 1 tsp (125 g) milk

⅓ cup + 1⅓ tbsp (125 g) condensed milk

1 tsp agar

Strawberries, for garnish

Fennel seeds, toasted, for garnish

Microgreens, for garnish

For the Flan Mix. In a heatproof bowl, mix the cornstarch and all-purpose flour. In a saucepan, heat the milk, cream and vanilla to a boil. Begin pouring the heated cream into the flour mixture a little at a time, mixing well to avoid lumps. Strain this mixture into a saucepan, and continue to cook over medium heat until it turns thick enough to coat a spoon. That's when we add in the granulated sugar and stir until it's fully dissolved. Turn off the heat and allow the mixture to cool before resting it in the refrigerator overnight.

For the Pie Dough. In a stand mixer with a paddle attachment, mix the butter with the salt, icing sugar and almond flour. Gradually add in the egg and mix until the ingredients feel well combined. Proceed to fold in the all-purpose flour to form a nice, even dough. Place this between two sheets of baking paper and flatten it a little before resting it in the refrigerator for 2 hours. Grease the ring with extra butter and place it on a tray lined with baking paper. Roll the dough out into a sheet ⁵⁄₃₂-inch (4-mm) thick, and cut out a 9-inch (23-cm) disc of dough for the base. Place the disc inside the greased ring and press gently, starting from the bottom and working your way up the sides. If the edges are above the rim, carefully trim them with a small knife, then pop it in the refrigerator for at least 1 hour, or until you're ready to bake.

For the Condensed Milk Gel. Place the milk, condensed milk and agar in a saucepan over medium heat. Bring the mixture to a vigorous boil for about a minute, then turn off the heat and allow to cool before using a hand blender to whip it to a creamy consistency.

Time for assembly. Preheat the oven to 338°F (170°C). Pour the flan mix into the lined ring, filling the pie base almost to the top. Go ahead and bake the pie for 60 to 70 minutes. During the course of baking, the flan will rise and turn a dark brown, and then eventually it will collapse on itself—that's when you know it's done. After the flan is baked, you can either finish it up immediately if you're in a hurry, or allow it to cool and leave it in the refrigerator for 4 hours to set beautifully.

Bring out that perfectly baked flan pie, arrange some sliced strawberries across the top surface and drizzle condensed milk gel over it all. Garnish with a bit of toasted fennel and microgreens to make things extra special. We're sure Grandma approves of your fabulous flan. Slice and serve it chilled. You can store it in the refrigerator for up to 2 days.

BEACH-SIDE PAVLOVA

Yield: 10 pavlovas

Named after a Russian ballerina extraordinaire, pavlovas prove to be among the most elegant, light desserts in human history. They're traditionally presented with a dainty chantilly cream, but we wanted a pavlova that could be served at a beach-side pop-up . . . hence the coconut rum ganache and exotic fruit confit. You're going to have a great time making these, and everyone who tastes it will know why the pavlova is undoubtedly the queen of meringues.

Coconut Rum Whipped Ganache

⅔ cup + 2 tsp (120 g) white chocolate, chopped

6 tbsp (90 g) coconut cream

1½ tsp (10 g) corn syrup

1 tsp invert sugar

¾ cup + 1 tbsp + 1 tsp (200 g) heavy cream, cold

1 tbsp (15 g) white rum

French Meringue

2 egg whites

¼ cup + 2½ tsp (60 g) granulated sugar

½ cup (60 g) icing sugar, sifted

Exotic Fruit Confit

1½ tsp (3 g) gelatin

1 tbsp + ½ tsp (18 g) cold water

¼ cup (45 g) passion fruit purée

¼ tsp salt

1 tbsp (20 g) corn syrup

2½ tbsp (35 g) coconut purée

1 tsp pectin NH

2 tbsp + 1 tsp (30 g) granulated sugar

⅓ cup (50 g) pineapple, chopped

¼ cup (50 g) banana, chopped

¼ cup (50 g) mango, chopped

2 tsp (10 g) lime juice

Tempered white chocolate, for garnish (see Quick Reference Notes, page 219)

Edible flowers, for garnish

Fresh coconut, for garnish

For the Coconut Rum Whipped Ganache. In a heatproof bowl, add the white chocolate. In a saucepan, add the coconut cream, corn syrup and invert sugar, and heat them to a boil. Pour the hot mixture into the bowl containing the white chocolate, allowing it to melt. Use a hand blender to get a beautiful, smooth consistency. To finish off, gently fold in the heavy cream and white rum for a boozy touch. Let's keep this in the refrigerator overnight to form a perfect ganache.

For the French Meringue. Preheat the oven to 176°F (80°C). Line a tray with baking paper. In a stand mixer with a whisk attachment, start by whipping the egg whites on a low speed until they're white and foamy. Add in the granulated sugar gradually, one spoonful at a time to ensure that it dissolves properly. Continue whipping until it turns glossy and the meringue forms stiff peaks. Finish by gently folding in the icing sugar with a spatula. Use a piping bag with a round tip nozzle to pipe the meringues onto the prepared tray. Try and keep your hands steady above the surface and form nice, large 2½-inch (6-cm) kisses. Dip a small spoon in warm water and use it to carve out the tops of each meringue, forming small indents that can hold the confit. Proceed to dehydrate them by placing them in the oven for 3 hours until they're perfectly crisp.

For the Exotic Fruit Confit. In a small bowl, add the gelatin and water, letting the gelatin bloom for 5 minutes, until it absorbs the water and swells. In a saucepan over medium heat, mix the passion fruit purée, salt, corn syrup and coconut purée. When the mixture turns nice and warm, add in a combination of the pectin NH and granulated sugar and continue to stir until it reaches a boil. That's when we drop in the chopped fruits, and allow it to cook for another minute. Turn off the heat and add in the bloomed gelatin and lime juice, making sure they're well dissolved.

Time for assembly. Spoon a little exotic fruit confit into the indent on each meringue. Whip the ganache a little to get it light and airy, and use a star nozzle to pipe the ganache in a circular motion around and over the confit, forming a glorious peak. We've used white chocolate sticks as an elegant decoration. If you'd like to do the same, just spread tempered white chocolate on an acetate sheet, and allow it to cool. While the chocolate is still semi-set, use a knife and scale to cut it into nice thin sticks. Place these at angles on the ganache, and sprinkle some edible flowers and sliced fresh coconut to finish up. These light and regal desserts are best served immediately. You can store them in the refrigerator for up to 1 day.

PECAN GREEN APPLE CHOUQUETTE

Yield: 20 pastries

Recipes are a continuous evolution. There was a super-buttery chocolate pecan pie we used to make back in the day—one of those classic recipes reminiscent of American pie culture. But for this book we decided that the next evolution of that recipe was to have a bite-size version, and suddenly this choux was born. It's full of the flavors of autumn: stewed apples, pecan crunch, and a homemade praline that brings it all home!

Pecan Whipped Ganache

¼ cup + 2 tsp (50 g) white chocolate, chopped

1 tsp gelatin

2½ tsp (12 g) cold water

1 cup + 2 tsp (250 g) heavy cream

3 tbsp (45 g) pecan praline paste

Zest of 1 lemon

Choux Paste

½ cup + 1 tbsp + 1 tsp (140 g) water

3 tbsp (45 g) milk

¼ tsp sea salt

1 tsp granulated sugar

¼ cup + 1 tbsp + ¾ tsp (75 g) butter

⅞ cup (110 g) all-purpose flour, sifted

3 eggs

Caramelized Apples

2 Granny Smith apples

1 tbsp + ¼ tsp (15 g) butter

1 tbsp + 2 tsp (35 g) honey

Green Apple Gel

1½ tsp (3 g) gelatin

⅜ cup + 1 tsp (93 g) water, divided

⅔ cup (175 g) green apple purée

1½ tsp (4 g) pectin NH

1 tbsp + 2 tsp (20 g) granulated sugar

1¼ tsp (6 g) lemon juice

Caramelized apples

Pecan Crunch

⅞ cup + 1½ tsp (90 g) pecans

¼ cup + 1 tsp (45 g) milk chocolate, melted

1 tbsp + ¼ tsp (15 g) butter

1¼ cups (35 g) crispy rice cereal (We recommend Rice Krispies)

Pinch of sea salt

Pecan Praline Paste

1 cup + 3½ tbsp (120 g) pecans

¼ cup + 2 tbsp + 1 tsp (80 g) granulated sugar

Pecans, toasted and chopped, for garnish

For the Pecan Whipped Ganache. In a heatproof bowl, add the white chocolate. In a small bowl, add the gelatin and water, letting the gelatin bloom for 5 minutes, until it absorbs the water and swells. In a saucepan, heat the cream until it reaches a simmer, then stir in the bloomed gelatin to dissolve it completely. Pour this into the bowl containing the white chocolate, allowing it to melt, and use a hand blender to get a luscious, creamy consistency. Now add in the measured pecan praline paste and lemon zest, and continue to blend. Keep this in the refrigerator overnight so the fats have time to properly crystallize.

For the Choux Paste. Preheat the oven to 356°F (180°C). Line a tray with baking paper. In a saucepan, boil the water together with the milk, salt, granulated sugar and butter. Bring the pan off the heat just to add in the all-purpose flour, and mix, making sure there are no lumps. Then resume cooking until you get a thick dough that pulls easily away from the sides of the pan, leaving a thin skin at the bottom. Transfer this over to a stand mixer with a paddle attachment and start to slowly incorporate the eggs, a little at a time. Now, on the prepared tray, it's time to start piping mounds of choux, each about 1½ inches (3.8 cm) in diameter. Pop the tray into the oven, leaving it to bake for 30 to 40 minutes, until the choux rises and forms a lovely crispy top.

For the Caramelized Apples. Cut the apples down into small, ³⁄₁₆-inch (5-mm) cubes. In a saucepan over low heat, melt the butter, then toss in the apple cubes and honey. Cook until the apples turn perfectly tender and are well-coated with juices, then set it aside until assembly.

(continued)

For the Green Apple Gel. In a small bowl, add the gelatin and 1 tablespoon + 1 teaspoon (18 g) of cold water, letting the gelatin bloom for 5 minutes, until it absorbs the water and swells. In a saucepan, heat the green apple purée and ¼ cup + 1 tablespoon (75 g) of water to get it nice and warm. Add in a combination of the pectin and granulated sugar, and bring the mixture to a boil. Add the lemon juice and stir in the gelatin, making sure it's fully dissolved. Then turn off the heat and use a hand blender to bring it all together to a smooth emulsion. Finally, fold in the caramelized apples gently so they're evenly distributed. Spoon this into 2-ml demisphere molds, and freeze for 4 hours until the gel is properly set.

For the Pecan Crunch. Preheat the oven to 320°F (160°C). Toast the pecans for 10 minutes, then blend them in a food processor to get a 100 percent nut paste. In a bowl, add the milk chocolate, butter, crispy rice cereal, salt and the pecan paste we just made. Mix well and reserve it for filling inside the baked choux.

For the Pecan Praline Paste. Line a tray with baking paper. With the oven still at 320°F (160°C), toast the pecans for 10 minutes, and spread them out on the prepared tray. In a saucepan, heat the granulated sugar, stirring continuously until it caramelizes to a light golden brown, and pour it over the toasted pecans. Allow it to cool down and harden, then break it into pieces, and toss those in the food processor to get a nutty praline paste.

Time for assembly. Carefully slice off the upper portion of each choux using a small knife, and keep that top portion aside for now. Let's also whip the pecan ganache before we start, so it's nice and airy. Sprinkle a layer of pecan crunch into the choux, and pipe a little bit of that pecan whipped ganache over it. Carefully demold the green apple gel spheres and insert them into the choux. Then use a piping bag fitted with a star nozzle to pipe the ganache in a circular motion to form a peak, and drizzle over some pecan praline paste. Finish by sprinkling some toasted chopped pecan, and placing the choux caps right back on top.

These perfect puffs are decadent enough to satisfy you, but light enough to have you reaching for another. Once the choux are assembled, make sure to finish them off within a day while they're at their tastiest.

RED VELVET PROFITEROLE

Yield: 20 pastries
Mold: 7-inch (17½-cm) round cake tin

Inspired by the ever-fashionable and instantly recognizable red velvet cake: a fine-textured cake that feels like velvet, and looks like . . . red. So when we made our own striking choux pastry, we loaded it with bits of red velvet cake, a light cream cheese chantilly and hints of refreshing raspberry gel. They say you can't have your cake and eat it too. But now you can have your red velvet cake, and eat a choux!

Cream Cheese Chantilly

1¼ cups (300 g) cream cheese, softened

1 tbsp (6 g) gelatin

2 tbsp + 1 tsp (36 g) cold water

1¼ cups (300 g) heavy cream

¼ cup + 1 tsp (55 g) granulated sugar

1 vanilla bean pod (see Quick Reference Notes, page 219)

Craquelin

2 tbsp + 1½ tsp (37.5 g) butter

⅓ cup + 1 tsp (45 g) all-purpose flour

3 tbsp + 2 tsp (45 g) granulated sugar

4-5 drops of natural red food coloring

Choux Paste

½ cup + 1 tbsp + 1 tsp (140 g) water

3 tbsp (45 g) milk

¼ tsp sea salt

1 tsp granulated sugar

¼ cup + 1 tbsp + ¾ tsp (75 g) butter

⅞ cup (110 g) all-purpose flour, sifted

3 eggs

Red Velvet Cake

2 tbsp (30 g) butter, plus more for greasing cake tin

¼ cup + 1½ tbsp (78 g) milk, divided

1¼ tsp (6 g) vinegar, divided

¼ cup + 2½ tsp (60 g) granulated sugar

¼ tsp vanilla extract

½ cup (60 g) all-purpose flour

¼ tsp salt

1 tsp cocoa powder

¼ tsp baking soda

⅛ tsp natural red food coloring

Raspberry Gel

2 tbsp (25 g) granulated sugar

⅕ tbsp agar

⅓ cup + 1½ tbsp (100 g) raspberry purée

Red velvet crumbs, dried, for garnish

Edible flowers, for garnish

For the Cream Cheese Chantilly. In a medium bowl, add the cream cheese. In a small bowl, add the gelatin and water, letting the gelatin bloom for 5 minutes, until it absorbs the water and swells. In a saucepan, heat the cream along with the granulated sugar and vanilla, and bring the mixture to a steady simmer. That's when we stir in the bloomed gelatin and make sure it dissolves completely. Pour this into the bowl containing the cream cheese, and use a hand blender to emulsify it into a lovely, smooth consistency. Store this in the refrigerator overnight before using.

For the Craquelin. In a bowl, paddle together the butter, all-purpose flour, granulated sugar and red food coloring to get a dough. Place that between two sheets of baking paper, and roll it out into a super-thin ⅓₂-inch (1-mm) sheet, then freeze for 1 hour. Cut out 2½-inch (6-cm) discs, a little larger than the choux we're planning, so they'll fit over nicely.

(continued)

For the Choux Paste. Preheat the oven to 356°F (180°C). Line a tray with baking paper. In a saucepan, boil the water together with the milk, salt, granulated sugar and butter. Pull the dish off the heat just to add in the flour, and mix, making sure there are no lumps. Then resume cooking until you get a thick dough that pulls easily away from the sides of the pan, leaving a thin skin at the bottom. Transfer this dough to a stand mixer with a paddle attachment and start to slowly incorporate the eggs, a little at a time. Now on the prepared tray, it's time to start piping mounds of choux, each about 1½ inches (3.8 cm) in diameter, and covering the tops with discs of craquelin. Pop the tray into the oven, leaving it to bake for 30 to 40 minutes, until the choux rises and the craquelin forms a lovely crust on top.

For the Red Velvet Cake. Preheat the oven to 338°F (170°C). Grease the cake tin with extra butter. Then, in a small bowl make a quick buttermilk by stirring together ¼ cup (55 g) of milk and 1 teaspoon of vinegar until it starts to curdle. Set this aside to use in the cake. In a stand mixer with a paddle attachment, cream the butter with the granulated sugar to get it light and fluffy, then gradually add in the vanilla extract and 1½ tablespoons (23 g) of milk a little at a time to form a nice batter. In a small bowl, mix together the all-purpose flour, salt and cocoa powder, and start adding this into the batter in small portions, alternating with the buttermilk to keep the texture feeling great. Finally, add in ¼ teaspoon of vinegar, the baking soda and the food coloring, and combine well. Pour this into the prepared cake tin and bake for 25 minutes. Use a cake tester to check if the baking is done, or use a probe thermometer to know when the cake reaches 203°F (95°C). Allow the cake to cool, and use a 1-inch (2.5-cm) cookie cutter to cut out little chunks of red velvet cake.

For the Raspberry Gel. In a bowl, mix the granulated sugar and agar together. In a saucepan, add the raspberry purée, then dissolve the agar mixture into it. Heat this mixture until it reaches a vigorous boil, then turn off the heat and leave it in the refrigerator for 2 hours to set. Use a hand blender to bring this to a creamy consistency before we use it.

Time for assembly. In a stand mixer with a whisk attachment, whip the cream cheese chantilly to get it light and airy. Carefully slice off the upper portion of each choux using a small knife, and pipe some of that cream cheese chantilly into them. Place a disc of red velvet cake inside and pipe a generous portion of chantilly to form nice peaks on top of each choux bun. Use a melon-baller or small spoon dipped in warm water to carve a small indent in the top of the cream. Finish things off by piping a bit of raspberry gel into the indent, and garnish with cake crumbs and edible flowers for a natural look.

These perfect puffs are decadent enough to satisfy you, but light enough to have you reaching for another. Once the choux are assembled, make sure to finish them off within a day while they're at their tastiest.

VANILLA PISTACHIO BERRY SANDWICH

Yield: 6 pastries
Mold: 12 x 16-inch (30 x 40-cm) frame

The concept of sandwiches has been around forever, but they seem to have got their name from an English nobleman from a town called Sandwich, who loved them because they allowed him to eat while doing other things. And clearly he was on to something, because since then there's been cookie sandwiches and ice cream sandwiches and croissant sandwiches, just to name a few of our favorites. This delicate sandwich is made from soft slices of cake with a minty berry jam inside and a light pistachio ganache on top. Who said sandwiches had to be horizontal?

Pistachio Chantilly

1 tsp gelatin

2½ tsp (12 g) cold water

¼ cup + 2 tsp (50 g) white chocolate, chopped

3 tbsp + 1 tsp (50 g) pistachio paste

1 cup + 2 tsp (250 g) heavy cream

Pistachio Sablé

½ cup (115 g) butter

⅔ cup + 2 tsp (85 g) icing sugar

1 tbsp + 1 tsp (20 g) milk

1⅓ cups + 1 tsp (170 g) all-purpose flour

½ cup + 1 tsp (50 g) pistachio flour

Pinch of sea salt

Pinch of ground cinnamon

Rolé Cake

3 tbsp (45 g) milk

3½ tbsp (50 g) butter

1 tbsp (20 g) invert sugar

4 drops natural red food coloring

½ cup + 1 tbsp (70 g) all-purpose flour, sifted

1 egg

4 egg yolks

4 egg whites

¼ cup + 2½ tsp (60 g) granulated sugar

1 tsp cream of tartar

⅓ tsp sea salt

1¼ tsp (3 g) beetroot powder

Strawberry Jam

1½ cups + 1 tbsp (225 g) strawberries, chopped

1 tsp pectin NH

2 tbsp + 1 tsp (30 g) granulated sugar

½ tsp sea salt

½ tsp lime juice

Zest of 1½ limes

3½ tbsp (20 g) mint leaves, minced

Vanilla Ganache

1⅜ cups + 1½ tbsp (250 g) white chocolate, chopped

¾ cup + 2 tbsp + 2 tsp (225 g) heavy cream

¼ tsp sea salt

1 vanilla bean pod (see Quick Reference Notes, page 219)

1½ tsp (10 g) corn syrup

Strawberries, for garnish

For the Pistachio Chantilly. In a small bowl, add the gelatin and water, letting the gelatin bloom for 5 minutes, until it absorbs the water and swells. In a heatproof bowl, add the white chocolate and pistachio paste. In a saucepan, heat the cream to a simmer, and stir in the gelatin, making sure that it fully dissolves. Pour this hot cream into the bowl containing the chocolate mixture, allowing it to melt. Use a hand blender to get a perfectly smooth emulsion, which we will keep in the refrigerator overnight.

(continued)

For the Pistachio Sablé. Line a tray with baking paper or have two perforated silicon mats ready to use. In a stand mixer with a paddle attachment, cream the butter and icing sugar together. Gradually add in the milk, and mix until it's fully incorporated. Follow that by gently folding in the all-purpose flour, pistachio flour, salt and cinnamon to get a nice sablé dough. Place this between two sheets of baking paper and flatten it a little with a rolling pin before resting it in the refrigerator for 2 hours. Preheat the oven to 320°F (160°C). Roll the dough out into a sheet ⁵⁄₃₂ inch (4 mm) thick, then cut 6 (1½-inch [3.8-cm]) squares and 6 (3 x 1½–inch [75 x 38–mm]) rectangles. Put them back in the refrigerator to set for 30 minutes, then transfer them onto the prepared tray. Bake these for 12 minutes, until they're golden brown.

For the Role Cake. Preheat the oven to 338°F (170°C). Line two frames with baking paper. In a saucepan over medium heat add the milk, butter, invert sugar and food coloring. Gently fold in the all-purpose flour and mix well, making sure there are no lumps. Continue to cook until enough moisture evaporates and you get a thick dough that pulls easily away from the sides of the pan, leaving a thin skin at the bottom. Transfer this dough to a stand mixer with a paddle attachment and gradually add in the whole egg and egg yolks one at a time, mixing well until fully incorporated. Set this aside to cool. Then with the stand mixer fitted with a clean bowl and whisk, let's make a meringue by whipping the egg whites together with the granulated sugar, cream of tartar, salt and beetroot powder until it forms medium peaks. Once the dough has cooled, carefully mix in the meringue using a spatula. Pour this into the prepared frames to get ½-inch (1.3-cm)-thick layers in each, and bake them for about 7 minutes, until the top of the cake feels bouncy to the touch.

For the Strawberry Jam. In a saucepan, heat the strawberries. In a bowl, combine the pectin, granulated sugar and salt, mixing it well. Bring it all to a boil for 1 to 2 minutes, until a nice jam begins to form. Turn off the heat and add in the lime juice. Allow the jam to cool before gently folding in the lime zest and mint leaves for that special flavor.

For the Vanilla Ganache. In a heatproof bowl, add the white chocolate. In a saucepan, heat the cream, salt, vanilla and corn syrup to a steady simmer. Pour this hot mixture into the bowl containing the white chocolate, and allow it to melt. Then use a hand blender to bring it to a luscious, creamy emulsion.

Time for assembly. Once the baked cakes are out of the oven and cooled, pour a layer of vanilla ganache into the frames. Make sure the ganache is at 81°F (27°C) for it to work best. Now put both trays in the freezer to set. Bring one of the trays back out after 1 hour and use a palette knife to spread a layer of strawberry jam over it, then pop it back into the freezer for another 2 hours. By now they should both be set enough for us to easily demold. Place the sheet with just ganache over the one with strawberry jam so it forms a nice layered cake, and start cutting out 3-inch (7½-cm) sandwiches. Place these cake sandwiches vertically onto the rectangular sablé bases.

Fill a piping bag with pistachio chantilly, and use a petal nozzle to create a delicate ruffle pattern across the top of each sandwich. Drop a few sliced strawberries on top of the chantilly, and add a sprinkling of pistachio powder. Finally take those sablé squares out, and place them on the side of each cake to give it a unique, artsy look.

Enjoy these delicious cake sandwiches while you work or out at the park. You can store them in the refrigerator for up to 2 days.

CRANBERRY MATCHA CAKELET

Yield: 16 pastries
Mold: 3-inch (7½-cm) oval cutter

Over the years Japan has given us some of the most innovative and interesting foods and flavors imaginable, and of those almost none have become as wide-spread and popular as matcha. It's a stone-ground green tea powder, and we love its sharp, toasty complexity. This little tart is all about finding a perfect balance between the matcha sponge, tangy lemon marmalade and vanilla cream seasoned with fresh yuzu zest.

Cocoa Shortbread

⅓ cup + 1 tbsp (90 g) butter

3 tbsp + 2 tsp (45 g) granulated sugar

¾ cup (90 g) all-purpose flour

4½ tsp (15 g) rice flour

¼ tsp sea salt

1 tbsp + 2½ tsp (10 g) cocoa powder

½ cup (60 g) all-purpose flour

3 tbsp + 1 tsp (20 g) matcha powder

½ cup + 2 tsp (120 g) butter, melted

Matcha Sponge

⅞ cup (150 g) white chocolate

4 eggs, separated

1 tbsp + ¾ tsp (25 g) invert sugar

Zest of 1 lemon

⅓ cup (65 g) granulated sugar

⅓ tsp sea salt

1 tsp cream of tartar

Vanilla Cream

1¼ tsp (2.5 g) gelatin

1 tbsp (15 g) cold water

2 egg yolks

1½ tbsp (12 g) cornstarch

2 tbsp + 1 tsp (30 g) granulated sugar, divided

½ cup + 1 tbsp + 2 tsp (150 g) milk

¼ vanilla bean pod (see Quick Reference Notes, page 219)

1 tbsp + ¼ tsp (15 g) butter

½ cup (120 g) heavy cream

Macerated Cranberries

⅜ cup + 2 tsp (100 g) water

½ cup (100 g) granulated sugar

¾ tbsp (10 g) citric acid

⅔ cup (100 g) fresh cranberries, small dice

Lemon Marmalade

2 (approximately 110 g) lemons, whole

Pinch of sea salt, plus more for salting water

¼ cup (60 g) lemon juice, divided

½ vanilla bean pod (see Quick Reference Notes, page 219)

1 tsp pectin NH

½ cup (100 g) granulated sugar

Tempered white chocolate, for garnish (see Quick Reference Notes, page 219)

Edible flowers, for garnish

Yuzu zest, for garnish

For the Cocoa Shortbread. In a stand mixer with a paddle attachment, cream the butter and granulated sugar. Then gently fold in the all-purpose flour, rice flour, salt and cocoa powder to get a nice dough. Place this between two sheets of baking paper, and roll it into a sheet ⅛ inch (3 mm) thick, then rest it in the refrigerator for 2 hours. While it's resting, preheat the oven to 320°F (160°C). Line a tray with baking paper. Use an oval cutter to make neat discs of dough, and place them on the prepared tray, then put the tray in the oven for 15 to 18 minutes. Use a cake tester to check if it is done, or use a probe thermometer to know when the shortbread reaches 203°F (95°C).

For the Matcha Sponge. Line a 10-inch (25-cm) square cake tin with baking paper. Preheat the oven to 320°F (160°C). In a bowl, melt the white chocolate. In another bowl, use a hand whisk to whip the egg yolks, invert sugar and lemon zest until the mixture turns light and fluffy. Now, in a stand mixer with a whisk attachment, whip the egg whites, along with the granulated sugar, salt and cream of tartar to create a meringue with medium peaks. Add the yolk mixture into the meringue, then start mixing this into the melted white chocolate. Gently fold in the all-purpose flour and matcha powder, and finish by mixing in the butter. Pour this into the prepared cake tin so the batter is about 1 inch (2.5 cm) thick. Bake for 25 to 30 minutes. Use a cake tester to check if the baking is done, or use a probe thermometer to know when the cake reaches 203°F (95°C). Allow it to cool before using cookie cutters to get discs of sponge the same size as the shortbread discs.

(continued)

For the Vanilla Cream. In a small bowl, add the gelatin and water, letting the gelatin bloom for 5 minutes, until it absorbs the water and swells. In a mixing bowl, add the egg yolks, cornstarch and 1 tablespoon + ½ teaspoon (15 g) of granulated sugar, and mix to form a paste. Then in a saucepan, heat the milk with the vanilla and the remaining 1 tablespoon + ½ teaspoon (15 g) of granulated sugar until it's warm. Pour one-third of it into the yolk-mix, while stirring continuously to help it temper the eggs. Then strain that mixture back into the saucepan containing the rest of the milk, and cook until it begins to boil and thicken. Turn off the heat, add in the gelatin and butter, and allow this to cool in an ice bath while stirring continuously. Once the mixture has chilled, whip the cream a little and fold that in as well. Keep this in the refrigerator until we're ready to assemble.

For the Macerated Cranberries. In a saucepan, add the water, granulated sugar and citric acid. Bring it to a boil until it's fully dissolved, then cool it down using an ice bath. Drop the cranberries into the syrup, letting them soak for a good 10 minutes. Strain the macerated cranberries out, and keep them aside for a bit.

For the Lemon Marmalade. Pierce the lemons with a knife, and toss them in a saucepan with salted water. Heat to a boil, then drain the water out, and replace it with more salted water. Once it reaches a boil again, replace the salted water a third time and wait until it boils before draining the water out. Now we can cut the lemons in halves and remove the seeds. Run the lemons in a food processor along with 2 tablespoons (30 g) of lemon juice. Transfer this into a saucepan over medium heat, and add in the remaining 2 tablespoons (30 g) of lemon juice and the vanilla. Let's get it nice and warm. In a bowl, combine the pectin and granulated sugar, then add that to the saucepan, making sure it dissolves completely. Continue to boil the mixture, cooking until it thickens into a delightful lemon marmalade. Then turn the heat off and allow it to cool.

Time for assembly. Place the matcha sponge disks onto the shortbread bases. Fill a piping bag with the vanilla cream, and use a round tip nozzle to pipe kisses of cream around the edge of the cakes. Spoon some lemon marmalade into the center and place the macerated cranberries on top.

For the garnish. We've used white chocolate rings as an elegant decoration. If you'd like to do the same, just take tempered white chocolate in a piping cone, make rings on an acetate sheet, and allow them to cool. Once fully set, place them on top of the cakes, and add edible flowers and yuzu zest (or a citrus flavor of your choice) to finish the dessert.

These matcha cakelets are ready to be eaten and they're sure to keep you satisfied until your next visit to a Japanese tea house. You can store them in the refrigerator for up to 2 days.

Quick Reference Notes

This section is for the slightly more curious among us. It has little explanations on some of the more uncommon ingredients in the book, and a couple of general techniques that apply to many different types of recipes.

Agar. Extracted from red seaweed, this stuff maintains a perfect gel consistency even at a temperature as high as 176°F (80°C).

Cake Testing. If you're a baker with many years of experience you start developing a sort of sixth sense for knowing when a cake is done, but we still recommend using good tools to be more precise. Use a cake tester to poke into the center of the cake and see whether it comes out dry. You could also use a probe thermometer to know when the cake's internal temperature reaches 203°F (95°C)—that's the magic number to know that it's done!

Caramelized White Chocolate. To caramelize white chocolate, start by spreading finely chopped white chocolate on a tray lined with baking paper, then put it in an oven set to 194°F (90°C) for about 50 minutes. During this time, you'll need to prevent the chocolate from burning by stirring the white chocolate at 10-minute intervals, until it caramelizes to a perfect light brown. Transfer the melted chocolate over into a narrow container and emulsify it using a hand blender, then pour it into a tray lined with baking paper and put it in the fridge to set for 30 minutes. Once it's solidified, chop it into small pieces and keep that ready in a medium-sized bowl.

Corn Syrup. A type of invert sugar also used to prevent recrystallization, but it has a higher moisture content and is sweeter than liquid glucose.

Dextrose. This is a type of sugar that comes from corn, and is used in a wide variety of confections when the recipe calls for something slightly less sweet as compared to regular sugar.

Gelatin. Gelatin powder can't be used as is; it needs to be activated first. In a small bowl, leave the powder to soak in 6 times its weight of ice-cold water. The gelatin will absorb the water and start to swell in a process called blooming, which takes about 5 minutes. When using bloomed gelatin in a recipe, it's best to add it to a hot liquid to help it dissolve easily, and make sure not to overheat it after that. In case you have gelatin leaf, use a food processor in blitz mode to form a fine powder, then proceed to bloom it and use it in the same way.

Gellan. A heat-resistant gelling agent that can be heated without losing its shape, which is so useful! It helps us create heat-resistant jellies which are perfect for baked goodies.

Guar Gum. Harvested from the endosperm of seeds from the guar bush, this is used as a thickener, emulsifier, stabilizer and fat replacer, so it's super useful for pastry chefs.

Isomalt. A sugar substitute made from beets that absorbs less moisture, retains heat, remains clear for longer and doesn't caramelize.

Liquid Glucose. Widely used for a lot of confections and pastry production, this nifty little ingredient helps prevent the recrystallization of sugars.

Manié Butter. Just paddle together a combination of all-purpose flour (¾ cup [90 g]) and butter (2 cups [500 g]) and use the mixture to grease your molds so the cakes you bake can be demolded with ease.

Melting Chocolate and Cocoa Butter. Often when making dessert, we need to melt chocolate before we use it. The easiest way is to chop the chocolate up into a microwave-safe bowl and pop it in the microwave for 40 seconds. Then give it a little mix before heating for another round of 40 seconds. Repeat this process of heating and mixing until the chocolate looks and feels evenly melted. Melting cocoa butter can be done using the same process, but you'll want to chop it up more finely just to help the melting process go faster.

Nut Powder and Paste. To make these, roast the nuts in the oven at 320°F (160°C) for 10 to 15 minutes. Don't rush this by turning up the heat; keep it low and slow as this will help bring out the natural flavors of the nut. Once they're done, drop them in the food processor and blitz them at short intervals to get a nut powder. Now, if you want a nut paste instead, continue to run the food processor for a few more minutes, until a paste consistency forms.

Oven Door. One personality trait that really seems to help bakers is patience. That's most apparent when it comes to opening an oven door. When you put a cake in to bake, remember to not open the oven door for the first 20 minutes while baking. We know how exciting it is to bake a new recipe, to see and smell and touch what you're making, but opening the oven door means the hot air and moisture that had built up until then is immediately lost! Your cake could start sinking or even collapse. So have some patience; the results are going to be worth it.

Pectin. Pectin is a naturally occurring starch from the cell walls of citrus fruits. When cooked to a high temperature, in combination with acid and sugar, it forms a gel. In fact, this is exactly what makes jams and jellies develop that semi-solid texture when they're cool.

Pectin NH. This is a type of modified pectin made to be thermally reversible. We use it in our jellies as a thickening and setting agent.

Resting Batters. Resting batter helps with proper hydration and it gives your cakes and cookies better structure while baking. It also gives certain ingredients time to mature, and might be just what your product needs to get that next-level taste! Resting time can vary quite a bit depending on who you ask; we prefer letting many of our batters rest for a full 12 hours before baking.

Resting Ganache. Being a mixture of chocolate and cream, ganache needs to sit in a refrigerator so the crystals in the chocolate form a stable chain. This process can take anywhere from 2 to 12 hours, and helps the ganache get that thick, luscious, creamy consistency we're hoping for.

Storing Products. Storing and serving your pastries at the right temperature is what takes the pastry to the next level. Make sure to use airtight containers or cling film when storing anything; it helps retain the moisture of your products as well as helps increase their shelf life.

Surface Wrap Ganache. If you've ever noticed those weird skins that form over your cup of milk or tea, a similar thing happens to ganaches and custards, and it's not the most pleasant texture to deal with. When storing these components, make sure to wrap them such that the cling film gently touches the full surface of the ganache. Then when you unwrap it, you'll still have a smooth, silky mixture with no skin.

Tempering Chocolate. Tempering involves managing the temperature of melted chocolate to stabilize the fat crystals. There are many ways to temper, with the popular ones being tabling or seeding. The seeding method is the simplest: let's take chocolate in a bowl and melt it to 113°F (45°C). Then start adding chopped chocolate in parts to help it cool, while mixing and periodically checking the temperature till it reaches 80°F (27°C). At this point we'll need to use a microwave to get specific temperatures based on the type of chocolate: ideally dark chocolate should be 88°F (31°C), milk chocolate 86°F (30°C) and white chocolate 84°F (29°C). These are known as the "working temperatures," where we can safely use the chocolate for various garnishes and molded chocolates.

Trehalose. Similar to dextrose, except this one is only 45 percent as sweet as regular sugar. This helps give it a lower freezing point so it stays in liquid form for longer.

Vanilla Pods. To extract the vanilla from the pod, use a knife to split it open lengthwise and scrape all those tiny vanilla seeds out from both sides to use in our recipe. You can also use the scraped pods themselves—let them soak in warm milk or a jar of sugar until the flavors transfer over. Then use those ingredients in anything else to get an added vanilla aroma.

Xanthan Gum. This is a polysaccharide gum with thickening power. It acts as an emulsifier that can bind together fat and water-based solutions that don't usually mix. Xanthan gum is also widely used in gluten-free baking as a thickening agent.

Yeast. If your recipe calls for a certain amount of fresh yeast and you have only instant yeast, just use half the amount. In case you only have active dry yeast, then use three-fourths the amount instead.

Acknowledgments

Making a cake and making a book are similar in a lot of ways: They both take inspiration, effort and patience, and bring you deep satisfaction in return. The main difference is you can easily bake a cake alone if you want, but it takes a kitchen-full of talented people to make a book!

A massive thank you to the management and team of chefs at Lavonne for giving us their hearts and time in tasting, testing and tweaking these recipes to perfection. They stepped up and proved why they're the best in the business. So many people helped us in big and small ways but we'd like to extend some extra tight hugs to:

Nandheetha Varadaraj & Anosh Ranbhise for heading the production and managing the superb team of chefs during the photo shoot: Sujit Seshadri, Vaishnavi Ram Murthy, Pallavi Sethi, Amrutha Varshini, Arielle Varghese & Mili Panjwan.

Prathana Narang & Upamanyu Urs for fact-checking the writing and making sure all our madness actually makes sense.

Raj & Swathi from Arka Photography for setting scenes, adjusting lights and photographing our desserts like they were supermodels.

Nitish Ayyodh from LimeSoda Photography & Sarabjeet Singh from Slurp Studio for making us pose for photos at every window, market and street corner in Bangalore.

Shailesh Johny for coordinating between all the chefs, photographers and locations so every shoot went off without a hitch.

Manek D'Silva for guiding the language and image styles so all these little pieces can finally come together as one vision.

Page Street for guiding us through the process of taking this book from concept to reality.

To every chef that has left an imprint in our hearts and in our work, we honor you through these pages and hope we did you proud.

And finally, thanks to you the readers; we can't wait to see all the insanely delicious cakes you make!

About the Authors

VINESH JOHNY

Vinesh Johny is the co-founder of Lavonne Academy of Baking Science & Pastry Arts, India's first international specialized baking academy, as well as the Executive Pastry Chef of the award-winning patisserie under the same brand. He worked in the pastry kitchens of multiple luxury hotel properties before finding his calling to be an educator, and now Lavonne Academy graduates over 1,200 students every year through various programs. Vinesh was featured on the inaugural *Forbes* "30 Under 30 Asia" and CNN's prestigious "20 Under 40" lists, and was also part of the *Forbes* "All Star Alumni" in 2017 and 2019. After mentoring Team India to a historic silver-medal win in the pastry category at WorldSkills Abu Dhabi, he took the position of Chief Expert at WorldSkills, ensuring that upcoming pastry chefs have the training and platform they need to shine. Both as an educator and firebrand pastry chef, Vinesh is known for his engaging personality, rebellious creative style and mind-bending product ideas, including sensations like the BucketCake and Moodpills.

ANDRÉS LARA

Andrés Lara is a pastry maestro with global exposure, having honed his skills over years of constant traveling making desserts. After training at the prestigious French Pastry School in Chicago, he had the opportunity of working with renowned chefs from all over the world. Andrés gained immensely valuable experiences at Michelin-starred restaurants such as Bagatelle in Norway, ElBulli in Spain, Noma in Denmark and Iggy's in Singapore. After being part of the opening team for Cacao Barry in Tokyo as their Regional Chef for Asia Pacific, and greatly inspired by a combined love for learning and travel, Andrés went on to teach pastry classes and demonstrations all over the continent and beyond, to Europe, North and South America. He then continued with Cacao Barry to be Canada's Creative Innovation Chef. Over the years of research and travel, Andrés has developed a unique style, respecting and combining the food cultures of the world, while reflecting sophistication and elegance in every creation.

Index